The Catholic Biblical Quarterly
Monograph Series
25

Speech and Response

A Rhetorical Analysis of the Introductions to the Speeches of the Book of Job (Chaps. 4–24)

BY

John E. Course

The Catholic Biblical Quarterly
Monograph Series
25

Produced in the United States

Library of Congress Cataloging-in-Publication Data

Course, John E.
Speech and response : a rhetorical analysis of the introductions to the speeches of the Book of Job, chaps. 4-24 / by John E. Course.
p. cm. — (The Catholic Biblical quarterly. Monograph series ; 25)
Includes bibliographical references and index.
ISBN 0-915170-24-8
1. Bible. O.T. Job IV-XXIV—Criticism, interpretation, etc.
I. Title. II. Series.
BS1415.2.C675 1994
223'.1066—dc20 94-26566
CIP

Contents

Acknowledgments

I express my gratitude first of all to my father-in-law and mother-in-law, D. Whiting and Margaret H. Lathrop, for opening their home to our family for five years. Without their financial and moral support, graduate study would have remained an impossible dream. My thanks also to my wife, Anna, for child care, typing, insightful editorial suggestions, and her consistent encouragement and confidence throughout the entire academic process. Finally, to my advisor Prof. Gerald T. Sheppard, I extend my appreciation for his guidance and counsel during the writing of this work. Special thanks also to my readers, Professors Brian Peckham, William H. Irwin, Anthony R. Ceresko, and Tom Dozemann, for their suggestions with regard to refinement and clarification.

CHAPTER 1

Introduction

Biblical scholars have published a great deal of literature on the Book of Job in recent years.[1] The problems inherent in the present arrangement of the book,[2] difficulties of translation arising from the frequent use of words with uncertain meanings, and the study of the presentation of the subject matter in itself, to name a few areas of interest, continue to attract the interest of both teacher and student alike.

One area of research, which is recently receiving attention, focuses on the possibility that Job and his friends actually respond to one another through their speeches despite a fairly widespread scholarly consensus to the contrary. This consensus is not too surprising as there is no clear point-by-point rebuttal in the speeches. Nor is there an obvious argument which is then resolved in the course of the debate, although W. A. Irwin has argued otherwise.[3] In the context of his rejection of Irwin's

[1] For a review of some of the publications on Job see R. J. Williams, "Current Trends in the Study of the Book of Job" in *Studies in the Book of Job* (Studies in Religion Supplements; Waterloo: Wilfrid Laurier University, 1985) 1–27.

[2] E.g., the dislocations of the third cycle of speeches, the purpose of the Yahweh speeches, and the integrity of the Elihu speeches.

[3] W. A. Irwin, "An Examination of the Progress of Thought in the Dialogue of Job," *JR* 13 (1933) 150–64. Briefly, Irwin argues that in response to the friends' advice to repent, Job, who is convinced of his innocence, is driven to seek one who will represent him before God (19:23–29). Herein Irwin finds the climax to the book and the solution to the problem of Job's suffering. The major problem with Irwin's thesis is that the idea of a redeemer is a fleeting hope for Job which is dropped in favor of Job himself standing before God (23:3–7).

position, M. H. Pope speaks against the viewpoint that the speeches of Job and his friends respond to each other:

> Actually it is scarcely appropriate to call this section of the book a dialogue. There is not here the give-and-take of philosophical disputation aimed at the advancement of understanding and truth. Rather each side has a partisan point of view which is reiterated ad nauseam in long speeches. There is no real movement in the argument.[4]

The three standard works on wisdom literature in the OT present a similar argument. Von Rad writes:

> As they listen to each other, both partners in the dialogues scarcely have more than very loose connections with individual, characteristic hypotheses. In their own train of thought they do not adhere closely to that of the other. This means that, on one hand, the argument often fails to advance and that, on the other, the intellectual ground covered becomes more and more extensive. The speeches are repetitive and, to a certain extent, move forward only in a circular fashion.[5]

R. B. Y. Scott comments:

> Accusers and accused restate their respective positions with increasing vehemence, making little or no attempt to meet the arguments of their opponents.[6]

And J. L. Crenshaw advocates:

> . . . the various responses frequently ignore the addresses they purport to answer, giving the impression that Job and the friends talk past one another.[7]

In agreement with these scholars, the speeches do create a circular argument in which both sides consistently reiterate their own particular point of view. Thus it would appear at first that no effort was expended by the writer to engage the speakers in at least some measure of a response to each other. Nevertheless, every speech of the Book of Job is prefaced

[4] M. H. Pope, *Job* (AB 15; 3d ed.; Garden City, NY: Doubleday, 1973) lxxv.

[5] G. von Rad, *Wisdom in Israel* (London: SCM, 1972) 210.

[6] R. B. Y. Scott, *The Way of Wisdom in the Old Testament* (New York: Macmillan, 1971) 154.

[7] J. L. Crenshaw, *Old Testament Wisdom: An Introduction* (Atlanta: John Knox, 1981) 106.

with a brief statement which identifies the speaker and appears to mark the speech as a response to what was previously said.[8] In chaps. 4–26 these statements are constant in form and consist of two verbs, *'ānâ* ("to answer") followed by *'āmar* ("to say") with the "consecutive" *waw* prefixed to them both. These verbs frame the name of the speaker and in the case of the friends, their tribe as well. The pattern remains much the same for the Elihu speeches, the Yahweh speeches and Job's replies to God's part in the book.[9]

Job's complaint of chap. 3, however, is introduced with a relatively lengthy narrator's comment, "After this Job opened his mouth and cursed his day. And Job answered and said" (vv 1–2). The first verse forms a link with the prologue through the phrase "after this." Yet the second verse, "And Job answered and said," is curious, for it is written in 2:13 that no one spoke to Job. On this basis, and with the support of only extra-biblical references from Ugaritic writings, Fohrer concludes that

[8] On one occasion this type of statement announces the conclusion to Yahweh's first speech (40:1).

[9] In Elihu's last speech (36:1), the pattern is broken with the substitution of the verb *yāśap* ("to continue") for *'ānâ*, perhaps to acknowledge that this speech is the fourth of a series. A minor variation occurs in 32:6; 34:1; 35:1. In his first speech (32:6), Elihu's father's name and tribe are listed alongside of the speaker's name, whereas in the latter two references only Elihu's name is recorded with the announcement of his speech. The statement prefacing the Yahweh speeches is identical in 38:1 and 40:6 and is similar to the corresponding verses of chaps. 4–26, yet is more detailed as it indicates the addressee as well as the location from which God speaks. Similarly, in Job's replies (40:3; 42:1), the verbs *'ānâ* and *'āmar* are used along with the name Yahweh which identifies the person addressed. The major exception to the above similarities is 27:1 and 29:1 where it is written, "And Job continued with his *māšāl* ("discourse") and said." The idea of continuity is probably expressed here as chaps. 27 and 29 immediately follow Job's speech of chap. 26 (see the assessment of 36:1 above). Also the verb *'ānâ* is not present because chaps. 27 and 29 are intended for the court and not primarily as a response to the friends in particular. The term *māšāl* is used here of Job's oath to set it apart from his previous disputation speeches (cf. Habel, *The Book of Job* [OTL; Philadelphia: Westminster, 1985] 379). The verbs *'ānâ* and *'āmar* (in this sequence) are also used consistently for the Satan in his exchange with God in the prologue (1:7b, 9; 2:2b), whereas the verb *'āmar* is used solely for God (1:7a, 8, 12; 2:2a, 3, 6). On two occasions (1:12; 2:6) God's directives issued to the Satan could be read as replies to his requests. In this context, one might have expected to see the verb *'ānâ* used in conjunction with *'āmar* as with the Satan. Perhaps *'āmar* is used alone to ensure that God is seen as the initiator of the dialogue with the Satan and that God is understood as responsible for what is about to happen to Job. As the Satan is presented as a respondent, he appears less accountable for Job's forthcoming misery.

the statement "And he answered and said" is simply a conventional introduction to a speech.[10] A survey of OT texts, however, reveals that the verbs *'ānâ* and *'āmar* are commonly used to introduce direct speech in response to conversation (e.g., Exod 4:1; Num 11:28; Deut 1:14; Josh 7:20).[11]

In addition, on at least three occasions (Gen 31:36; 1 Kgs 13:6; 1 Chr 12:18) these two verbs are used to introduce direct speech not in reply to a spoken word but in response to an action or event. In 1 Kgs 13:1–6, for example, there is recorded an incident involving a man who prophesied against the altar at Bethel in the presence of Jeroboam. The king, on ordering the man's arrest, put out his hand against him, and as a result it is recorded that his hand was stricken. In response to this sudden ailment, Jeroboam asks that his hand be healed. Interestingly enough, this request is introduced with the statement, "And the king answered and said" (1 Kgs 13:6). The second example concerns David's response to the warriors who came to join his ranks (1 Chr 12:17–18). According to this passage, David is the first to speak when he goes to meet with some troops. Here he issues a warning introduced with the words, "and he answered and said."

The remaining example is from Gen 31:36, where Jacob is said to have become angry presumably as a result of Laban's search of Jacob's belongings for his family gods. Consequently, the statement, "And Jacob answered and said," which introduces his angry outburst (v 36), probably should be understood as a reaction to Laban's invasion of his privacy and to the fact that he was pursued. In the light of these three passages where the clause, "And he answered and said," is used in response not to a spoken word but to an action or event, it appears that Job 3:2 would best be understood as introducing a response to: (a) his friends' expressions of solidarity with him (2:12–13) and (b) the severity of his suffering.

In sum, the purpose of this formula ("And he answered and said") in the Book of Job is threefold: (a) it indicates the beginning of a new speech except on one occasion where it sets off the conclusion to a speech (40:1); (b) it identifies the speaker; and (c) it marks the speech as a response to the previous speaker's discourse or to a preceding action or event as

[10] G. Fohrer, *Das Buch Hiob* (KAT 16; Gütersloh: Gütersloher, 1963) 115. The Ugaritic texts Fohrer cites are: 51, II,20; IV,30; 129,16; and *'nt* (pl. IX) 11,17.

[11] Cf. R. L. Harris *et al, Theological Wordbook of the Old Testament* (Chicago: Moody, 1980) 2. 681. The verb *'ānâ* may also be used on its own to mark a response to direct speech (e.g., Gen 23:5; Exod 19:8; Num 32:31; Judg 18:14). The same is true for *'āmar* (e.g., 2 Sam 1:4; 1 Kgs 11:22; 2 Kgs 1:8; 2:13).

in the case of 3:1–2.[12] Thus the narrator's line at the beginning of each speech gives some warrant to reading the speeches primarily as a response to what was previously said. The fact that several scholars argue against such a possibility suggests that if the speeches do respond to one another it must be in a subtle, indirect and therefore easily overlooked manner. Such a feature might be part of the rhetorical aesthetic and intended not to advance any overall argument, but rather to create a bickering type of atmosphere for the debate in which one speaker would be understood as adopting a word, phrase or idea from a previous speaker in order to exploit it for his own purposes. Unfortunately, the consensus that there is no substantial relationship between the speeches of Job and his friends has, on the whole, discouraged scholars from researching the possibility of connections based on shared words, roots and recurrent themes. At the same time, some scholars have recently supported the idea that the speeches do, at least to some degree, interrelate. A critical review of their work is necessary to evaluate the quality of literature published on this subject. Of special interest are the flaws in the research which, when isolated, will hopefully be avoided in this work.

R. Gordis pursued the possibility of connections between the speeches in his illuminating chapter on the use of quotations in Job in his book, *The Book of God and Man: A Study of Job*.[13] The passages Gordis identifies as quotations are not marked as such but, as he observes, stand out from their context by virtue of providing a variant opinion or change in mood. Consequently, Gordis notes that a verb of speaking (e.g., "you said") or thinking (e.g., "I thought") needs to be supplied in the translation for purposes of clarity. Moreover, Gordis stresses that they are not word-for-word citations but are paraphrases of a previous speaker's thoughts.

Of the several kinds of quotations Gordis isolates in Job, the citation from the argument of an opponent is of particular interest. The most striking evidence of this kind put forward by Gordis is from the latter half of Job's seventh speech (21:19–34).[14] Three of his most astute obser-

[12] In recognition of the importance of "c" in particular to the argument such verses will be designated as an "announcement of response." As this type of verse belongs to the narrator, it will not be considered part of the introduction to a speech.

[13] R. Gordis, *The Book of God and Man: A Study of Job* (Chicago: University of Chicago, 1965) 169–89. See also R. Gordis, "Virtual Quotations in Job, Sumer and Qumran," *VT* 31 (1981) 410–27.

[14] Gordis, *The Book of God and Man,* 185–186.

vations will be mentioned. First, Gordis notes that in 21:19a Job quotes the orthodox view of his friends that children are punished for the sins of their father (see 5:4; 18:12; 20:10) so as to reject it in 21:19b–21. Second, as Gordis points out, the friends have argued that God's wisdom is beyond the reach of humanity and therefore his treatment of humanity is above criticism (4:17; 11:6–12; 15:14, 18). Gordis, then, observes that Job quotes this view in 21:22 only to criticize it with his belief that God treats humanity poorly (21:23–26). Third, this scholar also presents the rhetorical question of 21:28, which assumes that the wealthy sinner will eventually experience his or her demise, as a citation based on the friends' teaching (see 5:3–7; 8:22; 11:20; 15:32–35; 18:5–21; 20:26) which is then refuted in vv 29–33. Gordis' work on quotations not only clarifies the meaning of obscure passages but also builds support for the idea that the speeches do interact with one another in a manner that is often unrecognized.

In addition, two dissertations which deal with the use of irony in Job make a significant contribution toward an appreciation of the connections between the speeches at a deeper level. The first, *A Study of Irony in the Book of Job*,[15] written by W. J. A. Power, explores the incidence of different types of irony in Job. Of the three types of irony discussed in this dissertation, Power's classification of "verbal irony," defined as that in which the author creates a meaning opposite to the literal sense, is most relevant to this study.[16] Within this category Power includes sarcasm, hyperbole and its opposite, understatement, as well as what he calls "ironic interplay."[17] This latter term Power uses to describe the various ironic connections which he argues exist between the speeches.

Power's most convincing evidence for ironic interplay may be seen in those cases in which he isolates a specific word shared by two passages and draws out the implications of his finding. The use of the verb *ḥānan* in 9:15b as a sarcastic response to Bildad's recommendation that Job appeal for mercy (*ḥānan*) to Shaddai (8:5b) is an example of Power's better

[15] W. J. A. Power, *A Study of Irony in the Book of Job* (Ph.D. Dissertation, University of Toronto, 1961).

[16] The remaining two types of irony discussed by Power are: (1) "Socratic irony" or feigned ignorance, a method of instruction used especially by the Greek philosopher, Socrates; and (2) "irony of events" in which the audience alone is made privy to information important for a character's true understanding of his or her situation (Power, *A Study of Irony in the Book of Job*, 20–21, 24–26).

[17] Power, *A Study of Irony in the Book of Job*, 22, 30.

evidence.[18] All too often, however, Power's evidence is rather weak. Further, the vague manner in which he sometimes presents his evidence does not strengthen his case.

In two texts separated by a number of speeches, for example, Power simply cites Bildad's question, "Can papyrus grow without marsh?" (8:11a), alongside of Job's statement, "He uproots my hope as a tree" (19:10b), which he identifies as a response. Beyond the shared image of plant life devoid of the necessary growing conditions, there is nothing obvious in these texts which indicates that the latter should be interpreted as a reply to the former. Yet Power makes no attempt to explain why 19:10b should be read as a response to 8:11a, nor does he state how this so-called response might be understood as ironic. In spite of such difficulties in many of his examples, Power's dissertation, on the whole, alerts the reader to the possibility that the speeches might in, in fact, respond to one another.

The second dissertation was written by J. C. Holbert[19] under the direction of Power. The focus of this work is on the incidence of formal and verbal irony which may be found in those passages influenced by the genre of complaint (*Klage*). Of special interest is the attention Holbert gives to "verbal irony" which he defines as:

> . . . a description of those instances where words and/or phrases occur in the mouths of different participants in the book to comment, usually ironically, on one of the other participant's use of the same word and/or phrase.[20]

Holbert makes an effort to concentrate on repeated words and phrases which are used in different speeches and pursues the significance of these connections in greater detail than Power did in his earlier study. Further, he does not argue every case with equal force but admits when an example may be less clear and inconclusive. The result of Holbert's attention is an argument which is generally more precise and convincing than that of Power. Holbert's treatment of the "verbal ironies" he finds in 4:7–11 of Eliphaz's speech is representative of his better evidence. He highlights

[18] Power, *A Study of Irony in the Book of Job,* 65.

[19] J. C. Holbert, *The Function and Significance of the "Klage" in the Book of "Job" with Special Reference to the Incidence of Formal and Verbal Irony* (Ph.D. Dissertation: Southern Methodist University, 1975).

[20] Holbert, *The Function and Significance of the "Klage,"* v.

four words, three of which are significant from the standpoint of Job's complaint of chap. 3 and one which may be understood as ironic from the perspective of the prologue.[21] For Holbert these "ironies" indicate that Eliphaz has already condemned Job as a wicked person.[22] Nevertheless, there remain several examples of rather unconvincing evidence which could be presented in this review. One, however, will suffice. From 9:17–18 Holbert isolates the word for "storm" (*śĕʿārâ*) and relates it to Eliphaz's vision of 4:12–17 where this word is used with the meaning of "hair" (4:15b). The irony which Holbert sees in this supposed connection is that Eliphaz's "hair" which a "breeze" (*rûaḥ*) has stood up on end has, in his words, "become God's 'awful storm.'"[23] This example is unconvincing as it is based on a connection between a word used in these two texts in a vastly different way. It is highly unlikely that the reference to a "storm" was even subtly intended to remind the reader of Eliphaz's "hair" upraised as a fearful reaction to a vision.

A further point might be raised over the understanding of "verbal irony" or "ironic interplay" as used in both Power's and Holbert's dissertations. Power speaks of this type of irony in terms of an intended meaning which is opposite to the literal sense. Similarly, Holbert clarifies in his conclusion that "verbal irony" exists in those ". . . instances where words and phrases mean something other than an obvious reading would yield."[24] Irony, understood in this fashion, is defensible yet prone to a certain amount of ambiguity. It is not altogether clear how several of the examples presented, especially by Holbert, may be understood as ironic because a meaning other than an "obvious" sense is a vague concept; and, as he concedes in his definition of "verbal irony," his purpose is to explore those repetitions which comment "usually ironically" on a previous speaker's words.[25] Although irony is a critical feature of Job, not every example

[21] The words or roots which Holbert (*The Function and Significance of the "Klage,"* 120–23) treats as significant are: *ʾābad,* "to perish" (used by Job in 3:3a and by Eliphaz in 4:7a, 9a, 11a), *ʿāmāl,* "trouble, misery" (used by Job in 3:10b and 20a, by Eliphaz in 4:8b), *šaʾăgât,* "groaning, roaring" (used by Job in 3:24b, and by Eliphaz in 4:10a), and *yāšār,* "upright" (used of Job in 1:8 and 2:3 of the prologue, and by Eliphaz in 4:7b).

[22] Yet in agreement with N. C. Habel (*The Book of Job* [1985] 121) Eliphaz is probably best understood as a friend rather than an accuser at this point in the book. Perhaps these indirect connections would be more accurately approached as doubts Eliphaz harbors concerning the moral character of Job which are, then, clearly stated later in the dispute.

[23] Holbert, *The Function and Significance of the "Klage,"* 164–65.

[24] Holbert, *The Function and Significance of the "Klage,"* 281.

[25] Holbert, *The Function and Significance of the "Klage,"* v.

of an interplay between speeches may be understood as ironic. Thus, in this study, proposals for connections between speeches will be examined simply as responses but without reference to irony unless it is obvious and requires comment.

Two articles published in Hebrew by N. Klaus are of direct interest for this study.[26] His aim, as stated in the first article, is to discover "associative-verbal connections" which link the various speeches together.[27] In these two articles, Klaus focuses on the speeches of the first cycle (chaps. 4–14). Both articles follow the same format. In terms of method, Klaus lays out the two related texts with the shared lexicographical items highlighted. Following this display, Klaus usually makes a brief comment on his interpretation of the correspondence, although on occasion he simply makes an observation of how the word(s) is used in each context and leaves the reader to draw his or her own conclusions. Many of Klaus' examples of responses are convincing[28] but his strong examples are, on the whole, weakened by the presence of less convincing proposals which are given equal weight. In general, Klaus' arguments for a response based on word repetition are strongest, but there are several instances where his argument appears forced. Not every incidence of word repetition should be understood as purposeful. After all, the vocabulary of any given language is finite. Consequently, certain words may be repeated in different speeches as a matter of course. Two examples from Klaus' work illustrate this point. After highlighting the word *rûaḥ* from 4:15a and 7:7a, Klaus comments:

> Job uses an identical word that Eliphaz used in the description of his vision of the night. In both cases the word *rûaḥ* is given two meanings: "wind" (7:7a) and "spirit" (4:15a).[29]

[26] I express my gratitude to Anna Urowitz who translated N. Klaus' first article, "Between Job and His Friends," *Beth Mikra* 31 (1985/86) 152–68, and to Ahouva Shulman for the translation of "Joban Parallels to Job," *Beth Mikra* 32 (1986/87) 45–56.

[27] Klaus, "Between Job and His Friends," 153.

[28] A sample of Klaus' better proposals might include: (a) the linkage of the word *ṣēl* ("shadow") which is given to Bildad in 8:9b after this word is used by Job in 7:2a (Klaus, "Between Job and His Friends," 162); (b) Zophar's use of the verb *šûb* ("to hinder, stop") in 11:10b which follows from 9:12a where this verb is put on Job's lips (Klaus, "Joban Parallels to Job," 47); and (c) Zophar's quip concerning a *pere'* ("wild donkey," 11:12b) which relates to Job's query about a *pere'* in 6:5a (Klaus, "Joban Parallels to Job," 48).

[29] Klaus, "Between Job and His Friends," 159.

In this example, Klaus only informs the reader how the word is used in the context of each speech and falls short of explaining how he understands this word might function as a response to Job. Above all, the fact that this word is used with two different meanings in two very different contexts makes it quite unlikely that an interplay was ever intended. It is more logical to assume that this occurrence is simply a case of a common word coincidentally used in two successive speeches.

A second example of a weak proposal based on word repetition involves the expression *mî-yittēn* ("O that") as it occurs in 6:8a and 11:5a. On this correspondence, Klaus comments: "Zophar answers the challenge and says to him: 'May God grant your request, and then you will realize that your punishment is very small compared to your sin.'"[30] Klaus' explanation makes some sense but one is hesitant to ascribe such significance to two distant texts which are linked only by the words *mî-yitten*. If such a response was intentionally built into the text, then one would expect a better clue such as a partial quotation or a paraphrase which would link these two passages together in a more obvious manner. Previously, it was stated that the connections between the speeches are typically subtle, indirect and therefore easily overlooked. Yet there must be limits to this subtlety, especially when dealing with passages which are separated by intervening speeches.

Finally, in his most recent commentary on the Book of Job, N. C. Habel gives attention to the interrelationships between the speeches themselves and the links between the speeches and the prologue and epilogue, all of which he refers to as "literary connections." On this subject Habel writes:

> Contrary to the opinion of some scholars, the book of Job is not a disparate collection of narration and speech materials with relatively little internal cohesion or connection. We have argued above that the underlying narrative plot of Job provides an integrating framework for the book as a whole. To this argument can be added evidence from the author's technique of verbal allusion and motif repetition. The artist's way of integrating materials does not reflect a pedantic, point-for-point correspondence between argument and rebuttal, or between challenge and response. The approach is tangential; verbal associations are made by indirect allusion; and literary connections are often playful.[31]

[30] Klaus, "Joban Parallels to Job," 47.

[31] Habel, *The Book of Job* (1985) 50–51.

As Habel observes, the speeches do not follow the format of a modern debate where a speaker will quote systematically from an opponent to refute his or her arguments. Rather in this work subtlety and indirection are the norm for response, and for this reason the connections are easily and often overlooked. Unlike Power's and Holbert's sometimes loose and consequently weak examples of ironic interplay, Habel's examples are for the most part based on clear word repetition which carry more weight. From the many instances presented by Habel, the table of the various connections between the latter half of Zophar's first speech (11:13–20) and Job's previous speeches adequately illustrates his position.[32] In his subsequent section entitled, "Message in Context," Habel comments on the significance of these connections.[33] A typical example of Habel's approach is his observation concerning Zophar's assurance that Job will be able to lift (*nāśā'*) his face if he will turn to God (11:15a). In Habel's view, this comment stems from Job's previous complaint that he is not able to lift (*nāśā'*) his head due to his shame (10:15b).[34]

Habel's sensitivity to the presence of such connections and sound judgment, evident from his explication of their significance, makes his commentary the most solid work in this area of research. Although his verbal associations are not always accepted, and the implications he draws from accepted associations are not necessarily affirmed, his outlook and approach remain a positive influence on this study.

Over and above the manner in which the published findings have confirmed a suspicion of subtle links between the speeches themselves, and between the speeches and the narrative portions of the book, this review has isolated three of the pitfalls associated with this type of research. First, unless the evidence for a response is particularly strong an appeal to texts separated by one or more speeches should be avoided. Second, some proposals for a connection between texts will be clearer and stronger than others. If all the evidence is argued for with equal force, the less convincing examples will weaken the overall argument. In order to build the strongest possible argument, it is expedient to present the most convincing evidence first and to follow with examples which are less

[32] Habel, *The Book of Job* (1985) 205–6.
[33] Habel, *The Book of Job* (1985) 206–11.
[34] Habel, *The Book of Job* (1985) 210.

convincing on their own.[35] If a convincing case can be built on the strength of the clearest evidence, then it follows that the less obvious proposals might also be conceivable as part of the overall pattern of responses. Third, one must remain open to the possibility that a word repetition between two speeches may simply be coincidental. After all, every language has a limited vocabulary at a given time and biblical Hebrew has a relatively restricted number of words. Further, if a word occurs frequently throughout the disputation, then it is unlikely that a convincing case can be made for a specific connection unless it is one of two or more words which together form the response.[36]

In addition, one must guard against reading too much into a vague correspondence which requires an excessively complicated and unnatural explanation. One may argue that the poet purposefully and artfully composed each speech in view of what precedes it, but the significance of a specific response should be such that an alert reader, who is open to this possibility, would be able to make sense out of them in a straightforward manner.

As can be seen from the work of those scholars who tie the speeches together, connections are not restricted to any one subsection of the speeches. To identify and discuss the significance of every conceivable connection within the Book of Job would be an exhausting task and lies beyond the scope of this study. At the outset the researcher must make a choice as to what portions of the book will be covered. One could pursue the connections which might be uncovered within a major section of the book such as the first cycle of speeches, or one could examine a specific portion of each speech from the three cycles for the possibility of a response to previous texts. If the speeches do in fact show some measure of a response to each other, then it is conceivable that developments along these lines may present themselves in an approach which examines a larger

[35] If none of the examples from a given passage stands out as stronger than the others, then in this study they will be approached in sequential order.

[36] For this reason certain word repetitions will be rejected as insignificant and recorded as such in the footnotes. For the information of the reader, whenever word repetition is cited as evidence for a response, a note will follow indicating how often a word occurs in Job. Unless there is good reason to relate a word with an earlier occurrence of the same word separated by one or more speeches, the repetition will be treated as insignificant. However, as any words which occur in earlier chapters could, for argument's sake, affect the significance of a later occurrence of that word, these earlier references will be cited by chapter and verse.

portion of the book as opposed to one which is restricted to one particular cycle of speeches. With this possibility in mind, the focus of this research will be on a specific subsection from the speeches of chaps. 4–24.

In my preliminary research, several instances were observed where the opening lines of one speech related to something the speaker of the immediately preceding speech said in his opening lines. Job's wish that the friends would be "silent" (*ḥāraš,* 13:5a), for example, relates to Zophar's inference that Job's speeches have effectively "silenced" (*ḥāraš,* 11:3a) Eliphaz and Bildad. As the introductory verses of at least a few of the speeches provide some evidence of connections between the speeches, and as these verses may be isolated from their respective speeches as literary units, the focus of this study will be on these units with a view to how they might respond to previous statements or texts within the Book of Job. For practical purposes these introductory units or strophes will be referred to as "introductions." This designation, however, does not imply that these units have a common, predictable form or structure. It simply means they fall at the beginning of a speech or poem.[37]

This work builds on the research of Gordis, Power, Holbert, Klaus, and Habel. Consequently, some of the proposals put forward below will not be original to this study. Yet, as the introductory portions of the speeches or of the major subsections within a speech will be studied in greater detail than in the work by the above scholars, the reader will find that the majority of proposals for connections are new to this work. The appendix will show the connections made by the above scholars prior to this research as well as the connections proposed by the present writer.

Moreover, as this study will examine the speeches as responses to preceding speeches, chap. 3 will be dealt with indirectly as it is the opening discourse of the disputation, and only insofar as Eliphaz's first speech (chaps. 4 and 5) appears to offer a response to it. Also, the speeches of chaps. 25, 26 and 27 will not be studied as explained in chap. 4, as this portion of the book is problematic. In addition, no clear examples for a response are apparent in the sections of these speeches which might be approached as introductory units. In addition, so as not to overlook further possibilities of connections between texts, each introductory unit of a speech will be closely scrutinized for links to the whole of the

[37] Three of the speeches which will be dealt with (chaps. 4–5, 6–7, 12–14) may be divided into two or three subsections which will be called "poems." It follows that each poem will have its own particular "introduction" or "introductory" strophe.

immediately preceding speech as well as to any other earlier speeches and to the prologue.

The approach best suited for this study is that known as "rhetorical criticism." First advocated by J. Muilenburg in his presidential address delivered at the 1968 annual meeting of the Society of Biblical Literature,[38] this distinctive method aims to move beyond the general and typical features of the text as highlighted by form critical studies to its "individual, personal and unique characteristics."[39] A form-critical analysis of the passages of interest is useful for drawing out their common characteristics but is not well suited for the pursuit of their more idiosyncratic features; and it is through these more atypical features that literary connections are established between passages.

The rhetorical critic is concerned with the structure of a clearly delimited passage and so focuses his or her attention on the various rhetorical devices which give the literary unit its shape. One device of interest to the rhetorical critic is the repetition of a key word which, as Muilenburg observes, gives the passage its "unity and focus."[40] C. Isbell, for example, explores the role such key words play in the various literary units which make up the first two chapters of the Book of Exodus.[41] He also focuses on key words shared by more than one literary unit. To differentiate between these two kinds of key words, he calls the former type "intra-unit key words" and the latter "inter-unit key words."[42] Our primary interest is not so much with "inter-unit *key* words" but simply with "inter-unit words" which connect various texts in the Book of Job in such a way that they form the basis of a response.

The evidence for a response in the Book of Job, however, is sometimes more subtle than the adoption of a specific word or phrase. One must therefore watch also for synonyms and thematic correspondences which hint at a response in a more indirect manner. A specific word or root repetition will, in general, be viewed as the strongest evidence for a response as it is the clearest. The term "allusion" will be used to denote

[38] J. Muilenburg, "Form Criticism and Beyond," *JBL* 88 (1969) 1–18.

[39] Muilenburg, "Form Criticism and Beyond," 5.

[40] Muilenburg, "Form Criticism and Beyond," 17.

[41] C. Isbell, "Exodus 1–2 in the Context of Exodus 1–14; Story Lines and Key Words," in *Art and Meaning: Rhetoric in Biblical Literature* (ed. D. J. A. Clines *et al;* JSOTSup 19; Sheffield, England: JSOT, 1982) 37–59.

[42] Isbell, "Exodus 1–2 in the Context of Exodus 1–14," 38.

a synonym which appears to tie two passages together. Unless fairly strong, an allusion will usually be accorded less weight than word repetition. The least weight will be given to a thematic connection, the term which will be used to indicate a link between two passages on the basis of similar subject matter rather than by shared vocabulary or through the employment of synonyms.

In order to build the argument that the speeches do in some way respond to one another, the evidence must be approached systematically. First, and central to the method of rhetorical criticism, is the delimitation of the passages of interest. Once the limits of a passage are clarified, the translation will follow accompanied with text-critical notes. Next, attention will be given to the form and structure of the passage, the purpose of which is to facilitate the discussion of the features which the introductory units have in common in the final chapter of this study.[43] The following section for each passage studied will be entitled "rhetorical analysis" and will consist of two subsections. In the first subsection, the

[43] In terms of genre, scholars do not agree on the overall form of the book. W. Whedbee ("The Comedy of Job," *Semeia* 7 [1977] 1–39) considers Job a comedy in the classical sense of the term. C. Westermann (*The Structure of the Book of Job: A Form Critical Analysis* [Philadelphia: Fortress, 1981] 12) classes this work as a lament, although he admits that it is ". . . depicted as a disputation." H. Gese (*Lehre und Wirklichkeit in der alten Weisheit* [Tübingen: Evangelische, 1958] 64–66) sees it as a "*Klageehörungsparadigma*," i.e., a "paradigm of an answered lament." H. Richter (*Studien zu Hiob,* Theologische Arbeiten 11 [Berlin: J. C. B. Mohr, 1959]) stresses its legal nature and classes it as a judicial work, as does B. Gemser ("The *rīb*-or Controversy Pattern in Hebrew Mentality," VTSup 3 [1960] 134–35) who speaks of it as a *rîb* or court trial. G. Fohrer (*Das Buch Hiob,* 50–53) recognizes the weakness of stressing one aspect of the work to the exclusion of others and writes that Job is a mixture of genres and that the speeches draw on elements from law, wisdom and the Psalms. Aware of the different genres inherent in this work, Pope (*Job,* xxxi) wisely stresses its unique character by referring to it as a *sui generis.* Alternatively, if one takes the work as a whole and makes allowance for its pecularities it may be compared with the Mesopotamian disputations such as the "Tamarisk and the Palm," "The Ox and the Horse," and "The Fable of the Fox" (see W. Lambert, *Babylonian Wisdom Literature* [Oxford: Oxford University, 1960] 151–64, 175–85, 186–209 for a translation of these writings) which have in common a mythological introduction and conclusion, a disputation, and an appearance by the deity who resolves the problem under discussion (cf. J. L. Crenshaw, *Old Testament Wisdom: An Introduction* [Atlanta: John Knox, 1981] 121 and Habel, *The Book of Job* [1985] 45). In this study, the Book of Job is approached as a disputation and in the overall context of the work each individual speech is understood to function as a disputation speech, although as isolated units some of Job's speeches may appear as complaints.

evidence of a response to the arguments uttered by one or more of the opponents will be presented. Incidences where a speech might refer to the prologue will also be noted as such connections strengthen the overall argument for a relationship between the speeches. The second subsection will offer an overview of the passage under study particularly from its perspective as a response to previous texts. The bulk of this work will consist of three chapters each devoted to a study of the introductions from chaps. 4–24 which belong to the three speech cycles of Job and his friends. The final chapter will consist of a conclusion preceded by a general discussion of the type of responses uncovered, the pattern of the connections presented (i.e., the idea that the introductions might be linked to the introduction(s) of the immediately preceding speaker will be assessed), and the form of the introductions studied including the subgenres present in their composition.

CHAPTER 2

The First Cycle

The First Speech of Eliphaz (chaps. 4–5) His Response to Job

Eliphaz's first speech consists of forty-eight lines and is by far the longest of any of the friends' contributions to the dispute.[1] On the basis of its exceptional length, Skehan and Murphy could well be correct that chaps. 4 and 5 fall into two major sections, although their dividing point and supporting argument is questionable.[2] E. C. Webster suggests, on thematic

[1] The second longest speech also belongs to Eliphaz (chap. 15 at thirty-four lines). Zophar's second speech (chap. 20) ranks third with twenty-eight lines. Most of the remaining speeches of the friends range from nineteen to twenty-one lines in length. In the Book of Job, a speech is understood as a major unit of poetry set off by the narrator's introductory line which identifies the speaker.

[2] See P. W. Skehan, "Strophic Patterns in the Book of Job," in *Studies in Israelite Poetry and Wisdom* (CBQMS 1; Washington: The Catholic Biblical Association of America, 1971) 97–108. R. E. Murphy, *Wisdom Literature* (FOTL 13; Grand Rapids, MI: Eerdmans, 1981] 19) adopts Skehan's approach to the structure of chaps. 4 and 5.

Skehan argues that the speeches of chaps. 4–14 are composed in units corresponding to the length of the Hebrew alphabet (i.e., on a twenty-two or twenty-three line pattern). In accordance with this hypothesis, Skehan considers chaps. 4 and 5 to consist of two "alphabet-length" compositions. The first piece, claims Skehan ("Strophic Patterns," 99 and 102), is a twenty-two line structure which extends from 4:2–5:2. The second piece (5:3-27) is classed by Skehan as a "twenty-three line plus one type composition."

There is, however, a lack of clear evidence concerning the supposed acrostic features of chaps. 4 and 5. Skehan ("Strophic Patterns," 101), for example, cites the initial consonants of the lines which form the first and fourth strophes of chap. 4 as evidence for

grounds, that Eliphaz's first speech consists of two poems corresponding to the chapter divisions. He states that the first poem (chap. 4) opens with Eliphaz's message of compassion and encouragement and concludes with his vision. The second poem (chap. 5), he writes, contrasts the fate of the fool with that of the righteous.[3] The divergent subject matter, cited by Webster as a basis for dividing this speech into two poems, is by itself admittedly weak. If this speech does in fact consist of two poems in agreement with the chapter division, as is suspected, then each poem should begin with an introductory strophe. After the delimitation and study of these two tentative strophes, further evidence will be offered to justify a division of this speech into two poems in support of Webster's position.

---

an "artificial pattern." The consonants in question read as follows: *h, h, k, k, h* (4:2–6); and *h, h, ', m, h* (4:17–21). Skehan ("Strophic Patterns," 98) states that "certain letters of the alphabet are favored to mark off beginnings of stanzas and compositions: *aleph,* for obvious reasons; *he,* more obscurely, but it is an observable fact." Even if it could be accepted that the first *he* of these strophes is significant for an acrostic arrangement, it is indeed difficult to see a clear acrostic pattern supportive of Skehan's position in the initial consonants of these two strophes. Further, Skehan ("Strophic Patterns," 102) maintains that "Four five-line strophes in this part [chap. 5] begin with *aleph.*" The first two strophes, which begin at vv 3 and 8, open with an *aleph,* but Skehan resorts to the excision of the *hinnēh* of v 17 as a gloss to obtain a leading *aleph* for this strophe. The fourth five-line strophe (vv 22–26), however, begins with *lamedh* and not an *aleph* as Skehan assumes. Hence one looks in vain for a fourth strophe opening with an *aleph.* Skehan's argument for an alphabetic pattern in these four strophes is weak as only two of three strophes feature a leading *aleph* as they stand. Finally, Skehan's approach to this speech leads him to make an unnatural division in the text. In order to attain a twenty-two line structure for chap. 4, he is compelled to take 5:1–2 as a strophe and append it to the preceding piece, whereas it is generally accepted that this unit extends to at least v 5 of chap. 5. See, for example, G. Fohrer (*Das Buch Hiob,* 135) and E. C. Webster ("Strophic Patterns in Job 3–28," *JSOT* 26 [1983] 39) who take 5:1–5 as a strophe. A. Weiser (*Das Buch Hiob* [Göttingen: Vandenhoeck and Ruprecht, 1951] 50–51), S. Terrien (*Job* [CAT 13; Paris: Delachaux et Niestlé, 1963] 74), F. Horst (*Hiob 1–19* [BKAT 16; Neukirchen-Vluyn: Neukirchener, 1968] 63), Habel (*The Book of Job,* 118), P. van der Lugt ("Stanza-structure and Word-repetition in Job 3–14," *JSOT* 40 [1988] 8–9), and D. J. A. Clines (*Job 1–20* [WBC 17; Dallas: Word Books, 1989] 119) extend this unit to the end of v 7.

[3] Webster, "Strophic Patterns in Job 3–28," 38. Based on his analysis of the poetic structure of chaps. 4 and 5, P. van der Lugt ("Stanza-structure and Word-repetition in Job 3–14," 6–9) concurs with Webster's decision that Eliphaz's first speech consists of two poems. Following Webster and van der Lugt, the term "speech" will be used for the entire message attributed to a particular speaker. When a speech may be broken down into two or more major units these passages will be called "poems."

The first poem obviously begins with 4:2. Of those scholars who divide the poetry of the Book of Job into strophes or sections, there are basically two viewpoints. F. Horst, H. H. Rowley, and N. C. Habel divide the first portion of the speech into a fairly lengthy section extending to the end of v 11.[4] Yet, G. Fohrer, S. Terrien, P. W. Skehan, E. C. Webster and P. van der Lugt believe the introductory strophe ends with v 6.[5] A comparison of 4:7 with 5:1 is helpful for deciding where this strophe should end. Most scholars agree that 5:1 marks the beginning of a new strophe.[6] The first verse of chapter 5 opens with an imperative, to which is linked the particle *nā'*, followed by two rhetorical questions. As 4:7 and 5:1 are composed in a similar manner, it is likely that both of these verses mark the first line of a new strophe. In addition, 4:7 introduces a new theme—that of retribution—a further indication that this verse stands out as the beginning of a new strophe.[7] Thus, in agreement with Fohrer *et al.* (above), the introductory strophe to the poem of chap. 4 likely incorporates only vv 2–6.

With regard to the opening of the second poem to this speech, Fohrer and Webster take v 5 as the end of the first strophe in chap. 5, although Weiser, Terrien, Horst, Habel, and van der Lugt extend the strophe to the end of v 7.[8] In view of the fact that the sayings of vv 6–7 are based

[4] Horst, *Hiob 1–19,* 63; H. H. Rowley, *Job* (NCB; London: Marshall, Morgan and Scott, 1976) 45; and Habel, *The Book of Job,* 118. D. J. A. Clines (*Job 1–20,* 119) takes vv 2–11 as a major strophe which may be divided into smaller units of vv 2–6 and 7–11.

[5] Fohrer, *Das Buch Hiob,* 134; Terrien, *Job* (1963) 134; Skehan, "Strophic Patterns," 99; Webster, "Strophic Patterns in Job," 38–39; and van der Lugt, "Stanza Structure and Word-Repetition in Job 3–14," 6–7.

[6] Fohrer, *Das Buch Hiob,* 135; Webster, "Strophic Patterns in Job 3–28," 39; Weiser, *Das Buch Hiob,* 50–51, Terrien, *Job,* 74; Horst, *Hiob 1–19,* 63; Habel, *The Book of Job* (1985) 118; and van der Lugt, "Stanza-Structure and Word-Repetition in Job 3–14," 8–9.

[7] Note W. G. E. Watson's (*Classical Hebrew Poetry* [JSOTSup 26; Sheffield, England: JSOT, 1984] 163) observations on strophic division:

> It is generally agreed that (a) stanza division tends to be based on content, (b) that there are certain stanza-markers showing where stanzas begin and/or end . . . and (c) there are no hard and fast rules which can be applied to all cases. It is, to some extent, a matter of feel.

(Note that Watson prefers to use the word "stanza" for the major divisions within a poem and reserves "strophe" for the subdivisions within a stanza. As the majority of scholars prefer the term "strophe" for the thematic subsections of Hebrew poetry, this term is adopted for this work.)

[8] See the references listed at the end of n. 2.

on the observations concerning fools (vv 3–5), we concur with the decision of these latter scholars. In addition, since Eliphaz's counsel to appeal to God in v 8 (which in turn introduces a hymnic portrayal of God's power on earth [vv 8–16]) marks a shift in theme, v 7 is best taken as the close of the first strophe of chap. 5.

With the limits of these two passages (4:2–6; 5:1–7) clearly established, they will now be studied in greater detail so as to establish how they respond to Job's complaint of chap. 3.

The Introduction to Part I of the First Speech of Eliphaz (with the Narrator's Opening Statement)

4:1 Then Eliphaz the Temanite answered and said:
2 If one dares a word with you, could you bear it?
But who is able to refrain from speaking?
3 Look, you have instructed the elderly[9]
and strengthened weak hands.
4 Your speech uplifted those who stumble
and braced those with bent knees.
5 But now it happens to you and you falter;
it touches you and you are horrified.
6 Should not your fear (of God)[10] be your confidence
and your hope the very[11] integrity of your ways?

Form

Fohrer is of the opinion that this passage can either be considered as wisdom disputation or court disputation.[12] Murphy classifies both chaps.

[9] The noun *rabbîm* refers to the elderly in 32:9. In view of the reference to "weak hands" in v 3b, it is conceivable that *rabbîm* has the same meaning here. See M. Dahood, "Hebrew-Ugaritic Lexicography V," *Bib* 48 (1967) 425; A. R. Ceresko, *Job 29–31 in the Light of Northwest Semitic* (Rome: Pontifical Biblical Institute, 1980) 156–57; and W. L. Michel, *Job in the Light of Northwest Semitic* (Rome: Pontifical Biblical Institute, 1987) 81.

[10] The noun *yir'â* means "piety" and is elliptical for the "fear of God" (cf. 6:14b).

[11] The *waw* can be read emphatically (R. J. Williams, *Hebrew Syntax: An Outline* [2d ed; Toronto: University of Toronto, 1976] §438). Cf. A. C. M. Blommerde, *Northwest Semitic Grammar and Job* (Rome: Pontifical Biblical Institute, 1969) 40. The adjective "very" is adopted from Habel's translation (*The Book of Job* [1985], 115).

[12] Fohrer, *Das Buch Hiob,* 134. The former category he calls a "*Streitgespräche der Weisen*" and the latter a "*Parteireden vor der Rechtsgemeinde.*" For a brief discussion of these forms see pp. 50–51 of his commentary.

4 and 5 under the general category of "disputation speech." This decision, as Murphy explains, avoids the pitfalls associated with proposing a specific setting for the various subgenres employed in this speech and exhibits a sensitivity to the "broad perspective" of the work as a whole.[13] Thus, following Murphy, it is preferred to view 4:2–6 as a segment of a larger disputation speech.

Verse 2 consists of a twofold rhetorical question composed in indirect speech. As Westermann observes, this verse functions as a "pardoning introduction."[14] Eliphaz reminds Job of his past exemplary service in vv 3–4 as a means to influence his present behavior (v 5). The rhetorical questions of v 6 recommend a specific course of action. Fohrer identifies vv 3–6 as a warning.[15] Eliphaz, however, does not make threats, nor does he speak of the danger of Job's current state in these verses. This section, therefore, is best approached as Eliphaz's counsel or advice offered to Job. The structure of 4:1–6 may be outlined as follows:

	Announcement of response: Eliphaz replies to Job		(4:1)
1	Pardoning remarks (in the form of indirect rhetorical questions)		(2)
	(a)	Request for permission to speak	(2a)
	(b)	Compulsion to speak	(2b)
2	Advice		(3–6)
	(a)	Reminder of past service	(3–4)
	(b)	Description of present behavior	(5)
	(c)	Recommended course of action (rhetorical questions)	(6)

[13] Murphy, *Wisdom Literature,* 24. Murphy (pp. 175–176) defines a "disputation" as:

> An argument between two or more parties, in which differing points of view are held. The disputation is an overarching genre that can designate the discussions of wise men (cf. Job), or parties in court, or prophet and people (cf. Jer 2:23–28).

In the disputation itself, a vast array of subgenres can be employed, drawn from judicial practice, worship, the world of wisdom, etc. In his discussion of genre, Murphy observes that several such elements exist in Job but warns that one must avoid taking them out of their present context and speculating on a possible original setting (pp. 16–20). Of elements drawn from a judicial setting, Murphy writes (p. 18):

> This is particularly true of the legal subgenres; we have no real knowledge of due process in ancient Israel, and to reconstruct it from Job is working in a vicious circle. The speeches of Job and his friends can rightly be classified as DISPUTATION SPEECHES [capitals his], which employ various subgenres.

[14] Westermann, *The Structure of the Book of Job,* 20.

[15] Fohrer, *Das Buch Hiob,* 134, 135–36.

In agreement with Murphy, we approach the Book of Job as a disputation which draws upon the wisdom tradition, the Psalms, and judicial practice. As the evidence needed to establish a specific, original setting (wisdom or judicial) is inconclusive, the speeches or parts thereof studied will be identified simply as disputation.

Rhetorical Analysis

(1) The Connections between 4:2–6 and Previous Passages

A careful reading of 4:2–6 reveals three words (*tiqwâ* and *derek* of v 6b, *bāhal* of v 5b) which link this introduction to Job's complaint of chap. 3[16] and three words (*nāga*ʿ of v 5b; *yir'â* of v 6a; and *tōm* of v 6b) which recall the prologue.

The clearest example of a relationship between 4:2–6 and chap. 3 involves the nouns *tiqwâ* ("hope") and ("way") of 4:6b and their roots, which occur in 3:9b and 3:23a respectively. In 3:9 Job uses the verb *qāwâ* ("to hope") in his wish that the hope for light by the day of his birth be frustrated.[17] For Job this is a hopeless situation. In contrast, Eliphaz is given a response to this wish (4:6b) which advises Job not to give up but to "hope" for restoration (cf. 4:7).[18] Next, the term, *derek*, is uttered by Job in 3:23a, where he accuses God of blocking his "way" or "life purpose."[19] The reader is to understand that Eliphaz rejects Job's contention of 3:23a, for in his speech *derek* is used in a positive context consonant with his hopeful stance.[20] Thus Eliphaz recalls Job's past so

[16] An additional noun, *birkayim* ("knees"), appears only in 3:12a and 4:4b of Job. In the former reference, Job questions why "the knees" of his parents received him if his life was to come to such misery. In the latter reference, Eliphaz, in his reply, also uses this word when he recalls Job's past actions of strengthening those who were weak in "the knees." The context of each occurrence, however, does not support an interplay.

[17] The verb *qāwâ* occurs five times in Job, four of which appear in passages following Eliphaz's first speech.

[18] The noun *tiqwâ* appears twelve times in Job. Beyond the two occurrences in Eliphaz's first speech (4:6; 5:16), the remaining references are found in the following chapters. The use of *tiqwâ* in 5:16a, although with reference to the poor, could also be read in relation to Job's feelings of hopelessness (3:19) as a recommendation that Job, like the poor, should have hope.

[19] The translation "life purpose" is adopted from Habel, *The Book of Job* (1985) 111–12.

[20] The noun *derek* is a fairly common word in Job, occurring a total of thirty-two times. All but two of these occurrences (discussed above) are found in passages following chap. 5.

as to recommend that the integrity of his "way" be a source of "hope" in his time of trial (4:6b). The nouns *yir'â* ("fear") and *tōm* ("integrity") in v 6 strengthen this interpretation as they serve to remind Job of the type of person he was once reputed to be as written in the prologue: a "blameless (*tām*) man who "feared" (*yr'*) God (1:1, 8; 2:3). The logic of the dialogue presumes that Job's reputation was known to his friends. That Eliphaz speaks of Job's tragedy as "touching him" (*nāga'*) is ironic, however, since unbeknownst to Eliphaz it recalls the prologue where Yahweh grants the Satan permission to "touch" Job and his possessions (1:11; 2:5).

Given the correspondences between 4:2–6 and chap. 3 afforded by the nouns *tiqwâ* and *derek,* it is conceivable that the verb *bāhal* (v 5b)[21] might relate to Job's expressions of fear (*yāgōr, pāḥad;* 3:25),[22] as a further response, by way of allusion. It is evident in chap. 3 that Job believes his fear is a legitimate expression of his trauma. Eliphaz, however, speaks of Job's fear in a critical manner in 4:5–6. The proximity of *bāhal* (v 5b) to *yir'â* (v 6a) is significant and in the light of the connection of *yir'â* with Job in the prologue, it is likely that Eliphaz, mindful of Job's attitude toward his fear, recommends that the only fear Job should experience is the "fear of God."

(2) An Overview of 4:2–6 with Attention to the Proposed Connections

With the request for permission to speak (v 2a), the poet creates the impression that Eliphaz is sensitive to his friend's plight. That Eliphaz is given indirect speech at the outset furthers the initial, conciliatory tone and marks a cautious entry into the dispute. Such an urbane and tactful opening adds a note of realism to the debate as it should be understood as an attempt to placate Job so that he might be more receptive to Eliphaz's advice.

The second rhetorical question is also worded impersonally and reveals a compulsion to speak. The impersonal aspect of this question suggests

[21] In the contents preceding chap. 6, the verb *bāhal* occurs only in this one text. Elsewhere in Job it appears five times.

[22] The verb *yāgōr* occurs in Job only here and in 9:28. The verb *pāḥad* is used in 3:25, 4:14, and in 23:15. The second reference speaks of Eliphaz's reaction to his vision and does not directly tie in with Job's fear.

that anyone who might have heard Job's opening speech would be driven to reply. Hence this question highlights the provocative nature of Job's complaint in chap. 3.[23]

The verb *lāʾâ* (4:2a, 5a) means essentially "to be tired, exhausted." The clause of v 2a, therefore, literally reads, "would you be exhausted?" The second time Eliphaz employs *lāʾâ* (v 5a), it appears to mean "to falter" in the sense of a moral failure. In the light of this rebuke, it seems that Eliphaz's real concern of v 2a is that the message he delivers might be offensive to Job and consequently ignored—thus the translation, "could you bear it?" Under the surface the poet signals to the reader that Eliphaz is prepared for a confrontation.

In the first section of this introduction (v 2), Eliphaz begins with an attempt to pacify Job. He also alludes to the offensive nature of Job's opening speech which prepares for the advice of the second part of this text (vv 3–6). In this section Eliphaz first reminds Job of his exemplary past service administered to those in need. As the aged (v 3a) are reputed to be wise (cf. 12:12), Job's capacity to guide them indicates that he is even wiser than they. In v 5 Eliphaz focuses on Job's current state and rebukes him for failing to cope with his own plight.

In W. J. A. Power's opinion, Eliphaz insinuates "that Job's religion and piety were faked . . . that his righteous acts were hypocritical."[24] This interpretation is too extreme. Eliphaz does not reject Job's past as mere fakery but exploits it in an effort to call him back or shame him to emulate his true self. This approach is clearly evident in vv 5 and 6 which reflect details from the prologue and aspects of Job's opening speech. Thus Job should abandon his "fear" (3:25) and reclaim the "confidence"[25] which results from the kind of piety (i.e., one's "fear" of God) Job once practiced (1:1, 8; 2:3). Further, Eliphaz's positive references to the "hope" offered by the "integrity" of his "ways" hark back both to the negative

[23] The curse on one's own life, to mention one source of irritation to Eliphaz, could be considered an indirect curse against one's creator.

[24] W. J. A. Power, *A Study of Irony in the Book of Job,* 41.

[25] Y. Hoffman ("The Use of Equivocal Words in the First Speech of Eliphaz [Job 4–5]," *VT* 30 [1980] 114–19) argues that *kislâ* is one of several ambivalent words that possibly reveals Eliphaz's true stance toward Job. As Hoffman points out, the root *ksl* can mean either "stupidity, folly" or "confidence, hope." The former definition, according to Hoffman, yields the meaning "was not your awe of God, your honesty, your hope, just a result of your stupidity" (pp. 115–16)? Hoffman's suggestion is unlikely because Eliphaz's counsel (4:3–6) is based on Job's past faithfulness.

connotations attached to these terms in 3:9b and 3:23a (respectively) and to Job's recent past as recorded in the prologue (1:1, 8; 2:3). An appreciation of the uplifting manner in which these words are employed in 4:6b draws out the pastoral tone of Eliphaz's initial counsel.

The Introduction to Part II of the First Speech of Eliphaz

5:1 Call now! Will anyone answer you?
To which of the holy ones will you turn?
2 Surely indignation slays the fool,
and passion kills the simple.
3 I saw a fool taking root,
and immediately I said his dwelling would be cursed,[26]
4 his sons would be far from safety,
crushed in the gate without a deliverer,
5 the Hungry One would consume his harvest,
the Dry One would take his possessions,
the Thirsty One would pant after his wealth.[27]

[26] The MT reads *wā'eqqôb. As v* 3 relates an experience, it is likely that vv 4–5 provide the supposed details rather than the components of an actual curse (against Michel, *Job in Light of Northwest Semitic,* 107). Scholars deal with this text in various ways. Pope (*Job,* 42) follows the LXX and construes the verb as a passive. A. Guillaume (*Studies in the Book of Job, with a New Translation* [Leiden: Brill, 1968] 81) reads the root as *'qb* and derives its meaning from the Arabic *waqaba* ("to become rotten"). He also draws on the Arabic *nawhun* ("shoot," of a plant) for the meaning of *nāwēhû* and translates, "And suddenly his shoots rotted" (p. 22). The verb is intelligible, however, as *qābab* and following R. Gordis (*The Book of Job: Commentary, New Translation, and Special Notes* [New York: Jewish Theological Seminary of America, 1978] 42) makes good sense as a declarative: "But I declared folly's dwelling to be cursed." Cf. Habel, *The Book of Job* (1985), 117.

[27] As commonly asserted, this verse is difficult. Horst (*Hiob 1–19,* 59) omits it from his translation (p. 94). With the mythological reference in v 7b ("sons of Reshef"), Habel's suggestion (*The Book of Job,* 117) of *rā'ēb* as "the Hungry One" (v 5a) and *ṣammîm* (revocalized as *ṣĕmē'îm*) as "the Thirsty Ones" (v 5c) is favored. Following Michel (*Job in the Light of Northwest Semitic,* 110), however, we prefer to read *sammîm* as a "majestic plural." N. H. Tur-Sinai (*The Book of Job* [Jerusalem: Kiryath Sepher, 1957] 96) redivides the text of v 5b to yield *wĕ'ulām* and *ṣinnîm* and relates *'ulām* to *'ûl,* a variant of *'ĕyāl,* "strength." Since *'ulām* is parallel to *ḥêlām,* Tur-Sinai reasons that it likely means "power, possession, wealth." The word *sinnîm* probably vocalized as *ṣānnîm,* in his opinion, derives from the root *ṣānam* "to dry up." Hence his translation: "And death taketh their possessions" (p. 94). Tur-Sinai's approach is helpful, yet if one takes into account Michel's

6 Indeed[28] evil comes from the dust,
and trouble sprouts from the ground.
7 For a human is born to trouble
as[29] the sons of Reshef[30] fly upward.

Form

As with 4:2–6, this passage is a subsection of the disputation speech which takes in chaps. 4 and 5. The opening imperative of the first colon issues a challenge to call out for help. The following rhetorical questions imply that there is no one who will respond. Fohrer suggests that the verbs *qārā'* and *'ānâ* should be understood as legal terms,[31] but without further corroborating evidence from this passage these words are best considered typical of disputation in general.

It appears that v 2 may be a quotation of a wisdom saying (cf. Prov 14:30; 27:3).[32] As with most example stories (e.g., Prov 7:6–23; 24:30–34;

suggestion (*Job in the Light of Northwest Semitic,* 110) that "hunger" and "thirst" be understood as epithets of Mot, it is possible that "dry" might also connote Mot. (Note that the abode of the dead was thought to be a dry, waterless waste [Jer 2:31; Joel 2:20; Job 12:24–25], a place of dust [Pss 22:16c, 30b; Job 7:21; 17:16; 20:11; 21:26] and thirst [Isa 5:13–14; Jer 17:13b].) Thus we would have a tricolon with parallel components. (For a discussion on Death as the "Hungry One," see N. J. Tromp, *Primitive Conceptions of Death and the Nether World in the Old Testament* [Rome: Pontifical Biblical Institute, 1969] 107–10.)

[28] In the context of v 7, the negative particle *lō'* reads best as the asservative *lū'* in agreement with Pope, *Job,* 42 (cf. Habel, *The Book of Job* [1985] 117). Michel (*Job in the Light of Northwest Semitic,* 112–13) follows the first edition of Pope's commentary (*Job* [1965] 43) and reads *lō'* as the negative component of a rhetorical question.

[29] Reading the simple *waw* as a comparative (Williams, *Hebrew Syntax,* §437).

[30] The noun *rešep* can also mean "sparks, flame, lightning" (cf. S. R. Driver and G. B. Gray, *A Critical and Exegetical Commentary on the Book of Job* [ICC; Edinburgh: T. and T. Clark, 1921] 52). Terrien (*Job* [1963] 75) follows the LXX (*gupos*) and translates "eagles." With the reference to "dust" (*'āpār*) in v 6a, which frequently refers to the place of the dead (7:21; 17:16; 20:11; 21:26), the expression *běnê-rešep* likely denotes the Canaanite god, Reshef. M. Dahood (*Psalms I* [AB 16; Garden City, NY: Doubleday, 1965] 235) notes a Ugaritic text (1001:3) which tells of "Reshef the archer" and a fourth century Phoenician inscription bearing the name, "Reshef of the arrow." Further, Pope (*Job,* 42) cites a Ugaritic list of gods which identifies Reshef with the Mesopotamian Nergal, the god of pestilence and the netherworld.

[31] Fohrer, *Das Buch Hiob,* 146.

[32] Cf. Murphy, *Wisdom Literature,* 24; Habel, *The Book of Job* (1985) 131; and J. E. Hartley, *The Book of Job* (NICOT; Grand Rapids, MI: William B. Eerdmans, 1988) 117.

Qoh 4:13–16), vv 3–5 employ the verb *rāʾâ* in the first person. Rather than rehearsing the details of a story set in the past as do the example stories listed above, this story, based on experience, relates the perceived probable result of a certain lifestyle. Thus it might be called a "hypothetical" example story. In this context the story serves to illustrate the point of the saying in v 2, and, as Fohrer suggests, functions as a warning against anger.[33] Verses 6 and 7 also seem to be wisdom sayings.[34] They form the conclusion to this strophe and with their references to the underworld are closely related to v 5. The introduction to this poem may be outlined as follows:

1	Imperative: Challenge to call for help	(5:1aa)
2	Rhetorical questions: No one will help	(1ab–b)
3	Wisdom saying: Passion destroys the fool	(2)
4	Example story: The end of a fool	(3–5)
	(a) Observation of a fool's good fortune	(3a)
	(b) Declaration that the family dwelling will be cursed	(3b)
	(c) Exploitation of the offspring	(4)
	(d) Robbed by Death	(5)
5	Wisdom sayings	(6–7)
	(a) The Netherworld is the source of evil	(6)
	(b) The inevitability of trouble	(7)

Rhetorical Analysis

(1) The Connections between 5:1–7 and Previous Passages

Four words from Eliphaz's second introduction (*qābab,* v 3b, *lāqaḥ,* v 5b; *ʿāmāl,* vv 6b and 7a; and *yālad,* v 7a) appear to play on related words from chap. 3.

Job complains in chap. 3 of the "trouble" (*ʿāmāl,* v 10b) which he has experienced and questions why a person who endures such *ʿāmāl* (v 20a) should even be granted life in the first place.[35] As a result of his agony,

[33] Fohrer, *Das Buch Hiob,* 135.

[34] Murphy, *Wisdom Literature,* 24; and Habel, *The Book of Job* (1985) 119.

[35] In Job *ʿāmāl* appears nine times, four of which occur in texts following chap. 5. Four of the remaining texts will be discussed below (3:10, 20; 5:6, 7) as the former two

Job wishes that he had not been born (*yālad, v* 3a).[36] These texts suggest that Job is of the opinion that he and other faithful human beings should be protected from such trouble throughout their lives. Eliphaz, however, with the aid of the wisdom sayings of 5:6–7, presents the opposite point of view: "humans are born (*yld*) to trouble (*'āmāl*)." Job's intense reaction to his plight is, in his own eyes, a legitimate expression of one who was wronged by life. Yet Eliphaz is not sympathetic to this overreaction because tragedy is, in his view, a normal and expected fact of life.

In view of the connections established between 5:1–7 and chap. 3 on the basis of the use of the noun *'āmāl* and verb *yālad,* it is conceivable that the presence of the verbs *qābab* and *lāqaḥ* in these two texts are significant from the standpoint of a response. The verb *qābab* is used in Eliphaz's declaration concerning the certainty of a curse falling on a fool's house (5:3b). Previously, Job called upon the cursers (*'rr*) of the day to curse (*qbb*) the night of his conception (3:8a). In the light of Job's request for a curse, it seems that Eliphaz comes close to pronouncing that Job is under a curse in the relating of his example story. Perhaps the poet has Eliphaz react to Job's anger in such a way which suggests that he believes Job deserves the curse he requested.[37] The second verb, *lāqaḥ,* refers to Death personified's action of taking away the possessions of the fool in 5:5b.[38] Job uses this verb in his request that the gloom "take away" the night of his conception (3:6a). In view of this reference, Eliphaz possibly responds to Job's request with a subtle warning: "You would call upon the gloom to take away the night of your conception, but Death is nearer than you think and has already taken your possessions."

Beyond the connections with chap. 3, the example story of 5:3–5, particularly the reference to the probability of the oppression of the sons (*bānîm,* 5:4a) in the gate, is reminiscent of the fate which befalls Job's

appear to relate to the latter two which are located in an introduction. The fifth text (4:8) occurs in the body of Eliphaz's speech and also seems to respond to 3:10 and 20. As a reply to Job's complaint of trouble, Eliphaz, with the aid of a farming metaphor, suggests that Job experiences trouble because he initiated it.

[36] In addition to the two passages under discussion, the verb *yālad* occurs once in the prologue (1:2) and seven times in the chapters following chap. 5.

[37] That the verb *qābab* occurs in Job only in these two texts lends support to the idea that the latter reference might play on the former.

[38] The verb *lāqaḥ* occurs fifteen times in Job. Beyond the two present texts under examination, it appears four times in the prologue and nine times in the chapters following Eliphaz's first speech.

sons (*bānîm*)[39] and daughters in the prologue (1:18). Further, the mention of the loss of the accursed man's harvest, possessions, and wealth (5:5) could also be understood as an allusion to Job's loss of servants and livestock at the hand of the Satan (1:14–17). When the example story is read in the light of the similar episode in the prologue it appears that the poet has Eliphaz insinuate not just that Job deserves his requested curse but that he is apparently already under a curse. The implication would be that Job's situation is grave and that an immediate change in attitude is required.

(2) An Overview of 5:1–7 with Attention to the Proposed Connections

The negative answers expected from the rhetorical questions of v 1 are intended to convince Job that, at least for the present time, there is no one who will answer him from the heavens. In the meantime Job has recourse only to Eliphaz and his other two friends. By this means Eliphaz obtains by default permission to begin his speech anew. This opening performs a similar function as that of his "request for permission to speak" in 4:2.

If the wisdom saying of v 2 had currency among the people, then it would carry the authority of the wisdom tradition. If not, then its weight rests solely on its reliability as a verifiable, experiential truth of human behavior.[40] In either case, this saying is cited with the hope that Job will see himself reflected in its truth and consequently resolve his anger. Example stories, like wisdom sayings and the other teaching vehicles of the wise, build on common experience. This story (vv 3–5), however, holds greater power than the simple message to Job that fools meet a disastrous end. Incorporated into it are certain details with which Job could identify, namely, the curse on the family dwelling, the fate of the offspring, and the loss of possessions.[41] As with the wisdom saying of v 2, these

[39] The noun *bēn* occurs nineteen times in Job, seven times in the prologue and eleven times in the chapters following chap. 5.

[40] For a discussion on the role of observation in the acquisition of knowledge see J. L. Crenshaw, "The Acquisition of Knowledge in Israelite Wisdom Literature," *Word and World* 7 (1987) 245–52, esp. pp. 247–50.

[41] Cf. Habel, *The Book of Job* (1985) 131. K. Fullerton ("Double Entendre in the First Speech of Eliphaz," *JBL* 49 [1930] 334) was also open to this possibility. He comments that *pit'om* (v 3b) may be an allusion to the swift "visitations" of the prologue. F. Horst's

allusions prove especially relevant to Job. The purpose of Eliphaz's insinuations is to mirror Job's situation to such an extent that he might see himself in this story and subsequently modify his behavior.

Further, the association between the verbs *lāqaḥ* and *qābab* of the example story and chap. 3 (vv 6a and 8a, respectively), and the similarities with the fool's demise (5:3–5) and Job's situation as described in the prologue, suggest that Job's misfortunes stem from his own foolishness. It appears then that Eliphaz is not supportive of Job's reaction to his suffering.

The original wisdom saying cited in v 6 likely draws on negative agricultural experiences but, as Habel observes, it may also allude to the myth of the accursed ground in Gen 3:17–19.[42] The following saying of v 7 expresses the truth of the inevitability of human suffering. Together they stress the idea that such hardship comes from the underworld. Previously Job used the words *yālad* (3:3a) and *ʿāmāl* (3:10b, 20a) in contexts where it is presumed that human beings, such as himself, should be spared from intense suffering. These two words are put on Eliphaz's lips in the sayings of 5:6 and 7 to counter Job's viewpoint. Hence, according to Eliphaz, Job's anger is not justified as all human beings should expect to experience tragedy.

(3) Additional Evidence to Support a Division of Chapters 4 and 5 into Two Poems

With the analysis of 4:2–6 and 5:1–7 complete, further evidence may be offered to justify a division of the first speech of Eliphaz into two parts, each beginning with an introductory strophe. If 5:1–7 is an introduction to the poem of chap. 5, then one might expect it to bear some similarities with its immediate precursor (4:2–6), i.e., assuming that the poet may

position (*Hiob 1–9,* 80) that vv 3–5 do not allude to Job's fate and that of his children's is surprising. Similarly, D. J. A. Clines ("Job 5,1-8: A New Exegesis," *Bib* 62 [1981] 194) writes:

> It is unlikely that Eliphaz identifies Job, or invites Job to identify himself, with the "fool" of these verses. . . It is true that in 6:2 Job will acknowledge his *kaʿaś* but such an emotion on Job's part can hardly be hinted at by Eliphaz in the present passage. It is much more likely that the fool and his anger in vv 2f have nothing to do with Job, even by way of allusion, but are simply illustrations of the principle of retribution.

[42] Habel, *The Book of Job* (1985) 132.

have the beginning of one structure in mind when composing another. Four such similarities may be identified. First, all of Eliphaz's speeches begin with rhetorical questions (4:2; 15:2; 22:2) as do most of the friends' (except 20:2 and the problematic 25:2). Chapter 5:1 repeats this pattern. Second, both passages open with a concern to obtain permission to speak (4:2a; cf. 5:1). Third, the theme of anger in the wisdom saying of 5:2 builds on the inappropriateness of Job's behavior as observed in 4:5. Fourth, Eliphaz recalls Job's earlier good works in 4:3–4 to dissuade him from his present behavior. The example story of 5:3–5 presents a hypothetical experience with strong allusions to Job's situation. The intention of 5:3–5 is similar to 4:3–4 in that it serves to persuade Job to change his present disposition. In addition, it is noteworthy that the body of the poem of chap. 4 (vv 7–21) opens with an affirmation of hope (v 7). If 5:1–7 is taken as the introductory strophe of the poem of chap. 5, then the body (vv 8–27) also begins with an affirmation of hope (v 8).

The Second Speech of Job (chaps. 6–7)
His Response to Eliphaz

Terrien divides chaps. 6 and 7 into three poems: the first as a soliloquy (6:2–13), the second as an "invective" (6:14–30), and the third as a prayer (7:1–21).[43] Webster divides the speech in a similar fashion but classes the first and last poem as laments, and the middle piece he considers an indictment of the friends.[44] In his view the first section of the third poem is addressed to the friends (7:1–10), whereas the second half (7:11–21) is directed to God. The singular imperative *zĕkōr* ("remember") of v 7a, however, indicates that the first half of the chap. 7 addresses God as well.[45] The whole of chap. 6, however, speaks of God in the third person (vv 4a, c, 8b, 9, 10c, 14b),[46] and the friends are addressed directly in the latter half of the chapter with several second person plural verb forms

[43] Terrien, *Job* (1963), 79.

[44] Webster, "Strophic Patterns in Job 3–28," 39. Clines (*Job 1–20,* 167–68) also follows these divisions but identifies this speech as an "appeal" in the sense of a lament.

[45] Cf. Murphy, *Wisdom Literature,* 26. Conversely, Horst (*Hiob 1–19,* 98) takes 7:1–11 as addressed to the friends and treats the address of God in 7:7 as incidental.

[46] Cf. D. Patrick ("Job's Address of God," *ZAW* 91 [1979] 269), who observes that Job mentions God only in the third person in chaps. 3 and 6, whereas "Job bursts into address of God in chapter seven."

(see vv 22–29). Rather than dividing chap. 6 into two poems (as do Terrien and Webster), one might take the reproof of the friends (vv 14–30) as a complaint motif. Hence the friends are analogous to the enemies of the complaints in the Psalter (cf. Pss 4:3–4; 6:8–9; 17:9–12; 31:12–14).[47] Chapter 6, then, could be considered a unified complaint addressed to the friends. On the basis of the different addressees in chaps. 6 and 7, it is suggested that chap. 6 be considered a poem distinct from chap. 7.[48] Further support for this position is provided with the recognition of the *inclusio* formed with the noun *hayyâ* in 6:2b and what is probably a byform of this word (spelled *hawwâ*) in 6:30.[49]

As with Eliphaz's first speech, one would expect the two poems of chaps. 6 and 7 to open with introductory strophes. Habel makes the first division of chap. 6 after v 7 on the basis that the following unit (vv 8–13) deals with the theme of hope.[50] Irwin and others split this unit into two strophes: vv 2–4 and 5–7.[51] The clarification of the subject, represented by the pronoun *hēmmâ* ("they," v 7b), however, rules out a division of vv 2–7 into two strophes. One clue to the identity of this pronoun is provided by the simile, (literally) "like the sickness of my bread" (*kidwê*

[47] Cf. Murphy, *Wisdom Literature,* 25.

[48] Cf. Hartley, *The Book of Job,* 130 and van der Lugt, "Stanza-Structure in Job 3–14," 10. Habel (*The Book of Job* [1985] 141) similarly posits that these two chapters consist of two major parts but does so on the basis that chap. 6 is an indictment of the friends and chap. 7 is a lament directed to God. Our criticism is directed against his understanding of chap. 6, particularly vv 5–6, which he interprets as a negative allusion to the comfort provided by the friends (p. 146). These verses, as we shall see, more likely refer to the poison of the arrows (v 4ab). Thus Habel's first section of chap. 6 (vv 1–7) should be approached as a complaint about God's treatment of Job but directed to the friends (see Murphy's outline of this speech in *Wisdom Literature,* 25).

[49] Skehan ("Strophic Patterns," 102) followed by Murphy (*Wisdom Literature,* 25) divides chaps. 6–7 into two "alphabet" length speeches (6:2–23; 7:1–21) with 6:24–30 as a "transitional" passage. Skehan states that vv 28–30 point forward to the poem on humanity's "misfortune" in chap. 7. With the acceptance of the aforesaid *inclusio,* however, 6:28–30 must be understood as an integral part of the poem of chap. 6.

[50] Habel, *The Book of Job* (1985) 142. Cf. Weiser, *Das Buch Hiob,* 57; Janzen, *Job,* 78; and Hartley, *The Book of Job,* 130. Van der Lugt ("Stanza-Structure in Job 3–14," 10) takes vv 2–7 as a "sub-stanza" of vv 2–13.

[51] W. A. Irwin, "Poetic Structure in the Dialogue of Job," *JNES* 5 (1946) 34; G. Fohrer, *Das Buch Hiob,* 165; Skehan, "Strophic Patterns," 99; Webster, "Strophic Patterns in Job 3–28," 40; and Clines, *Job 1–20,* 167. Horst (*Hiob 1–19,* 98) approaches vv 2–4 and 5–7 as separate strophes but believes they function together as a larger unit incorporating vv 2–7.

laḥmî), which seems to refer to spoiled or diseased food. As the consumption of such food could bring illness or death through food poisoning, the most obvious antecedent for *hēmmâ* would be the poison arrows of v 4ab. Three further reasons in support of this hypothesis may be adduced as evidence. First, the pronoun *hēmmâ* and the noun *ḥiṣṣîm* of v 4a agree in gender (masculine) and number (plural). Second, the noun for "poison" (*ḥēmâ,* v 4b) is drawn into the relationship between *hēmmâ* and *ḥiṣṣîm* by virtue of its rhyme with *hēmmâ*. Third, the fact that *rûaḥ* (v 4b) and *nepeš* (v 7a) sometimes occur as a word-pair (e.g., Job 7:11 and 12:10) suggests a further association between vv 4 and 7, which is strengthened by the observation that these two nouns are used in this passage with the first person singular pronominal suffix. In the light of this argument and with the acceptance of Habel's rationale for considering vv 8–13 a separate unit, vv 2–7 will be treated as the introduction to the poem of chap. 6.

One possible objection to the proposed link between vv 4 and 7 is the apparent contradiction of meaning in vv 4b and 7a. Verse 4b states that Job's spirit consumes the poison of the arrows, yet in v 7a his *nepeš* ("soul, person") refuses to "touch" (*nāgaʿ*) them. The verb *nāgaʿ*, however, is capable of several meanings, and if it is interpreted with the sense "to reach" a new understanding is possible (see n. 61). In the opening complaint of chap. 3, Job expresses the desire to die. In 6:2–7 Job speaks as if God may be fulfilling his wish to die. It is likely, given the overall context of the issue, that the reader is to picture Job as refusing to reach for the arrows (in the sense of removing them), as he does not wish to take any action which may prolong his life.

Scholars generally divide the first portion of chap. 7 in four different ways. Fohrer and Horst class the first eleven verses as a major unit, but they disagree in their understanding of its strophic arrangement.[52] Second, according to Skehan, Murphy, and Webster, this passage is composed of three complete strophes: vv 1–3, 4–6, and 7–10 with v 11 opening a fourth.[53] The third approach, represented by Janzen and Hartley, advocates that the introductory unit encompasses the first six verses of the chapter.[54]

[52] Fohrer (*Das Buch Hiob,* 166) divides the passage into three strophes: vv 1–4, 5–8, and 9–11. Horst (*Hiob 1–19,* 98) has four strophes: vv 1–3, 4–5, 6–8 and 9–11.

[53] Skehan, "Strophic Patterns," 99; Murphy, *Wisdom Literature,* 25; and Webster, "Strophic Patterns in Job 3–28," 40.

[54] Janzen, *Job,* 80–81; and Hartley, *The Book of Job,* 142–43.

Lastly, Terrien and Habel extend the first division to v 8.[55] Terrien does not justify his decision, but Habel presents a convincing explanation of the unit based on his analysis of the entire structure of chap. 7.[56] He suggests that the chapter consists of three units (vv 1–8, 9–16, 17–21) framed with an opening axiom on the human condition (vv 1–2, 9–10, 17–18) and a closing taunt on the emptiness of life and the possible absence of Job (vv 7–8, 15–16, 21). On the basis of Habel's insightful analysis, the introductory strophe of chap. 7 is considered to consist of vv 1–8.

The Introduction to Part I of Job's Reply to Eliphaz (with the Narrator's Opening Statement)

6:1 Then Job answered and said:
2 If indeed[57] my indignation were weighed,
and all my ruin[58] laid on scales,
3 but now—it would be heavier than the sand of the sea;
therefore my words are rash.[59]
4 For the arrows of Shaddai are in me;
my spirit drinks their poison;
the terrors of Eloah are arrayed against me.
5 Does a wild ass bray over grass?
Does a bull bellow over fodder?
6 Can that which is tasteless be eaten without salt?
Is there flavor in slimy cream cheese?[60]

[55] Terrien, *Job* (1963) 79; and Habel, *The Book of Job* (1985) 153–54.

[56] See Habel, *The Book of Job* (1985) 153–55; Van der Lugt ("Stanza-Structure in Job 3–14," 12–13) adopts Habel's viewpoint and expands on his analysis of chap. 7.

[57] The conjunction *lû* expresses the optative mood "if only" (Williams, *Hebrew Syntax*, §460). The infinitive absolute of the root *šql* precedes the verb of the same root for emphasis. Hence the translation "if indeed."

[58] Although the LXX (*odunas mou,* "my pain, woe") and the versions read the *Qere, hawwātî* for *hayyātî,* the text may be explained as a byform of the *Qere.*

[59] The etymology of *lāʿû* is doubtful. Dhorme (*A Commentary on Job,* 76) suggests that the root is *lʿh* and draws on the modern Hebrew for the meaning "to be stammered out." N. H. Tur-Sinai (*The Book of Job,* 114) reads the root as *lwʿ*, yet similar to E. Dhorme, renders it "to stammer," based on his reading of Obad 16. Such a translation is inconsistent with the display of Job's eloquence in chap. 3. A more appropriate alternative is provided by Fohrer (*Das Buch Hiob,* 160), A. de Wilde (*Das Buch Hiob* [*OTS* 22; Leiden: Brill, 1981] 120), and Habel (*The Book of Job* [1985] 139), who derive the verb from the root *lʿʿ*, "to be rash," as in Prov 20:25.

[60] Scholars offer many translations for the obscure expression *rîb hallamût.* Gordis

7 My soul refuses to reach for[61] them;
they are like spoiled food.

Form

This passage, in which Job describes his distress, is a complaint addressed to the friends. Its purpose is to defend Job's "rash" words (v 3b) as appropriate given the extent of his suffering. The imagery of the hyperbole in vv 2–3 graphically conveys the severity of his "anguish" (v 2a). Similarly, the references to the poisoned arrows in Job and the description of the terrors of God set against him reinforce this point.

Verses 5 and 6 have the appearance of impossible questions. Such queries create a response of amazement that the question would even be asked.[62] Here they are obviously intended to elicit a positive and emphatic response from Eliphaz and the other two friends. But, as Crenshaw concedes, the import of these impossible questions is not clear in this context.[63] The problem arises from an abrupt transition from a scene of violence (v 4) to the subject of food (vv 5–7). As a result of this apparent incongruity, scholars hold divergent opinions as to the meaning of these questions. Driver and Gray, as well as Dhorme, interpret these references to food as symbols of Job's suffering.[64] Terrien, Gordis, and Habel suggest that

(*The Book of Job,* 71) translates it as "the juice of the mallows" (cf., "ist am Schleim des Eibisch Wohlgeschmack?" by Fohrer [*Das Buch Hiob,* 160]). Dhorme (*A Commentary on Job,* 78) has "the white of an egg," based on the Targum reading. Although no rendition offered thus far is completely convincing, Pope's (*Job,* 51) "slimy cream cheese" provides a reasonable alternative, especially in the context of "salt" in v 6a. For this translation, Pope draws on A. S. Yahuda's suggestion ("Hapax Legomena im Alten Testament," *JQR* 15 [1903] 702) that *ḥallāmût* might be related to the Arabic *ḥal(l)um,* a soft cheese. According to Pope, this cheese consists of a milky liquid before solidification which, due to its blandness, is then salted and flavored.

[61] The verb *nāgaʿ* is polysemic in nature and may mean "to reach" (cf., Lev 5:7; Isa 16:8; Jer 4:10,18; 48:32; 51:9; Job 20:7).

[62] As J. L. Crenshaw argues ("Impossible Questions, Sayings and Tasks," *Semeia* 17 [1980] 19–34), impossible questions deal with subjects whose answers are so obvious that the simple matter of posing the question elicits surprise. Such questions therefore appeal to an assumed consensus of opinion and evoke a predictable and emphatic response.

[63] Crenshaw, "Impossible Questions," 28.

[64] Driver and Gray, *A Critical and Exegetical Commentary on Job,* 61; and Dhorme, *A Commentary on Job,* 79–80. Similarly, F. Delitzsch (*Biblical Commentary on the Book*

these questions may allude to Job's cries of frustration over the lack of comfort provided by Eliphaz alone (Terrien and Gordis) or by his friends as a whole (Habel).[65] Pope's position mediates between both points of view. In his judgment v 5 refers to Job's suffering and v 6 is critical of Eliphaz's approach.[66]

If the argument for the relationship between vv 4 and 7 is accepted, then these verses provide an interpretative frame of reference for the impossible questions of vv 5 and 6. In v 5 Job likens himself to a wild ass and then a bull to make the statement that he would never complain over wholesome food. In the following verse he posits two questions on the topic of bland food to make the same point as v 5. Job's protest centers on the issue that his "food" is "spoiled" (*dĕwê,* v 7b), by which he means unfit for human consumption (v 4b). In conclusion, we agree with those scholars who view these references to food as symbols of Job's suffering but with the qualification that this "food" be understood as poison from the arrows of Shaddai.

In accordance with this position, the purpose of the impossible questions appear to be twofold: first, to awaken Job's friends to the possibility that he has good reason for his extreme reaction; and second, to impress upon Eliphaz, in particular, the fact that, in not grasping the seriousness of the issue, his friend is slow-witted. Lastly, v 7, when approached from this perspective, takes on the appearance of a death wish.

The structure of 6:1–7 may be seen in the outline below:

	Announcement of response: Job replies to Eliphaz	(6:1)
1	Description of the severity of Job's suffering as a justification for his complaint	(2–4)
	(a) An hyperbole of weight	(2–3)
	(b) Wounded by the poisoned arrows of Shaddai	(4ab)
	(c) Entrapped by the terrors of Eloah	(4c)
2	Further justification with the aid of two pair of impossible questions	(5–6)
	(a) Pertaining to animals	(5)
	(b) Pertaining to humans	(6)

of Job [Edinburgh: T. and T. Clark, 1966] 1. 111–12) and G. Fohrer (*Das Buch Hiob,* 169–70) take this point of view.

[65] Terrien, *Job* (1963), 80; Gordis, *The Book of Job,* 71; and Habel, *The Book of Job* (1985) 146.

[66] Pope, *Job,* 50–51.

3 Conclusion: Death wish
Job refuses to remove the arrows (7)

Rhetorical Analysis

(1) The Connections between 6:2–7 and Previous Passages

When this passage is examined for clues to a response to Eliphaz's first speech, several connections come to light. First and most obvious is the significance of the presence of the noun *ka'aś*[67] in 5:2a and 6:2a. In the former text, Eliphaz cites a wisdom saying, the first half of which states: "Surely indignation (*ka'aś*) slays the fool . . ." (5:2a). The meaning here is that "indignation" (in the sense of an angry disposition) has a negative effect on human life. When this word is put on Job's lips (6:2a), it refers not to his temperamental makeup but to his reaction to the series of tragedies which have befallen him. Even so, it draws attention to Eliphaz's saying which indirectly implies that Job's anger is characteristic of a fool. In response Job admits to his anger but, in the context of 6:2–7, defends it as justifiable in the light of the severity of his suffering, with the implication that his acute "indignation" should not be identified with that of a fool.[68]

Few scholars draw a connection between the "arrows"[69] of 6:4a and the reference to the "sons of Reshef" in 5:7b.[70] In the only appearance of the noun *rešep* in Job, Eliphaz states, with the wisdom saying of 5:6, that Reshef's sons bring trouble to humanity. As a reply to Eliphaz, Job seems to assert that he is victimized by more than the offspring of Reshef. To him it appears as if Shaddai has taken over the work of Reshef the archer and leads the attack against him.

The reference to the "terrors (*bi'ûtîm*) of Eloah" (6:4c) might be read as an allusion to Eliphaz's criticism of Job's reaction of horror (*bāhal*)[71]

[67] The noun *ka'aś* also occurs in 10:17 and 17:7.

[68] Klaus ("Between Job and his Friends," 156) notes this connection and writes, "For even if Eliphaz does not directly blame Job and does not directly call him a fool, Job recognizes the hint. Job therefore answers Eliphaz for his anger (*k'ś*) is great."

[69] In Job the noun *ḥēṣ* occurs only a second time in 34:6.

[70] Pope (*The Book of Job*, 50) merely notes that these two texts should be compared. Habel (*The Book of Job* [1985] 145), however, brings out the significance of this relationship along lines similar to the above.

[71] The verb *bāhal* also occurs in 21:6; 22:10; 23:15, 16.

in 4:5b.[72] The implication of such an allusion could be understood as a defense of Job's fear in view of his confrontation with the "terrors of Eloah" (6:4c) and, in the context of 6:4, with Shaddai his enemy. The root *bʿt* occurs also in 3:5c.[73] Gordis follows the lead of Rashi and Abraham Ibn Ezra, who relate this passage to the phrase *qeṭeb mĕrîrî* (Deut 32:24c). He translates this text as "the destruction of demons"[74] and on its basis renders 3:5c as, "and the demons of the day terrify it."[75] In Deut 32:24 *rešep, mĕrîrî* and *rāʾāb* (cf. 5:5a) occur together as agents of destruction. In view of this association, "the sons of Reshef" of Eliphaz's speech (5:7b) could be understood as a subtle reference to "the demons of the day" (3:5c). Job initially calls upon these demons to do away with the day of his birth. This text (3:5c), which may lie in the background of 5:7b, might suggest that it is Reshef's offspring who will fulfill this wish. The "terrors of Eloah" (6:4c) could then be seen as a collective reference to both the day demons and Reshef's offspring. The presentation of God as Job's enemy and the identification of these personified forces of evil as God's army serves to reinforce the idea that Job has good cause for his complaint of chap. 3.

One further reference might be understood as a response to Eliphaz's first speech. In what should be interpreted as an effort to influence Job's present behavior, Eliphaz appeals to Job's former "words" (*millîm,* 4:4a) or counsel which were, in his estimation, "instructive" (4:3a), "strengthening" (4:3b, cf. 4b), and "uplifting" (4:4a). As a response the noun *dābār* (6:3b), a synonym of *millâ,*[76] was conceivably placed on Job's lips. Through

[72] The thematic relationship between the roots *bhl* and *bʿt* finds support in 18:11a, "terrors (*ballāhôt*) frighten (*bʿt*) him."

[73] In 7:14 Job also uses the root *bʿt* in what appears as a further attempt to justify his fear. Later, in the book, this root occurs in 9:34; 13:11; 18:11; 33:7.

[74] Gordis, *The Book of Job,* 33.

[75] Gordis, *The Book of Job,* 33.

[76] The noun *dābār* occurs twenty-three times in Job. It is used ten times in chaps. 3–27 (4:2,12; 6:3; 9:14; 11:2; 15:3,11; 16:3; 19:28; 26:14). Half of these occurrences are found in introductory strophes (4:2; 6:3; 11:2; 15:3; 16:3) which take in much less than half the length of any one speech. Thus at the beginning of a speech there is a tendency for the speaker to refer to either his own words or to the words of one of his opponents. The fact that Job uses *dābār* in 6:3b, following Eliphaz's use of it in 4:2a and 12a, is not particularly significant to our discussion. It simply provides an example where both speakers refer to their own contributions as "words."

The noun *millâ* occurs more frequently in Job (thirty-seven times). It occurs nineteen

his admission that his "words" (*dĕbārîm,* 6:3b) are now "rash," Job appears to acknowledge the transition in his demeanor, observed by Eliphaz, but, as explained in 6:2–7, he has good reason for his change in attitude.

(2) An Overview of 6:2–7 with Attention to the Proposed Connections

Eliphaz tends to approach Job's problem impersonally through a discussion of the human condition in general (see esp. 4:7–8, 17, 19; 5:12–17).[77] Job, in turn, responds with a personal complaint which grounds the discussion in the pain and suffering of himself as an individual. In the context of a disputation, Job's answer should be understood as an attempt to force his friends to deal with the details of his particular case. When Eliphaz does address Job's situation, it appears that he underestimates the gravity of the problem. Eliphaz, for example, expresses surprise at Job's reaction to his suffering (4:5) and approaches Job's situation as though it were merely a matter of short-term discipline (5:17–26). That Job goes to such lengths to describe the degree of his suffering should be read as a reply to Eliphaz's lack of appreciation for his situation. Thus, in response to Eliphaz's implied criticism of Job's "indignation" (*kaʿaś,* 5:2a), Job defends his *kaʿaś* as appropriate to his predicament. Similarly, Eliphaz downplays the significance of Job's suffering with the wisdom saying which speaks of the inevitability of human suffering (5:7). Job's reference to poisoned arrows (6:4) ties in with the mention of the "sons of Reshef" (5:7b) and, in the context of 6:2–7, suggests that in comparison to the lot of human beings in general, Job's situation is excessive. Further, mention is made of "the terrors of Eloah" (6:4c) in defense of Job's fear in the light of Eliphaz's criticism of his "horror" in 4:5b. Finally Job's justification of his "rash words" seems to recall Eliphaz's praise of his former words of counsel (4:4a) in which he indirectly critiqued Job's current utterances.

---

times in chaps. 3–27, nine of which are found in introductions (4:2,4; 15:3; 16:4; 18:2; 19:2; 21:2; 23:5; 26:4). As with *dābār* it also exhibits a tendency to be used in the introductory strophes of the speeches. Similar to the use of *dābār* in 4:2a, 12a, and 6:3b, the occurrence of *millâ* in 4:2b is a further incidence of a speaker referring to his own speech.

[77] Although Eliphaz opens his speech with personal remarks directed to Job (4:2–6) and closes with a personal assurance of restitution (5:19–26), the bulk of the speech consists of impersonal argumentation.

The Introduction to Part II of Job's Reply to Eliphaz

7:1 Truly a mortal has a hard service on earth
and his days are like the days of a hireling.
2 As a slave who pants for shade,
and a hireling who hopes for his wages;
3 likewise[78] I am allotted months of emptiness
and nights of trouble are assigned to me.
4 When I lie down I say, "When will I rise?"
The night passes slowly and (I say),[79]
"I am sated with tossing till dawn."
5 The Worm has clothed my flesh,
Dust has touched my skin,
Tranquility discards (my skin).[80]
6 My days pass faster than a weaver's shuttle;
they go by without hope.
7 Remember, my life is just wind,
my eye will not again see good.
8 The eye which looks upon me will no longer see me.
Your eyes will be upon me, but I will be gone!

Form

As with the introduction to the first poem of this speech (6:2–7), the above passage is a complaint, but on this occasion it is addressed to God. It

[78] The preposition *kĕ* followed by *kēn* emphasizes agreement (cf. Isa 61:11; 64:14; Ps 83:15–16). See BDB 486.

[79] Following Dhorme (*A Commentary on Job,* 98) who recognizes the following as a quotation along with v 4a. Cf. Gordis, *The Book Job,* 80, and Habel, *The Book of Job* (1985) 152.

[80] This verse, especially the latter part, is difficult. Michel's suggestions (*Job in the Light of Northwest Semitic,* 159–63) make the most sense of any. He proposes that the words *rimmâ, ʿāpār,* and the root *rgʿ* be understood as terms of death and the underworld. Michel reasons that "tranquility" is an appropriate epithet for Sheol and consequently reads *rgʿ* as a noun. Rather than following the *Qere gûs,* "clod," for the *Kethib gîš,* Michel follows Tur-Sinai (*The Book of Job,* 136) and takes the root *gyš* as a verb related to *gš, gûš, gšš,* "to grope, touch." Further, Michel reads *ʿôrî* ("my skin") as the last word of the second colon. As he observes, this reading results in an unexpressed object for v 5c. He suggests that it might be *ʿôrî, bĕśārî* ("my flesh"), or *yāmay* ("my days") of v 6a. Yet *ʿôrî,* framed by the clauses of vv 5b and c, is most appropriately viewed as a double duty object.

consists of three parts: an opening axiom (vv 1–2), a complaint proper (vv 3–6), and a concluding taunt (vv 7–8).[81] The axiom describes humanity's oppression on earth. Job, next, turns from the condition of humanity in general to a more specific examination of his own troubles in vv 3–6. In the taunt which follows, Job begins with the suggestion that the life God gave him is nothing substantial but is simply "wind" or "emptiness." Then he threatens God with his absence, i.e., he will be dead and in Sheol away from God's watchful eye. Consistent with this overview, the passage may be laid out as follows:

1	Wisdom saying: Humans live an oppressed life	(7:1–2)
2	Complaint: A description of Job's distress	(3–6)
	(a) His life is full of emptiness	(3a)
	(b) His nights are sleepless	(3b–4)
	(c) His body is a living corpse	(5)
	(d) His days fly by without sign of hope	(6)
3	Taunt	(7–8)
	(a) His life is wind	(7a)
	(b) He threatens God with his death	(7b–8)

Rhetorical Analysis

(1) The Connections between 7:1–8 and Previous Passages

With the complaint of 7:1–8, Job appears to respond to Eliphaz's first speech in four ways. The opening verse of this introduction provides a clear example of a reply to Eliphaz's wisdom sayings of 5:6 and 7 and will be dealt with first. Both sets of statements agree that humanity is destined to live a difficult life, although each speaker is given a different vocabulary to convey this theme. Eliphaz's sayings are introduced with an emphatic *kî*. Job, in turn, uses the emphatic expression *hălōʾ*. By this means attention is drawn to the saying as a strong positive response to Eliphaz. Eliphaz speaks of "evil" (*ʾewen,* 5:6a) and "trouble" (*ʿāmāl,* 5:6b) that come from the "dust" (*ʿāpār,* 5:6a) or "ground" (*ʾădāmâ,* 5:6b) as a plague against "humanity" (*ʾādām,* 5:7a). Similarly, Job speaks of a "hard service" (*ṣābāʾ,* 7:1a) which "mortals" (*ʾĕnôš,* 7:1a) must endure

[81] I wish to express my indebtedness to Habel (*The Book of Job* [1985] 153–56) for the understanding of the structure of this passage and of chap. 7 as a whole.

upon "earth" (*'ereṣ,* 7:1a). Unlike Eliphaz, Job does not explicitly identify the source of humanity's trouble, although the comparisons to hirelings and slaves point to an oppressive overseer who must be understood as God.

The image of Job as a living corpse (7:5) serves to underline the fact that Job's condition cannot simply be addressed as a normal case in the life of humanity. Here the word "dust" (*'āpār*) comes into play. This noun occurs four times in these two speeches (4:19; 5:6; 7:5, 21), however, the similarities between 5:6–7 and 7:1 discussed above suggest an association between the two introductions (5:1–7; 7:1–8). On this basis the repetition of *'āpār* in 5:6 and 7:5 is most significant for our discussion.[82] Eliphaz cites the wisdom saying that "evil comes from the dust" (5:6a). In response, Job paints an horrific picture of himself coated with death's "dust" (7:5b). The point made is that it is not particularly helpful for an observer such as Eliphaz to quote various sayings about Sheol when Job knows firsthand what it is like to experience the "dust of death."

A further incidence of a possible response to Eliphaz's first speech involves the root *qwh.* In Job's speech of chaps. 6 and 7, the verb *qāwâ* occurs twice (6:19b; 7:2b) as does its related noun *tiqwâ* (6:8b; 7:6b). Eliphaz uses only the noun *tiqwâ* in two places of his first speech (4:6b and 5:16a). On the basis of the occurrence of *tiqwâ* in 6:8b, Habel takes 6:8–13 as a response to 4:2–7.[83] The sixfold use of the root *qwh* in these two speeches suggests that the relationship between these texts is more complicated than Habel allows.

In 4:6b Eliphaz recommends that Job should place "hope" in his integrity. Then, in 5:16a, he speaks of the "hope" for protection the poor place in God with the implication that Job should also have such faith in God. As a response Job maintains, in 6:8b, that his "hope" is only that God will put him out of his misery. In his second reference to "hope" (6:19b), Job seems to be saying to Eliphaz and his friends that he put his hope initially in their counsel, but they disappointed him (if Eliphaz is any indication of the friends' support). The last two references to "hope" occur in 7:2b and 6b. In 7:2b Job compares himself to the servant who hopes for his wages which, if understood as symbolic of death and release

[82] In 4:19b *'āpār* refers to the mortality of human nature in general. The noun *'āpār,* in 7:21c, furthers Job's belief of his imminent death. This word occurs relatively often (twenty-one times) in the remaining chaps. of Job.

[83] Habel, *The Book of Job* (1985) 141.

from suffering, seem a long way off. Similarly, Job's desire for restoration seems remote (7:6b). When the theme of hope in Job's second speech is interpreted as a response to Eliphaz, it appears that Job does not accept Eliphaz's advice because he: (a) does not put great stock in God's perception of his integrity; (b) does not trust in the protective powers of God; and (c) does not trust the council of his friends.

The final possible connection involves the verb *šāʾap* which occurs in Job only in 5:5c and 7:2a. In the first reference, Eliphaz speaks of the "Thirsty One" who "pants" (*šʾp*) after the wealth of the fool. Following this use of the verb, Job describes the slave as "panting" (*šʾp*) for shade or death. For Eliphaz this word is used in the context of a curse to refer to the actions of a personified figure. As with Job's use of the word for dust, the reference to the "panting" of a slave indirectly describes Job's physical condition. Eliphaz may imply that a shadowy figure was "panting" after his wealth, but for Job the crux of the matter is that he is the one who is now doing the "panting." Once again the severity of Job's suffering is stressed through the adoption of a word used by a previous speaker.

(2) An Overview of 7:1–8 with Attention to the Proposed Connections

That the complaint of 7:1–8 is addressed to God would appear to be directly related to Eliphaz's recommendation to seek God (5:8). Nevertheless, this passage functions as an indirect response to Eliphaz's speech and describes the extent of Job's distress for two reasons: first, to persuade Eliphaz and the other friends to approach him on a personal level; and second, to correct Eliphaz's minimizing of the seriousness of Job's situation.

The present complaint opens, as Habel observes, with the axiom of vv 1–2 which sounds like a quotation or formula from traditional wisdom sources.[84] The similarities observed between the wisdom sayings of 7:1 and 5:6–7 demonstrate that both Job and Eliphaz share at least one common viewpoint: they agree that human life is full of hardship. The noun *ṣābāʾ* of v 1a means "army, warfare" and takes on the nuance of enforced labor in the sense of a military conscription (cf. 14:14; Isa 40:2).

[84] Habel, *The Book of Job* (1985) 157.

A "hireling" (*śākîr,* v 1b) is a freeman employed for a sum of money (Deut 24:14–15). The simile "like the days of a hireling" (v 1b) suggests that hardship, characteristic of life in general, is comparable to that of a hireling.

In the following verse, the relative clauses reveal the basis of the comparison: both the slave and the hireling desire something that comes at the end of the day. The slave, who labors under the hot sun, awaits the "shade, shadow" (*ṣēl*) of the evening, and the hireling works in expectation of "payment" (*pāʿāl*) at the day's end (cf. Lev 19:13; Deut 24:14–15). A double entendre comes into play in v 2a as the noun *ṣēl* may also connote the brevity of life (e.g., 8:9; 14:2).[85] The noun *pāʿāl* also likely represents death, as it appears that the hireling hopes for a release from his oppression at the end of his life.[86] By implication the mortals of v 1 similarly await a time when their death will release them from forced labor (cf. 3:17–19). The idea of the slave "panting" for shade (v 2a) aptly describes Job's state and likely derives from the use of this term in 5:5c of Eliphaz's speech. The adoption of Eliphaz's word serves to reinforce the seriousness of Job's condition.

With the opening particle *kēn* of v 3, the teaching of vv 1–2 is applied to Job. In the analysis of 6:2–7, I argued that 5:2 was approached as an allusion to Job, but with the rejection of the inference that he was a fool. Verses 3 and 4 support this view; for Job is shown to prefer to compare his life to that of a slave or a hireling rather than a fool. But, as opposed to the laborers; Job hopes ultimately not for death but for restoration to his former quality of life. He observes, however, that his days pass rapidly without any sign that his hope[87] will be fulfilled (v 6).[88] This

[85] Habel, *The Book of Job* (1985) 158.

[86] Habel, *The Book of Job* (1985) 157.

[87] Note the double entendre "hope/thread," which plays on *'ereg* ("weaver's shuttle") in v 6a.

[88] That Job's hope is for restitution has the support of the commentators (see Delitzsch, *Biblical Commentary on Job,* 121; Fohrer, *Das Buch Hiob,* 177; Terrien, *Job* [1963] 86; Horst, *Hiob 1–19,* 115–16; Gordis, *The Book of Job,* 80; de Wilde, *Das Buch Hiob,* 128–29; Habel, *The Book of Job* [1985] 159; and Hartley, *The Book of Job,* 145–46), yet none mention the transition from his desire for death in chap. 3 to his hope for a restored life in the first half of his second speech (6:7, 8–9). If not an inconsistency in composition, it might represent an attempt to portray accurately the attitude of a person under extreme duress and near death. Such persons are often ambivalent toward life and alternate between a desire to find release in death, and the hope that they might make an unexpected recovery.

idea of hope, as expressed in 7:6b and 2b (and in 6:8b, 19b), responds to Eliphaz's mention of the root *qwh* in 4:6b and 5:16a and makes the overall point that any hope Job might have seems fruitless at this time. In v 5 Job says he is clothed with both the "Worm" and "Dust" of death. Clearly the reference to "dust" recalls Eliphaz's use of this term in 5:6a and serves to underline the intensity of Job's suffering.

Job, then, looks ahead to his impending end in vv 7 and 8 and taunts God with his absence. In return to the previous theme of v 3a, he reminds God that his life is as empty as the "wind" (*rûaḥ,* v 7a).[89] The "eye" (*'ayin*) is the dominant image of vv 7 and 8. Job first speaks of his eye as not seeing good again (v 7b), and then comments that in death he will be safe from the scrutiny of God's eyes (v 8). With this taunt Job makes it known to God that his "favorite object of surveillance"[90] will disappear at death. This threat, addressed to God, should perhaps be seen as a ploy to induce God to restore Job.

The introduction to chap. 7 is a fascinating piece of poetry. Repeated references to periods of time ("days", vv 1b [twice], 6a; "months," v 3a; "night(s)," v 3b, 4b; and "dawn," v 4c) interwoven with the theme of death, create an image of prolonged, intense suffering. "Hope" (vv 2b, 6b) is also a key concept in this passage, as Job compares his unfulfilled hope for restoration with the hopes of the slave and hireling.

This passage, in conjunction with 6:2–7, functions as a defense of Job's attitude toward suffering. In 6:2–7 Job argues that his anger is proportional to the degree of his ruin; and in 7:1–8 he maintains that his suffering exceeds by far humanity's expected norm. Thus, although Job may be seen to agree with the general truth of Eliphaz's statement in 5:7, he vigorously asserts that he has suffered unduly and beyond reasonable limits. The defensive tenor of both these introductions is attributed to Eliphaz's negative interpretations of Job's behavior in 4:5 and from his allusions to Job as a fool (5:2–5).

The First Speech of Bildad (chap. 8)
His Response to Job

The first speech of Bildad consists of twenty-one lines. Due to its uniformity, it will be treated as a single poem. With regard to its strophic

[89] For *rûaḥ* as signifying "emptiness," see Isa 41:29; Jer 5:13; and Qoh 1:14.

[90] Habel, *The Book of Job* (1985) 160.

divisions, scholars may be divided into two camps: those who divide the speech into relatively small units of six or seven strophes, and those who believe it consists of three major divisions. Fohrer and Skehan (followed by Murphy) propose seven three-line strophes (vv 2–4, 5–7, 8–10, 11–13, 14–16, 17–19, 20–22).[91] Webster's arrangement of six strophes (vv 2–4, 5–7, 8–10, 11–15, 16–19, 20–22) varies slightly from the above pattern.[92] The major problem with these arrangements is that they impose, in terms of length, a relatively constant pattern but with little attention given to the thematic structure of this piece.[93] As an example of insensitivity to content, Fohrer and Skehan treat vv 14–16 as a strophe. Yet v 14 continues with the description of the "godless" of v 13. Moreover, v 17 develops the narration on the plant of v 16. Webster's strophes of vv 11–15 and 16–19 satisfy these objections, although the larger issue of the relationship between the plants of vv 11 and 16 remains. Should they be approached as two different strophes or as one major strophe? A reading of the content shows that the teaching on the plants is attributed to the wisdom of the fathers (vv 8–10) and therefore belongs together as part of an ancient tradition. Consequently, this unit begins with v 8 and extends to at least v 19.

This assessment is shared by the second group of scholars mentioned above. Rowley, Horst, and de Wilde belong to this camp and posit three

[91] Fohrer, *Das Buch Hiob*, 186–87; and Skehan, "Strophic Patterns," 103. In addition, Skehan observes, "In this case it would be easy to press for larger units, as 8:2–7 and 14–19 especially would also make good 6-line strophes (p. 103)." He rejects this approach, however, on the basis of Bildad's second speech, which, in his view, is constructed in smaller units. Cf. Murphy (*Wisdom Literature*, 26). As previously pointed out, Murphy has largely adopted Skehan's alphabetic structure and strophic divisions for the Book of Job. Clines (*Job 1–20*, 200–1) proposes a similar strophic division with one exception. He puts v 16 with the sixth strophe. Despite these short strophes, Clines believes the speech divides into three larger units (vv 1–7, 8–19, 20–22) in agreement with Rowley, Horst, and de Wilde.

[92] Webster, "Strophic Patterns in Job 3–28," 41.

[93] Note Watson's comments (*Classical Hebrew Poetry*, 160):

> Another source of confusion is the preconception (based on Greek classical poetry) that the structure of strophes and stanzas has to be *regular* [italics his]. It would seem that the poets we are considering had a greater degree of freedom in this matter; once that is conceded a great deal of misunderstanding can be removed at one go.

uneven strophes (vv 2–7, 8–19, 20–22) for chap. 8.[94] Habel varies slightly in this arrangement with his reading of v 20 as the conclusion to the second strophe. The closing verses of the speech (vv 21–22) are understood by Habel as a "closing assurance."[95]

With regard to the contents of the introduction to chap. 8, the section on the two plants (vv 8–19 or 20) is clearly a separate topic from the preceding verses. This division, according to the above scholars, allows for basically two alternatives for the introductory strophe: vv 2–4 or vv 2–7. A review of vv 2–7 reveals the placement of the particle *'im* at the beginning of vv 4, 5, and 6. Whereas the first *'im* is likely emphatic and the latter two conditional, on a stylistic level the threefold repetition links these lines together. With the support of this observation and a rejection of what might be viewed as the "uniform approach to strophic division," vv 2–7 are proposed as the introduction to chap. 8.

The Introduction to the First Speech of Bildad (with the Narrator's Opening Statement)

8:1 Then Bildad the Shuhite answered and said:
2 How long will you say these things,
and[96] the words of your mouth be a great wind?
3 Does El pervert justice?
Does Shaddai pervert the right?
4 Your children have surely[97] sinned against him,
and he made them cross (the Channel) because of their wickedness.[98]

[94] Rowley, *Job,* 70; Horst, *Hiob 1–19,* 127–28; and de Wilde, *Das Buch Hiob,* 133. Cf. Terrien's division (*Job* [1963] 41) of four strophes: vv 2–7, 8–12, 13–17, 18–22. Van der Lugt ("Stanza-Structure in Job 3–14," 14–15), however, breaks the second strophe (vv 8–19) into two units: vv 8–13, 14–19.

[95] Habel, *The Book of Job* (1985) 168, 170–71.

[96] Driver and Gray (*A Critical and Exegetical Commentary on Job,* 75) recognize the ellipsis of v 2b and add in brackets to their translation, "how long will."

[97] As Gordis notes (*The Book of Job,* 88), *'im* cannot be conditional here, as the destruction of Job's children is not a hypothetical case but an event of the plot. Hence it should be understood emphatically. Cf. Habel, *The Book of Job* (1985) 169.

[98] L. G. Rignell ("Comments on some *cruces interpretum* in the Book of Job," *ASTI* 11 [1978] 111–12) suggests that *šālaḥ* is an ellipsis for "to cast out of His presence." But on the basis of 33:18, Dahood's translation ("Hebrew-Ugaritic Lexicography XI," *Bib* 54 [1973] 360), "he made them cross the infernal river," offers a better understanding of this

5 If you go early to El
and make supplication to Shaddai,
6 if you are pure and upright,[99]
he will now rouse himself[100] for you
and restore your righteous dwelling.
7 And though your beginning was small,
your end will prosper greatly.

Form

Verses 2–4 comprise an attack of Job's argument. With the rhetorical questions of v 2, Bildad first scolds Job for uttering such words (v 2a) and then specifically ridicules the content of Job's defense.[101] The rhetorical questions of v 3 presume that Job has previously maligned God's justice and are posed as a strong objection against such a view. The indictment of Job's children in v 4 illustrates God's justice and therefore supports the expected negative answer to the questions of v 3. Bildad, in vv 5–7, offers a conditional assurance of restoration. First, he states three conditions which must be met before any restoration may be granted (vv 5–6a).

text. Cf. Michel, *Job in the Light of Northwest Semitic,* 181 and Habel, *The Book of Job* (1985) 174.

[99] Dhorme (*A Commentary on Job,* 114) deletes v 6a as a gloss for two reasons: first, he argues that v 6, as the only tricolon in this speech, is too long; second, he believes the ethical dimension of v 6a, with its understanding that purity is a prerequisite for effective prayer, does not belong with the conditions of v 5 (cf. Fohrer, *Das Buch Hiob,* 184; and Horst, *Hiob 1–19,* 129). Since the publication of Dhorme's work, further research on both Hebrew and Ugaritic poetry has shown that in a series of bicolons a tricolon may unpredictably occur (see, for example, Watson's discussion on the tricolon in *Classical Hebrew Poetry,* 177–85). Hence Dhorme's first objection to the presence of v 6a may be discarded as dated. With regard to Dhorme's second objection, it may be contended that the focus of v 6a is not on any ethical prerequisites for effective prayer, which admittedly could be considered the work of a pious scribe. Rather v 6a should be read as the third of three conditions for Job's restoration listed in vv 5–6a. In addition, the deletion of this colon would destroy the balance between these three conditions and the three rewards of the assurance of vv 6b–7.

[100] Gordis (*The Book of Job,* 89) rejects the nuance "to arouse oneself from sleep" for the verb *'ûr* of the second colon of v 6 and attributes to it the derived meaning "to watch." Yet, in the context of the verb *šāḥar,* with its connotation of "earliness," *'ûr* is best understood as an anthropomorphism.

[101] Cf. Westermann, *The Structure of the Book of Job,* 21.

Then he pronounces an assurance of restoration accompanied with three promises pertaining to God's response (vv 6b–7). This introduction to the speech of chap. 8 consists of disputation as does the speech as a whole. The structure of 8:1–7 may be considered as follows:

	Announcement of response: Bildad replies to Job	(8:1)
1	Attack of Job's argument	(2–4)
	(a) Scolding of opponent (rhetorical question)	(2a)
	(b) Ridicule of opponent (rhetorical question)	(2b)
	(c) Bildad's argument: God is just (rhetorical question)	(3)
	(d) Support for argument: Punishment of Job's children for their sin	(3)
2	Conditional assurance of restoration	(5–7)
1	Conditions for restoration	(5–6a)
	(a) Job must seek God	(5a)
	(b) Job must pray for God's mercy	(5b)
	(c) Job must be of exceptional character	(6a)
2	Assurance of restoration	(6b–7)
	(a) God will act on Job's behalf	(6b)
	(b) God will restore Job's house	(6c)
	(c) God will reward Job	(7)

Rhetorical Analysis

(1) The Connections between 8:2–7 and Previous Passages

The introduction to the first speech of Bildad responds in several ways to Job's second speech. First, the reference to "wind" (*rûaḥ,* v 2b)[102] directly recalls Job's query of 6:26, "Do you think to correct me with words but count as wind (*rûaḥ*) the words (*'ēmer*) of a despairing person?" Bildad is portrayed as in agreement with this assessment and is given two terms

[102] The word for "wind" (*rûaḥ*) is used ten times in Job, four of which occur within the first eight chaps. (1:19; 6:2b; 7:7; 8:2). Although a case could be made that 8:2b plays also on 7:7a, in the sense that Bildad claims Job's words, like his life, are transitory and therefore carry no weight, the evidence favors a correspondence between 8:2b and 6:26 since both verses also speak of Job's words and have the term *'ēmer* in common. The reference to "wind" in the prologue is significant to the current discussion and will be discussed below.

(*'ēmer* and *rûaḥ*) from 6:26. Further, the incorporation of the adjective "great" stresses the degree of his agreement. This critique of Job's arguments must also be seen as a negative reaction to Job's evaluation of his discourses as "rash words" (*dĕbāray lā'û,* 6:3b) and as "honest words" (*'imrê yōšer,* 6:25a). Bildad rejects the idea that Job's words could be considered anything other than a "great wind."

Second, the verb *ḥāṭā'* and noun *pešaʻ* (both of v 4) recall 7:20a and 21a, respectively.[103] Job, in this passage, makes a hypothetical confession of sin (*ḥāṭā'*) in preparation for his mock demand for the forgiveness of his transgression (*pešaʻ*).[104] Bildad does not exclude the possibility that Job might be a sinner (note the conditional statement in v 6a) but applies these terms to Job's children to make the point that, in his view, they are clearly sinners, and that their death is confirmation of their evil ways.

A third connection involves the verb *šāḥar* (v 5a),[105] which also occurs in the concluding verses of chap. 7. Here, in 7:21, Job says of God, "You will seek (*šāḥar*) me, but I will be gone." As Rowley proposes, Bildad is given this term in 8:5a to suggest that it would be more appropriate if Job would seek God.[106]

The rhetorical questions of v 3 suggest that, according to Bildad, Job has impugned God's righteousness. Tur-Sinai suggests Job's complaint that God has "subverted" (*'āwat*) him and "justice" (*mišpāṭ*) is nonexistent (19:6–7) lies behind 8:3. Based on the correspondences between the two texts, Tur-Sinai proposes that in an earlier form of the book 19:6–7 must have preceded 8:3.[107]

An examination of Job's second speech, however, reveals one text in particular which may be understood as leading to 8:3. In 6:29–30 Job's testimony of his righteousness implies that God has attacked him unjustly. More specifically, in v 29b, Job requests of his friends, "Relent!

[103] The verb *ḥāṭā'* occurs ten times in Job five of which occur within the first eight chapters (1:5; 2:10; 5:24; 7:20; 8:4). The first three texts are relatively distant and are not likely related to this exchange. Further, only the second text (2:10) refers specifically to Job. The noun *pešaʻ* is also used ten times in the book but only occurs in these two places (7:21 and 8:4) in the first eight chaps.

[104] Following Habel's (*The Book of Job* [1985] 166) interpretation of this text as a form of mockery.

[105] The verb *šāḥar* occurs three times in Job (7:21; 8:5; 24:5).

[106] Rowley, *Job,* 71.

[107] Tur-Sinai, *The Book of Job,* 145.

I am still in the right" (*ṣdq*). It is quite possible that Bildad is portrayed as reacting to this assertion. If so, his twofold rhetorical question has this text in view. The presence of the root *ṣdq* in 6:29b and in 8:3b supports this viewpoint.[108] In addition, Bildad's query of 8:3 could be understood as an allusion to at least three other texts: (a) Job's statement of his faithfulness, "For I have not denied the words of the Holy One" (7:10c), which suggests that Job is not deserving of such treatment; (b) the parody of Ps 8 in 7:17–18 which also implies that Job believes he was mistreated; and (c) the threefold question of 7:20, which insinuates that God is overzealous in watching over human beings and punishes them for the smallest of offenses.

An appreciation of Job's argument in the introductions to the poems of chaps. 6 and 7 reveals an additional line of thought which may be interpreted as an affront to God's justice. In 6:2b–3 Job specifically stresses the severity of his suffering. As previously argued, Job implies that his suffering exceeds reasonable expectations for the normal course of human life. Since this line of reasoning follows Eliphaz's presentation of the doctrine of *mûsār* in 5:17–26, it suggests that Job believes God has overstepped the boundary which may be considered a just level of discipline. These examples of passages, where Job appears to criticize God's righteousness, are cited as possible evidence which underlies Bildad's charge against Job implicit in the rhetorical questions of 8:3. On the basis of this evidence, one can avoid Tur-Sinai's appeal to 19:6–7 as the text which led to the queries of 8:3 thereby eliminating the need to postulate a later reordering of the book.

Beyond the various ways in which the introduction to chap. 8 responds to elements of Job's second speech, there are three instances where vocabulary reminiscent of the prologue is put on Bildad's lips. First, there is the parallel between *rûaḥ kabbîr* (v 2b) and *rûaḥ gĕdôlâ* (1:19). With the reference to the fate of Job's children in 8:4 and the earlier disclosure that his children were destroyed by a "great wind" (1:19), it is likely that v 2b is an intentional literary link intended to convey the fact that Job's words are not merely empty but also destructive.[109] Second, the reference

[108] The root *ṣdq* occurs thirty-one times in Job, four of which occur up to this point in the dispute (4:17; 6:29; 8:3 and 6). The noun *ṣedeq* (8:6c), used in reference to Job's dwelling, is not significant to this discussion.

[109] Delitzsch (*The Book of Job,* 146) states that these two descriptive statements regarding

to Job's children in v 4, accompanied with the verbs *šālaḥ* and *ḥāṭā'*, remind the reader of the time when Job would send (*šālaḥ,* 1:5) for his offspring to purify them in case they might have sinned (*ḥāṭā'*, 1:5). With these connections in mind, it seems likely that the verb *šāḥar* ("to go early," 8:5a) is intended, by way of allusion, to remind Job of his former custom of rising early in the morning (*šākam*)[110] to offer sacrifices for his children (1:5).[111] It appears that, with this custom in mind, Bildad suggests Job should rise early but on this occasion to make supplication to God for himself.

The verbs *ḥāṭā'* and *šāḥar* were also discussed as indicators of a probable response to Job's second speech. Since these two verbs are used in both the introduction to chap. 8 and in the prologue, either with specific reference to Job's children or in the context of such a reference (as with *šāḥar* in 8:5a), it is probable that Bildad should be understood as responding to aspects of Job's second speech as well as to the prologue. Finally, Bildad's statement of 8:6, "if you are pure and upright" (*yāšār*), recalls Job's outstanding moral character (especially that of his "uprightness," *yāšār*) as described in the prologue, although the conditional aspect of his statement expresses some doubt concerning the true moral fibre of Job's life.

The purpose of the connections with the events of the prologue is likely related to Bildad's efforts of encouraging Job to seek restoration. Bildad reminds Job of the great wind which caused the death of his children not only to make the point that his words are destructive but also to remind Job of his offspring's tragic end. Similarly, the references to Job's former custom of rising early to offer sacrifices for his children serve to remind him of his love and devotion toward them. The intention of such reminders would be to exploit Job's grief so as to weaken his resistance to Bildad's advice. Further, the doubt cast on Job's reputation as the near-perfect man suggests that repentance might be necessary for his restoration. These references to Job's past, combined with promises

---

the wind are equivalent but then writes that the phrase of 8:2b signifies Job's speeches are devoid of content.

110 The verb *šākam* occurs in Job only in 1:5.

111 Habel (*The Book of Job* [1985] 175) observes what he calls a "literary link" between these verbs. All that he says of this link, however, is that the former verb (*šāḥar,* 8:5a) "extends back" to the latter (*šākam,* 1:5).

of an even greater future,[112] would make Bildad's council very attractive to Job.[113]

(2) An Overview of 8:2–7 with Attention to the Proposed Connections

The opening verse of Bildad's introduction is laden with sarcasm and contrasts sharply with the tactful beginning of Eliphaz in 4:2. Through the use of a twofold rhetorical question, Bildad expresses his impatience with Job's speeches in general and implicitly demands that Job cease from speaking. An appreciation of the significance of "great wind" (v 2b) in the light of Job's earlier statement (6:26) and with reference to the prologue (1:19) reinforces Bildad's disgust with his words. In the following verse (v 3), with the aid of a second pair of rhetorical questions, Bildad focuses on the specific issue to which he takes exception—the justice of God. These queries of v 3 expect a negative response. Bildad believes that Job has impugned God's righteousness and demands that he rethink his position. A search of Job's previous speech (chaps. 6–7) revealed several possible texts to which Bildad may be understood to have reacted as they all cast doubt on God's righteousness.

Tur-Sinai is of the opinion that it is unlikely for a writer to use the verb *'āwat* twice in the bicolon of v 3.[114] Yet further instances where a root is repeated in the same verse (cf. 6:2; 7:8; 22:2) suggest that this occurrence is deliberate and serves to express emphasis.

In this particular case the twofold occurrence of the verb *'āwat* creates a sense of alarm that anyone would question God's justice.[115] In addi-

112 Note that Bildad ironically predicts the outcome of the epilogue (42:10–17) in vv 6b–7.

113 Habel (*The Book of Job* [1985] 170) draws attention to the significance of the placement of the verbs *šālaḥ* and *ḥāṭa'* in this passage and in the prologue. These correspondences are, in his view, examples of dramatic irony, in that Bildad is not aware of how his thoughts relate to the prologue. That the friends were informed of Job's plight and travelled to console him for a substantial period of time (2:11,13), however, assumes an intimate relationship. An awareness of Job's reputation (cf. 4:3–4) and customs should be understood as common knowledge implied by this relationship. Yet, what is withheld from the friends are the details of the background scenes featuring the intrigue between God and the Satan.

114 Tur-Sinai, *The Book of Job,* 146. Here Tur-Sinai falls back on his theory that the Book of Job is a translation from an Aramaic text and suggests that he prefers a different verb such as *nāṭâ* ("to bend") or *sālap* ("to twist, pervert") in one of the members of the bicolon.

115 Cf. Fohrer, *Das Buch Hiob,* 184.

tion, from the responses expected by v 3, it is clear that for Bildad the righteousness of God is above question. After disclosing the basis of his argument, Bildad, nevertheless, does not discuss Job's personal morality as a case in point. Perhaps this avoidance is due to the fact that Job is still alive, and Bildad is portrayed as believing that God, in his justice, destroys the wicked (8:22b). If so, this character, therefore, is reluctant to condemn Job unequivocally as a wicked man, although he is equally hesitant to ascribe to Job anything more than a hypothetical morality (8:6a) in a reference that recalls Job's reputation of the prologue. Yet, the death of Job's children furnishes Bildad with clear evidence of their guilt. Thus he is given words (*ḥāṭā'* and *peša'*, 8:4) reminiscent of Job's hypothetical confession of sin (7:30a), which are used to confirm the evil ways of his children. Instances of vocabulary which recall the events of the prologue discussed above serve to remind Job of the loss of his loved ones. This reminder is intended to use Job's grief as a means to make Bildad's advice more palatable. It also serves as an indirect warning as to what might happen to Job if he does not fulfill the three conditions for restoration of vv 5–6a. The first condition, that Job must "seek" God (v 5a), was seen to play on an earlier statement in which Job speaks of God as "seeking" him (7:21). The threefold assurance of restoration (vv 6b–7) stands out as a promise of what God will do for Job if he does satisfy the requirements of vv 5–6a. Bildad, therefore, attempts to persuade Job to accept his advice with both a threat of punishment and a promise of reward.

The Third Speech of Job (chaps. 9–10) His Response to Bildad

No scholarly consensus has yet emerged concerning the structure of chaps. 9–10. Terrien proposes that this speech consists of four "poems" which develop the following themes: God as arbitrary (9:2–13), despot (9:14–24), inhuman (9:25–10:6), and creator (10:7–22).[116] Rowley is more cautious than Terrien and avoids a clear-cut division of the speech into separate poems. Nevertheless, he suggests that the speech consists of five "sections":

> The speech falls into the following sections, though they are not very sharply marked off: his recognition of the inscrutability and power of

[116] Terrien, *Job* (1963) 93–104.

> God (9:2–13); the impossibility of facing God in court (9:14–21); God's complaint (9:25–35); his review of God's dealings with him and longing for death (10:1–22).[117]

Fohrer divides the contents of chaps. 9 and 10 into three parts also according to theme. The first part (9:2–24), in Fohrer's view, deals with God's overwhelming strength; part two (9:25–35) speaks of Job's hopeless situation; and part three (10:1–22) describes God as his enemy and Job's desire for death.[118]

There are some similarities between these proposals but certainly no collective agreement. Rowley and Fohrer, for example, agree on the limits of the last two units, although there is a difference of opinion concerning the opening unit(s) of chap. 9. Conversely, Terrien and Rowley agree on the first section of the speech but are at variance over the remaining portions. These observations lead one to suspect that the contents of this speech are not composed in major units. An examination of the speech, as a whole, reveals a common thread of litigation woven through its contents. Habel highlights this fact and argues that this speech is essentially a unity composed on the theme of litigation:

> The design and rhetoric of this speech becomes apparent when we recognize its integrated thought progression, involving a subtle movement from Job's announcement on the futility of litigation to his considering the odds against litigation, God, and finally returning to futility.[119]

In support of his analysis of chaps. 9 and 10, Habel lists several "key legal expressions" which maintain the unity of this speech (e.g., *ʿnh* [9:3b, 14a, 15a, 32a], *ršʿ* [9:20a, 22b, 29a; 10:2a, 7a, 15a], and *ṣdq* [9:2b, 15a, 20a, 10:15]).[120]

Rather than arguing on the basis of theme, some scholars have supported their analysis with an appeal to forms of address. De Wilde, Webster and Clines use this approach and divide chaps. 9 and 10 into two poems: 9:2–24 as spoken to the friends and 9:25–10:22 as addressed

[117] Rowley, *Job,* 75.

[118] Fohrer, *Das Buch Hiob,* 201.

[119] Habel, *The Book of Job* (1985) 185. For a detailed overview of Habel's structure of chaps. 9 and 10 see pp. 186–87 of his book.

[120] Habel, *The Book of Job* (1985) 188–89.

to God.[121] The delimitation of the first poem is defensible as v 2 is clearly directed to the friends and all the references to God are in the third person. The contents of the second poem are less clear particularly with regard to 9:25–35. In this section, there are two second person (vv 28b, 31a) and five third person references to God.[122] The following section (10:1–22) is not under dispute as it consistently speaks of God in the third person.

Skehan divides chaps. 9 and 10 into three "speeches" (9:2–24; 9:25–10:1a; 10:1b–22) primarily on alphabetic grounds, but he also supports his decision with reference to the addressees.[123] Since the second unit contains only eleven lines, Skehan refers to it as a "transitional half-speech."[124] As to whom it addresses, Skehan focuses on the third person references and entitles this section "Job to himself."[125] He writes:

> It could be argued from vss. 28,31, that Job is already addressing God; but the fact that he speaks of God in the third person throughout the stanza 9:32–10:1a, shows that this is basically a soliloquy, in which Job is, of course, thinking of God, but addresses him only in hesitant asides.[126]

A division of this speech into two or more poems on the basis of the persons addressed is inconclusive particularly with regard to 9:25–35, as it contains references to both God and the friends. Therefore Habel's position that chaps. 9 and 10 are a unified speech is probably correct.

Of those scholars who divide the poetry of Job into strophic patterns, there is general agreement that vv 2–4 of chap. 9 form the introductory unit.[127] One dissenting view, however, should be noted. With the sup-

[121] De Wilde, *Das Buch Hiob,* 140; Webster, "Strophic Patterns in Job 3–28," 41, and Clines, *Job 1–20,* 223.

[122] Verse 32a opens with a verbless clause in a clear reference to God. The following verb *'ānâ* in this verse, speaks of God with the third person verbal suffix *-ennû.* There are two further references to God in v 34 and one in v 35a.

[123] Skehan, "Strophic Patterns," 103–4.

[124] Skehan, "Strophic Patterns," 104.

[125] Skehan, "Strophic Patterns," 104.

[126] Skehan, "Strophic Patterns," 104. Cf. Westermann (*The Structure of the Book of Job,* 51–52), who divides 9:25–10:1a as a "self-lament" from 9:2–24 and 10:16–22 on the grounds that these latter two sections are dominated with accusations against God.

[127] Delitzsch, *Biblical Commentary on Job,* 1. 147; Fohrer, *Das Buch Hiob,* 202; Terrien, *Job* (1963) 93; Horst, *Hiob 1–19,* 144; Skehan, "Strophic Patterns," 103; Webster, "Strophic Patterns in Job 3–28," 41; Habel, *The Book of Job* (1985) 185; and Clines, *Job 1–20,* 224.

port of K. Schlottman's commentary of 1851, van der Lugt argues that the first section of Job's speech extends to v 12.[128] This division is defensible as a major unit but an examination of its contents reveals that it may be broken down into three sub-units (vv 2–4, 5–10, 11–12) on thematic grounds. The first and third sections correlate as they focus on humanity's limitations before God, whereas the middle piece consists of a hymnic description of God's power in nature. Consequently, with the majority of the scholars, vv 2–4 are viewed as the opening strophe to Job's third speech.

The Introduction to Job's Response to Bildad (with the Narrator's Opening Statement)

9:1 Then Job answered and said:
2 Truly I know that this is so.
But how can a mortal be just before God?
3 If one wishes to enter into litigation with him,
he could not answer him once in a thousand charges.
4 He is wise of heart and mighty in strength.
Who could struggle against him and emerge unharmed?

Form

This introduction opens with an emphatic statement of knowledge (v 2a) and then develops into a discussion of the hopelessness of entering into litigation with God (vv 2b–4).[129] As shall be seen, the rhetorical question of v 2b reacts to previous questions raised by Bildad and Eliphaz in disputation style and provides the impetus for the following speech. This introduction belongs to the genre of disputation, although much of the speech consists of complaint (particularly 9:25–10:22).[130]

As the subject of v 3b is related to my understanding of the structure of 9:2–4, its ambiguity must be resolved before an outline may be

[128] Van der Lugt, "Stanza-Structure in Job 3–14," 16.

[129] Note the presence of legal language in this introduction (*ṣādaq,* v 2b; *rîb,* v 3a; and *'ānâ,* v 3b). Cf. Fohrer, *Das Buch Hiob,* 202; and Habel, *The Book of Job* (1985) 188.

[130] Cf. Murphy, *Wisdom Literature,* 28; and Fohrer, *Das Buch Hiob,* 201–2. Westermann (*The Structure of The Book of Job,* 51–53), however, considers the whole speech a complaint.

presented. Scholars have identified the subject of this clause as either God[131] or as a human being.[132] Habel argues for the former on the basis of Elihu's remark (33:13ff), which he believes is based on v 3b. While Habel's assumption of a related text seems warranted, that it affects the interpretation of v 3b depends on one's view of the integrity of the Elihu speeches. Habel argues that the Elihu speeches are "an integral part of the structure of the book of Job";[133] but if one views these speeches as a later interpolation, as do many scholars, then it is conceivable that 33:13b may be based on an incorrect interpretation of v 3b. In addition, it is best to support one's position primarily with the more immediate context of v 3b. Fullerton, almost fifty years before Habel's latest work on Job, argues from contextual grounds that the subject of v 3b is a human being. He bases his argument on two observations: (a) if a human being is understood as the subject of v 3b, then it is consistent with the subject of vv 2b and 3a; and God is, then, consistently understood as the object of these cola; and (b) this interpretation is supported by Job's remark that he would be unable to answer God's questions in a legal case (9:14).[134] But, as Hartley points out, Job also has difficulty believing that God would even hear his case (9:16, 19).[135] Instead of arguing to the contrary, however, Hartley also holds the position that the subject of v 3b is a human being. In his view Job's fear of his inability to answer God (9:14–16), coupled with his concern that his own mouth would prove him guilty (9:20), is "stronger than his doubt that God would not answer his case."[136] Essentially, Hartley argues on the same grounds as Fullerton[137] except for the fact that he also appeals to the climax of the book where God grants Job an audience and questions him. Job's inability to answer these questions is understood by Hartley as support for his interpretation.

Fullerton's and Hartley's arguments appear more convincing than Habel's reasoning. Further support for their position may be adduced

[131] Habel, *The Book of Job* (1985) 189; Dhorme, *A Commentary on Job,* 127; and Gordis, *The Book of Job,* 102.

[132] Fohrer, *Das Buch Hiob,* 204; Delitzsch, *Biblical Commentary on Job,* 147; Driver and Gray, *A Critical and Exegetical Commentary,* 84; and Hartley, *The Book of Job,* 167.

[133] Habel, *The Book of Job* (1985) 36.

[134] Fullerton, "Job, Chapters 9 and 10," *AJSL* 55 (1938) 231–32.

[135] Hartley, *The Book of Job,* 167.

[136] Hartley, *The Book of Job,* 167.

[137] Hartley (*The Book of Job,* 167) also presents the consistency of subject and object in vv 2b and 3a, to which he adds v 4b, as evidence for his position.

from our understanding of the role vv 3–4 play in this introduction. The key to the structure of these verses in question lies in v 4a. This text divulges the reason why a mortal would be unsuccessful in a lawsuit against God: the deity is too formidable an opponent in terms of wisdom and strength. This understanding, of course, depends on the translation of the verbs *qāšâ* and *šālēm*. Some scholars regard *qāšâ* as an ellipsis for the expression "to stiffen the neck" (e.g., 2 Chr 36:13) or "spirit" (Deut 2:30) and interpret the colon as an act of defiance.[138] Gordis rejects this meaning in favor of the mishnaic definition "to argue, dispute, raise a question."[139] Yet this verb is also used to denote the physical struggle of an unusually intense and difficult labor during childbirth (e.g., Gen 35:16, 17) or to describe a "physical" conflict with God as in the expression "his hand is heavy upon us" (1 Sam 5:7). The notion of "struggle" in 9:4b is appropriately complemented with the second verb of the colon *šālēm*, "to be unharmed, whole." Thus, in the context of the immediately preceding description of God's strength, it means that one could not possibly hope to engage in combat with the deity and emerge unscathed. Further confirmation of this reading is provided in the body of this poem, where Job states that if God entered into a physical conflict with him, Job would be injured (9:17). Hence Job says, "If it be a trial of strength—he is the mighty One (9:19a)!"[140]

The latter hemistich of v 4a, therefore, appears to function as the "reason" for the "probable result" of v 4b. This understanding leaves the first hemistich of v 4a hanging. Does it belong to the latter part of v 4a as an additional reason why Job might be hurt if he engages in a struggle with God? Or does it belong elsewhere? Later in this speech Job goes so far as to say that if he went to trial, then God would falsely prove him guilty (9:20). Thus, due to the deity's shrewdness, Job believes that a mortal cannot successfully enter into litigation with God. In view of the implications of v 20, the reference to God's wisdom in v 4aa might be understood as the "reason" for the "probable result" of v 3b, if it is assumed that a human being is the subject of v 3b.[141] When read in this

[138] Tur-Sinai, *The Book of Job,* 154. Cf. Driver and Gray, *A Critical and Exegetical Commentary on Job,* 84; and Hartley, *The Book of Job,* 167–68.

[139] Gordis, *The Book of Job,* 102.

[140] Habel's translation (*The Book of Job* [1985] 179).

[141] Note Fullerton's comment ("Job, Chapters 9 and 10," 283): "Man in the presence

manner, the symmetry of these verses becomes apparent: the two reasons why it is hopeless for a person to enter into litigation against God (vv 4aa, 4ab) are framed with two probable results (vv 3b, 4b) of such an undertaking.

With the subject of v 3b clarified as a human being and not God, the structure of this introductory strophe may be presented as follows:

	Announcement of Response: Job replies to Bildad	(9:1)
1	Emphatic statement of knowledge	(2a)
2	On the futility of litigation against God	(2b–4)
1	A mortal cannot hope to prove himself before God (rhetorical question)	(2b)
2	The outcome of litigation against God with explanation	(3–4)
	(a) Probable result: A mortal would be unable to answer	(3)
	(b) Reason: God is intellectually superior	(4aa)
	(c) Reason: God is superior in strength	(4ab)
	(d) Probable result: A mortal would lose such a contest (rhetorical question)	(4b)

Rhetorical Analysis

(1) The Connections between 9:2–4 and Previous Passages

Job's opening statement concerning that which he is certain of (v 2a) is most likely related to the theme of justice in v 2b. The rhetorical question of 8:3 also deals with the theme of justice (note the presence of the root *ṣdq* in 8:3b; 9:2b).[142] As we have seen, a negative answer is expected to his question. Job takes the position in chap. 9, however, that God perverts justice both in his personal life (9:17–20) and in the world

of God, becomes completely confused in his attempt to answer God's questions, seeing that God is all-wise."

[142] For the frequency of the occurrences of *ṣdq* in Job, see n. 108. In this section the occurrences of *ṣdq* in 4:17; 8:3, 7 will be discussed from the perspective of 9:2b. The presence of this root in three other places of this speech (9:15, 20; 10:15) follows from 8:3 and highlights Job's focus on his righteousness.

(9:22–24). In view of this development and taking into consideration the presence of the root *ṣdq* in 8:3 and 9:2, v 2a should be understood as an answer to 8:3 in which Job replies with a resounding, "Yes, truly I know that God perverts justice." Job, therefore, responds to Bildad's question with an unexpected affirmative answer. Rhetorical questions do not require a reply as only one answer is thought possible. An unexpected reply thus highlights the level of disagreement between Job and Bildad.[143]

One of the conditions Bildad sets for Job's restoration is that he must be "pure and upright" (8:6a). Job is portrayed as believing that he fulfills this condition, for he defends his innocence in chap. 9 (vv 15, 20–21) and plans to enter into litigation to prove this point. His query of v 2b raises the issue of how one is to proceed to prove this fact before such an unjust and formidable opponent in a court of law. The impossibility of fulfilling the condition of 8:6a before such a God along with Job's disagreement with Bildad over God's justice leads Job to the formulation of a question for Bildad. He asks in effect, "How can a mortal prove himself before a God who perverts justice?" Verse 2 is thus raised in response to Bildad's question of 8:3 and to the condition set forth in 8:6a.

In addition, as most scholars observe, 9:2b and a text from Eliphaz's first speech (4:17a) are remarkably similar:

ha'ĕnôš mē'ĕlôah yiṣdāq (4:17a)
ûmâ-yyiṣdaq 'ĕnôš 'im 'ēl (9:2b)

Both cola are rhetorical questions of similar length. They refer to human beings with the same word (*'ĕnôš*), have the verb *ṣādaq* in common, and both speak of God but with different names. In view of these similarities, 9:2b should also be seen as a response to 4:17a. In Eliphaz's speech this question, concerning whether or not humanity may be considered righteous before God, expects a negative answer. Job's position in 9:2b is very close to Eliphaz's in 4:17a but for different reasons. For Job the blame for humankind's apparent unrighteousness does not lie with human nature but with God's injustice. When read as a response to 4:17a, Job requests that Eliphaz reflect on the validity of his belief in a just God.

As to whom Job responds with the rhetorical question of v 2b, scholars

[143] Job disagrees with Bildad's position on the basis of personal knowledge (*yāda'tî*, 9:2a), on which he elaborates in 9:5–12.

hold one of three positions: (a) Job replies to Eliphaz;[144] (b) to Bildad;[145] or (c) to both Eliphaz and Bildad.[146] The last position—with the qualification that Job responds primarily to Bildad and only secondarily to Eliphaz—is probably correct. This reasoning is based upon a reading of both 9:2a and b as Job's answer to Bildad's queries of 8:3 and on the fact that Bildad strongly defends God's justice in the body of his first speech.

The verb *šālēm*[147] of 8:6c and 9:4b is also of significance for this discussion. Previously, as the second of his assurances, Bildad promises Job that God will restore (*šālēm*) his "righteous dwelling" (8:6c) if certain conditions are met. Job, in turn, speaks of the trial as a show of strength and argues that a mortal could not possibly win (*šālēm*) against such an opponent (v 4b). It follows from Job's argument that if a person cannot win the lawsuit, then his "righteous dwelling" will not be restored to him. Perhaps Job's dwelling as "righteous" (*ṣdq*) should be understood ethically, that is, as a reference to his supposed integrity. If so, 9:2b could be understood as a reaction also to 8:6c with the meaning, "How could I be rewarded with a dwelling distinguished by my righteousness if I cannot even prove my righteousness before God?" The major point is that the repetition of the verb *šālēm* in both these introductory strophes suggests that Job rejects Bildad's conditional offer of restoration on the grounds that it is impossible for him or any other mortal to fulfill the condition of righteousness before such an unjust God.

(2) An Overview of 9:2–4 with Attention to the Proposed Connections

The meaning of the opening statement, "Truly I know that this is so" (v 2a), is unclear as the object is unspecified. When it is read in the

[144] Dhorme, *A Commentary on Job,* 126; Driver and Gray, *A Critical and Exegetical Commentary on Job,* 84; Tur-Sinai, *The Book of Job,* 154; and Terrien, *Job* (1963) 93.

[145] Delitzsch, *Biblical Commentary on Job,* 147; Fohrer, *Das Buch Hiob,* 201; and Murphy, *Wisdom Literature,* 28.

[146] Horst, *Hiob 1–19,* 144; Rowley, *Job,* 75; Gordis, *The Book of Job,* 185; de Wilde, *Das Buch Hiob,* 140; and Habel, *The Book of Job* (1985) 185.

[147] The verb *šālēm* occurs nine times in Job but only in 8:5c and 9:4b thus far in the dispute.

context of the following query (v 2b) and as a response to Bildad's rhetorical question of 8:3, the meaning becomes clear: Job believes God perverts justice. The fact that Job is presented as adhering to this viewpoint means that one of Bildad's conditions for restoration (that Job be pure and upright, 8:6a) cannot be taken seriously. Verse 2b also echoes Eliphaz's rhetorical question of 4:17a with the implication that the fault lies not with humanity but with the justice of God.

Job next considers the expected result of entering into a lawsuit against God (9:3–4). As God is intellectually superior, Job reasons that a mortal would not be able to respond to his arguments (vv 3–4aa). Moreover, as God is the stronger of the two, Job states that a mortal would surely be overpowered if the litigation deteriorated into physical combat (vv 4ab–4b). The notion that a human being would not "emerge unharmed" (*šālēm*) from a physical struggle with God (v 4b) appears to be intended as a response to Bildad's conditional offer of restoration (*šālēm,* 8:6c). If this is the case, then the implication is that Job rejects Bildad's offer because it is fruitless to attempt to prove one's righteousness before an unjust God.

The First Speech of Zophar (chap. 11)
His Response to Job

Zophar's speech consists of nineteen lines. The impossible questions of vv 7 and 8 belong to vv 9–12 as a strophe outlining God's superior wisdom. The following strophe (vv 13–20) consists of a conditional assurance offered to Job complete with the details of the expected result of compliance with Zophar's advice. Two scholars in particular (Irwin and Fohrer) divide vv 2–6 into two strophes (vv 2–4, 5–6).[148] Verses 5 and 6, however, function as a refutation of the quotation in v 4 and therefore belong with vv 2–4. In sum, Zophar's speech falls into three strophes (vv 2–6, 7–12, 13–20).[149] The first strophe shall be considered the introductory unit of this speech.

[148] W. A. Irwin, "Poetic Structure in the Dialogue of Job," *JNES* 5 (1946) 34; and Fohrer, *Das Buch Hiob,* 223. Webster ("Strophic Patterns in Job 3–28," 41–42) divides vv 2–3 from 4–6. Cf. Weiser, *Das Buch Hiob,* 83–84. Yet v 4, at a minimum, belongs to the preceding verses as it highlights the type of speech which Zophar criticizes in vv 2, 3.

[149] Cf. Terrien, *Job* (1963) 105–8; Horst, *Hiob 1–19,* 165; Rowley, 87; and Clines, *Job 1–20,* 257. Hartley (*The Book of Job,* 193) cuts the first strophe short but otherwise

The Introduction to Zophar's Reply to Job (with the Narrator's Opening Statement)

11:1 Then Zophar the Naamathite answered and said:
2 Should a multitude of words go unanswered?
Should a verbose man be justified?
3 Your babbling may silence men.
You may mock and none shame you.
4 You may say, "My teaching is pure,
and I am clean in your sight."
5 But oh, if only Eloah would speak
and open his lips against you.
6 He would tell you the secrets of wisdom,[150]
for there are two sides[151] to understanding.
Know that Eloah overlooks part of your iniquity.

---

ends up with three similar units (vv 2–4, 5–12, 13–20). Habel (*The Book of Job* [1985] 204) divides this speech into only two sections (vv 2–12, 13–20). Fohrer (*Das Buch Hiob,* 223–224) divides this chapter into six considerably shorter strophes (vv 2–4, 5–6, 7–9, 10–12, 13–16, 17–20). Webster ("Strophic Patterns in Job 3–28," 41–42) also arrives at six strophes but with different divisions (vv 2–3, 4–6, 7–9, 10–12, 13–15, 16–20). Irwin ("Poetic Structure," 34) proposes eight strophes. His divisions correspond to those of Fohrer until the fifth strophe, which he takes as vv 13–15. From v 13 onwards, he divides the text into couplets. Skehan's discussion of chap. 11 ("Strophic Patterns," 105) is obscure. In his chart (p. 99) this speech is listed as twenty lines in length. Yet, since the introductory formula (v 1) is not normally counted in his analysis, this speech should be only nineteen lines long. This error is reflected in the strophic division of the lines of chap. 11 into three six-line units and one two-line unit. Murphy (*Wisdom Literature,* 29) does not recognize this oversight in his adoption of Skehan's work for the structure of chap. 11.

[150] On the basis of meter, Pope (*Job,* 84) omits *ḥokmâ,* as a scribal gloss which explains the obscure word *tûšiyyâ* in v 6b. Yet, as Habel points out (*The Book of Job* [1985] 203), extended lines are common in the poetry of Job. Further, the parallel structure of v 6 (*taʿălumôt* and *kiplayim* are paired along with *ḥokmâ* and *tûšiyyâ*) casts doubt on this emendation (cf. Michel, *Job in the Light of Northwest Semitic,* 254–55).

[151] Tur-Sinai (*The Book of Job,* 192) rejects *kiplayim* ("double") and redivides the text to read *kāpal yām* ("he has folded up the sea"). J. J. Slotki ("Job xi 6," *VT* 35 [1958] 230) transposes *kiplayim* to follow the *kî* of v 6c and reads, "And know thou that double (punishment) shall God exact of thee." Dhorme (*A Commentary on Job,* 159), Fohrer (*Das Buch Hiob,* 221), Gordis (*The Book of Job,* 121), Guillaume (*Studies in Job,* 89), and Horst (*Hiob 1–19,* 164) read *kiplāʾîm* ("wonders"). As the word makes sense as it stands in this context, the current text should be retained in agreement with Pope (*Job,* 84–85), Habel (*The Book of Job* [1985] 203), and Michel (*Job in the Light of Northwest Semitic,* 254–55).

Form

This introductory strophe consists of two parts (vv 2–4 and 5–6). The first section, with its ridicule of Job, indirect criticism of Eliphaz and Bildad, and summary of Job's position, functions as an attack against Job's argument and may well be reminiscent of litigation as Fohrer suggests.[152] The second section consists of a wish that God would respond to Job's argument. Wisdom motifs are evident in the references to the *taʿălumôt ḥokmâ* ("secrets of wisdom," v 6a) and *tûšiyyâ* ("understanding," v 6b).[153] This unit and chap. 11 as a whole consist of disputation. The structure of this passage may be outlined as follows:

	Announcement of response: Zophar replies to Job	(11:1)
1	Attack of Job's argument	(2–4)
	(a) Ridicule of opponent with rhetorical questions	(2)
	(b) Ridicule continued (v 3a) with accusation (v 3ba) and allusion to the friends' inability to counter Job's argument (vv 3a and 3bb)	(3)
	(c) Quotation summarizing Job's argument: Job maintains his innocence	(4)
2	Wish that God would refute Job	(5–6b)
	(a) The desire for God to respond	(5)
	(b) What God would reveal: hidden knowledge pertaining to Job's guilt	(6ab)
3	Assurance: Job's punishment is less than he deserves	(6c)

Rhetorical Analysis

(1) The Connections between 11:2–6 and Previous Passages

When this introduction is viewed against Job's immediately preceding speech, four words in particular[154] stand out as they appear to signal the

[152] Fohrer, *Das Buch Hiob,* 223.

[153] Cf. Murphy, *Wisdom Literature,* 29.

[154] The possibility of a meaningful link with a fifth word, the verb *yādaʿ*, is doubtful due particularly to its frequent use in different contexts in chaps. 9 and 10 (9:2a, 5a, 21b, 28b; 10:2b, 13b). It also occurs four times in preceding texts (5:24, 25, 27; 8:9), three times in chap. 11 (vv 6a, 8b, 11a) and forty-one times in the remaining chapters of the book.

possibility of a response by Zophar. The first involves the verb *ṣādaq* ("to be just, righteous").[155] In chaps. 9 and 10, it is used on four occasions (9:2b, 15a, 20a; 10:15b), each time with reference to Job's assumption of his innocence.[156] Zophar, in v 2b, is given this verb in a refutation of Job's claim. He is angered that Job's "babbling" and "mockery" were not silenced (v 3), as this failure makes it appear that Job is righteous after all. Zophar's position is that verbosity is no indication of one's innocence, and in Job's case the fact that it consists of "mockery" is further confirmation of his guilt.

The verb *lā'ag* ("to mock") also seems to form a link with the preceding speech.[157] Job employs this verb in 9:23b where he accuses God of making sport of the tragedies of the innocent. One might expect an opponent to react to such an extravagant claim. That this verb is put on Zophar's lips in an accusation against Job (11:3b) could be considered a sign of such a retort. When approached as such it appears that Zophar counters the charge made against God with one of his own—Job, not God, is the one who engages in mockery.

The root *ḥkm* occurs in 9:4a and 11:6a.[158] Job attributed to God wisdom and strength in the introduction to his last speech (9:4a). His overriding fear was that God would use his wisdom or cunning to distort Job's case and obstruct justice. Zophar is presented as adopting the motif of God's wisdom from 9:4a but purged of Job's view of wisdom's association with injustice. For Zophar, Job's guilt is real and could easily be exposed if God would intervene and make known previously unrevealed knowledge which has a bearing on Job's case. Zophar, in response to Job, seems to be saying that God, in his wisdom, is able to prove Job wrong not

[155] As we have seen, this verb also figures in Job's response of 9:2b (see pp. 60–62).

[156] In 9:2b the claim is more indirect. Although phrased in general terms, it is relevant to Job's case and presumes his innocence. The query merely raises the issue of how one such as Job can demonstrate his righteousness before God.

[157] The verb *lā'ag* occurs four times in Job (9:23; 11:3; 21:3; 22:19), two of which are found in the chapters up to and including chap. 11. These two references will be discussed below. The noun *lā'ag* occurs once in the book (34:7).

[158] The adjective *ḥākām* occurs eight times in Job. Two references are found within the first eleven chapters (5:13; 9:4). The noun *ḥokmâ* is used eighteen times, two of which (4:21; 11:6) occur in the first eleven chapters. The verb *ḥākam* is used twice in Job (31:9; 35:11). The two references in Eliphaz's first speech are too distant to be of relevance for this discussion.

through an obstruction of justice, as Job charges, but rather through an accurate portrayal of reality.

The fourth word, *ʿāwōn* ("iniquity") occurs twice in the body of Job's last speech (10:6a, 14b) and once in Zophar's introduction (11:6c).[159] In 10:6–7 Job describes God as searching for his "iniquity" despite an awareness of his innocence. If 11:6c is read as a response to this text, then Zophar may be understood as refuting Job's allegation with the assertion that he is not innocent but guilty of "iniquity." In the second text (10:14b), Job speaks of his "iniquity" as a hypothetical possibility. Zophar's assurance, as uncomforting as it is, can be understood from this perspective as a confirmation of the reality of Job's "iniquity." Both interpretations of 11:6c, as a response to 10:6a and 14b, yield the same conclusion: Zophar is convinced of Job's guilt.

Moreover, although Job has nowhere expressed himself in the words of the quotation in v 4, ("My teaching is pure, and I am clean in your sight") it does appear to allude to the several protestations of innocence in the preceding speech (9:15, 20, 21; 10:7). In two of the earlier introductions, the friends also make remarks about Job's moral character. Eliphaz provides the most positive character reference, as he recognizes Job's past record as exemplary (4:6), although in an allusion to Job's unbridled passion he also likens Job to a fool (5:3). Bildad is less certain of Job's character and couches his view in conditional language: "If you are pure (*zak*) and upright" (8:6a). Zophar is definitely the most negative of the three. He refers to the purity (*zak,* v 4a) of Job's teaching but in the form of a quotation from Job which effectively distances Zophar from Job's view of himself. Further, it is clear from 11:6c that Zophar sees Job as the guilty party.

(2) An Overview of 11:2–6 with Attention to the Proposed Connections

The rhetorical questions of v 2 focus on the verbiage of Job's speeches and expect a negative response. The first question expresses an obligation to speak.[160] The second question describes Job as a loquacious person

[159] Prior to chaps. 9–11 the noun *ʿāwōn* occurs once (7:21). Afterwards, it is used eleven times.

[160] Cf. Tur-Sinai, *The Book of Job,* 189.

(literally, "a man of lips"). The basis of this ridicule is justified as Job's speeches are consistently longer than those of the friends.[161] With these questions, Zophar impresses upon Job his duty to refute Job's arguments, lest it appear that Job is in the right. Here the verb *ṣādaq* (v 2b) comes into play as it recalls the occasions where it was used by Job in his previous speech (9:2b, 15a, 20a; 10:15b) in confirmation of his innocence. When put on Zophar's lips, however, it is used in reference to Job's guilt.

Previously, Eliphaz sought permission to speak (4:2) but in a tactful manner. The discourteous nature of Zophar's opening questions reflects an impatience and a desire to speak that is similar to Bildad's disposition in 8:2. As we have seen, Bildad critiques Job's words for their destructive quality. Zophar, by comparison, condemns Job's words first for their sheer volume and then in v 3 for their negative qualities. Along with this criticism, Zophar hints that Eliphaz and Bildad have unsuccessfully countered Job's arguments. They had the opportunity to speak before Zophar yet, according to him, were unable to "humiliate" (*kālam,* v 3b) Job and consequently were "silenced" (*ḥāraš,* v 3a). The fact that Zophar accuses Job of mockery (v 3b) has its roots in Job's allegation that God mocks the troubles of the innocent (9:23b). For Zophar this behavior is further evidence of Job's guilt.

Verse 4 summarizes Zophar's understanding of Job's position. It is worded as a direct quotation and introduced as such to ensure that this statement of innocence is understood as Job's and not as Zophar's assessment of him. Evident from the wish of vv 5–6b, Zophar desires that God would directly intervene to inform and convict Job with the "secrets of wisdom." This reference to "wisdom" (v 6a) stems from the mention of God's wisdom in 9:4a. The implication is that Zophar desires that God in his wisdom would prove Job guilty. The word *'āwōn* (v 6c) plays upon its use in 10:6a and 14b in the context of which Job assumes his innocence. In the light of the assurance of v 6c, it is clear that from Zophar's standpoint Job is guilty but receives lenient treatment from God. Hence Zophar obviously disagrees with Job's view of himself as cited in v 4.

[161] Cf. Skehan's comment ("Strophic Patterns," 98): "Job is always given a few lines more than the friend after whom he speaks."

The Fourth Speech of Job (chaps. 12–14)
His Response to Zophar

This speech is by far the longest of those belonging to chaps. 3–27. Those scholars who are sensitive to the structure of the speeches in Job generally divide this speech into three major units or poems,[162] but they do not agree on the specific points of division. Skehan approaches chaps. 12–14 as three speeches of "alphabetic" length: 12:2–25; 13:6–27; 14:1–22 (with 13:28 inserted after 14:3). The opening verses of chap. 13 (vv 1–5) are considered as a transitional unit by Skehan, which in his view, bind the first two "speeches" together.[163] One must remain skeptical of this approach as Skehan arbitrarily designates specific sections as "transitional" so as to arrive at poetic units of alphabetic length.

Webster divides this speech into three poems on thematic and form-critical grounds.[164] The first poem (12:2–25), in Webster's view, contrasts the fate of Job with the prosperity of the wicked (12:4–6) and then addresses the actions of God (vv 7–25). The following section (13:1–27) warrants a division, according to Webster, as the first part features a condemnation of the friends' words (13:1–16) and the second prepares to enter into litigation with God (vv 17–27). The third poem (13:28–14:22) is classed by Webster as a "lament." Rather than transpose 13:28, as do Skehan and others, Webster leaves it in its present position and views 13:28–14:2 as a strophe composed in a concentric pattern on the motif of death.[165]

Horst divides chaps. 12–14 into three poems using the same criteria as those of Webster. In Horst's view the first poem (12:3–13:2) deals with

[162] Terrien (*Job* [1963] 109–23) differs from this consensus with his division of the speech into four poems on the basis of thematic content: "l'expérience contre le dogme" (12:1–25), "le risque de la mort" (13:1–19), "l'invocation de la présence" (13:20–28), and "la prière pour la reconciliation dans l'au-delà" (14:1–28). Terrien overlooks the presence of the key word *pānîm* (13:8, 10, 15, 16, 20, 24) which binds the contents of chap. 13 into a unity and rules out the acceptance of a third poem (13:20–28) distinct from the rest of the chapter.

[163] Skehan, "Strophic Patterns," 105–6. Cf. Murphy (*Wisdom Literature,* 29–30), who consistently adopts Skehan's analysis.

[164] Webster, "Strophic Patterns in Job 3–28," 42–43.

[165] Webster, "Strophic Patterns in Job 3–28," 43.

the wisdom of God; the second (13:3–27) consists of disputation directed against the friends (vv 5–12) and God (vv 13–27)—the theme of which is announced in vv 3–4; and the third (14:1–22 with 13:28 inserted after 14:2) addresses the finite nature of man with 14:1–12 as an elegy on that theme and vv 13–22 as a complaint that Job's wish for death remains unfulfilled.[166]

Habel believes, as does Horst, that the first poem goes beyond the end of chap. 12 (though they disagree on how far it extends into chap. 13), but Habel leaves 13:28 in its present position in the MT. He argues that the "major speeches or sections" consist of the following: 12:2–13:5; 13:6–28; 14:1–22. Habel approaches the first section as Job's challenge to the claim of wisdom made by the friends; the second as a forensic, pretrial speech; and the third as a development of "Job's dream of post-mortem litigation and vindication."[167] Fohrer considers 12:7–11 and 12:12–25 as insertions.[168] Consequently, he believes the first part of the

[166] Horst, *Hiob 1–19,* 183–87.

[167] Habel, *The Book of Job* (1985) 236.

[168] Fohrer (*Das Buch Hiob,* 240) judges 12:7–11 an insertion because of the abrupt change from the third to the second person in this unit, the unexpected presence of the tetragrammaton in v 9b purposely avoided in the speech cycles, and the unconnected *zō't* of v 9b. Of these observations, the occurrence of the divine name "Yahweh" is the most serious evidence for an interpolation. Gordis (*The Book of Job* [1978], 138) notes the similarity of this verse with Isa 41:20 and argues that the poet was influenced by Deutero-Isaiah. As the poet consistently avoided the divine name in the speech cycles, it is unlikely that an outside influence could have led to this text. Habel (*The Book of Job* [1985] 214) suggests that "Yahweh" may be either a "lapse of the poet" or a later "correction" for Eloah, which is present in some MSS. This use of the divine name is unlikely a lapse of a writer who has demonstrated throughout this work an ability to handle detail in a meticulous manner. Habel's suggestion of a "correction" is unclear, as he offers no explanation why such a change was necessary. It seems best to view the presence of the divine name as the work of a later redactor who for some unknown reason altered the text.

Fohrer (*Das Buch Hiob,* 245) believes 12:12–25 is an insertion for three reasons: first, its theme of destruction is inconsistent with 12:6; second, it does not match the previous descriptions of God's power; third, the principle of v 12, that wisdom is associated with age, is not mentioned elsewhere by the friends but by Elihu in 32:6–9. In reply to Fohrer's three criticisms it may be suggested that against the first there is no consistency between 12:6 and 12:12–25 because the former passage speaks of the friends as allies of God and the latter refers to the leaders of the nations; against the second, this presentation on God's power may simply be seen as a new development; against the third, the correlation between wisdom and age may be assumed by the friends who argue on the basis of their years of experience. The overall problem with Fohrer's understanding of chap. 12 is that he

speech to have originally consisted of disputation directed against the friends (12:2–6; 13:1–12). The second (13:13–28) and third (14:1–22) parts of the speech are, in Fohrer's view, both addressed to God. Fohrer suggests that the second section consists of a challenge for God to enter into litigation against Job, and the third he classifies as a complaint on the fate of humanity.[169]

As noted in the above discussion, Terrien and Webster agree that the first poem ends with the close of chap. 12. Horst and Habel, however, argue that this poem concludes at 13:2 and 13:5, respectively. Habel's decision is based on a perceived *inclusio* (13:1–5 as a "balanced answer" to 12:2–4).[170] These sections are interrelated as Habel perceives, but not as opening and closing units. Rather they should be seen as two introductions which share common elements similar to 4:2–6 and 5:1–7.

The disagreement over the second division focuses on the present position of 13:28, which, admittedly, is rather loosely connected to the poem of chap. 13. Fohrer, Terrien, and Habel leave it in its present position, whereas Horst places it after 14:2,[171] and Skehan transposes it to the position following 14:3. Webster, however, leaves this verse in its present position and believes it opens the third poem of the speech. These scholars, who transpose 13:28 or view it as the beginning of a new poem, fail to recognize that this verse, in its present position with its depiction of death, is consistent with the trend exhibited by most of the speeches to the end of chap. 27—they almost all conclude on a note of death.[172] Verse 28, therefore, is best approached as the end of the second poem.

In sum, as is generally recognized, chaps. 12–14 consist of three poems. It is our contention that these poems coincide with the chapter divisions.[173] The first poem is composed on the theme of wisdom (cf. Horst and Habel, above); the second is a pretrial address which, following its introduction

---

fails to discern that this chapter is a unified piece composed on the theme of wisdom. Verses 7–11 contest the idea that the friends' wisdom is superior to Job's (cf. vv 2–3). Further, the key word *ḥokmâ* occurs first in v 2b and then in vv 12a, 13a, and 16a of Fohrer's presumed second insertion.

[169] Fohrer, *Das Buch Hiob,* 240–42.

[170] Habel, *The Book of Job* (1985) 215.

[171] Cf. Pope, *Job,* 106.

[172] See 4:19–21; 5:26; 7:21; 8:22; 10:21–22; 11:20; 14:20–22; 15:34; 16:22; 17:11–16; 18:5–21; 19:26–27; 20:26–29; 21:32–33; 23:24; 27:21–23.

[173] Cf. Rowley, *Job,* 91 and Van der Lugt, "Stanza-Structure in Job 3–14," 22–29.

(vv 1–5), is directed first to the friends (vv 6–16) and then to God (vv 17–28; cf. Horst and Habel, above); and the third focuses on the finite nature of human life and raises the hope of Job's vindication (cf. Horst and Habel, above).

Terrien, Skehan, and Habel take vv 2–6 as the opening unit of the first poem.[174] Fohrer and Webster divide these verses into two strophes (vv 2–3 followed by 4–6).[175] In support of these former scholars, the continuation of the first person subject in vv 3 and 4 suggests that these verses belong to the same strophe. In addition, as shall be argued below, vv 5–6, as a criticism of the friends, advance the opening remarks made against them in vv 2–3.

As to the introduction of the second poem, Skehan and Habel[176] approach 13:1–5 as a unit, whereas Irwin and Terrien[177] consider v 6 to belong to this unit as well. Fohrer and Webster split the first six verses into two three-verse strophes.[178] Verse 4, however, is addressed to the friends and belongs with v 3, which announces Job's intention to speak with God, for together these verses indicate to whom Job will direct his comments in the body of the poem (the friends in vv 6–16 and God in vv 17–28). Further, the desire for silence (v 5) logically follows from Job's declaration that he knows at least as much as his friends (vv 1–2). Hence, in support of Skehan and Habel, vv 4–5 should be taken as part of the opening strophe.[179] Against Irwin and Terrien, it is noted that the opening imperative *šimʿû* of vv 6 and 17 signals the beginning of the address of the friends and of God (respectively) and thus belongs to those sections. In conclusion, the opening strophe of the second poem runs from 13:1 to 13:5.

With regard to the introduction of the third poem, Irwin, Terrien and Habel treat 14:1–6 as a strophe.[180] Fohrer divides these verses into two

[174] Terrien, *Job* (1963) 108–9; Skehan, "Strophic Patterns," 105; and Habel, *The Book of Job* (1985) 215. Van der Lugt ("Stanza Structure in Job 3–14," 23) suggests 12:2–6 might be taken as a substanza of 12:2–13.

[175] Fohrer, *Das Buch Hiob,* 240–41; and Webster, "Strophic Patterns in Job 3–28," 43.

[176] Skehan, "Strophic Patterns," 106; and Habel, *The Book of Job* (1985), 215.

[177] Irwin, "Poetic Structure," 35; and Terrien, *Job* (1963) 114–15.

[178] Fohrer, *Das Buch Hiob,* 241. Webster, "Strophic Patterns in Job 3–28," 43.

[179] Van der Lugt ("Stanza-Structure in Job 3–14," 23, 25), however, considers the introduction to encompass vv 1–4.

[180] Irwin, "Poetic Structure," 35. Terrien, *Job* (1963) 120–21. Habel, *The Book of Job*

strophes (vv 1–3, 4–6) as does Skehan, although he inserts 13:28 after 14:3.[181] Similarly, Webster divides these verses into two strophes but at different points and with 13:28 as the opening line of the first strophe (13:28–14:2; 14:3–6).[182] We concur with the former scholars who treat 14:1–6 as a single strophe on the basis of the key word *yôm* ("day," vv 1b, 5a, 6b) which binds these verses together as a unit.

The Introduction to Part I of Job's Response to Zophar (with the Narrator's Opening Statement)

12:1 Then Job answered and said:
2 Truly you are the intelligentsia,[183]
and with you wisdom will die.
3 I have a mind as well as you;
I do not fall short of you.[184]
Who is not mindful[185] of these things?
4 A laughingstock to his friends I am,
A laughingstock—"The just and blameless one."[186]

(1985) 236. Van der Lugt ("Stanza-Structure in Job 3–14," 27–28) considers this unit a "sub-stanza."

[181] Fohrer, *Das Buch Hiob,* 242. Skehan, "Strophic Patterns," 107.

[182] Webster, "Strophic Patterns in Job 3–28," 43.

[183] Michel (*Job in the Light of Northwest Semitic,* 261–63) follows Dahood ("Ugaritic-Hebrew Syntax and Style," *UF* 1 [1968] 25, n. 1), who assumes the existence of a root *'mm,* "to be strong, wise." Hence Michel translates *'am* as "sagacity." Conclusive evidence, however, is wanting for this proposal. Pope (*Job,* 89) translates *'am* as "gentry," i.e., the upper-class landowners, "people of wealth, breeding, and education." (Cf. Gordis, *The Book of Job,* 136, who renders *'am* as "the people that count.") It is agreed that the term *'am* connotes a special category of people, but above all it must be stressed that their wisdom is the distinctive attribute in this context.

[184] Literally "I do not fall lower than you." This colon is often translated, "I am not inferior to you." So Gordis, *The Book of Job,* 130; Pope, *Job,* 88; Habel, *The Book of Job* (1985), 211; and the *NRSV.*

[185] The preposition *'et* with the nuance of "consciousness" (Williams, *Hebrew Syntax,* §347).

[186] Following Rowley (*Job,* 92), Habel (*The Book of Job* [1985] 213), and the *JPSV,* it seems best to interpret the derision of the friends (v 4bc) as a quotation. Although the root *'nh* is in the form of the *qal* theme, it is preferable to translate it as a passive (cf. Gordis, *The Book of Job,* 128 and the *JPSV*). As with Terrien (*Job* [1963] 110) and Guillaume (*Studies in Job,* 90), I take this root as *'nh* III, "to be afflicted" (see BDB 776).

5 For misfortune[187] there is contempt in the
thought of the comfortable,
a beating[188] for those whose feet slip.
6 The tents of the robbers are at peace,
and El's agitators[189] are secure,
whom Eloah leads by his hand.[190]

Form

The introduction and body to the poem of chap. 12 consist principally of disputation. Fohrer differentiates between legal disputation and wisdom argumentation in this unit. In his opinion vv 2 and 4–6 are drawn from legal practice and v 3 has its provenance in wisdom circles.[191] One wonders why Fohrer does not understand v 2 also as wisdom argumentation with its connection to the assertion of Job in v 3 and its reference to wisdom in v 2b. Further, vv 5 and 6 could be at home in either a wisdom or legal setting. Moreover, v 4, with its description of how others perceive the victim of misfortune, contains a complaint motif (cf. Pss 3:3; 13:5; 22:9; 31:12; 35:21; 41:6; etc.).[192]

[187] For *lāpîd* ("torch") read *pîd* ("misfortune, calamity") with the preposition *lĕ* as do Fohrer, *Das Buch Hiob,* 237; Pope, *Job,* 90; Habel, *The Book of Job* (1985) 213; Michel, *Job in the Light of Northwest Semitic,* 267; and others.

[188] Dhorme (*A Commentary on Job,* 170), Fohrer (*Das Buch Hiob,* 237), Terrien (*Job* [1963] 109), Horst (*Hiob 1–19,* 176), Gordis (*The Book of Job,* 136), de Wilde (*Das Buch Hiob,* 165) and Hartley (*The Book of Job,* 206) derive the noun *nākôn* from the root *nkh* ("to strike"). Delitzsch (*Biblical Commentary on Job,* 195), Driver and Gray (*A Critical and Exegetical Commentary on Job,* 113), Pope (*Job,* 88), and Habel (*The Book of Job* [1985], 213) take the root as *kwn* ("to be firm, ordered") and translate "ready, fitting." Either reading makes sense, yet the idea of violence fits well with the attitude of contempt in v 5a and in the context of affliction (v 4b).

[189] Following Michel's understanding of this text (*Job in the Light of Northwest Semitic,* 268) but as an allusion to the friends and not as a mythological reference.

[190] Dhorme (*A Commentary on Job,* 170), Pope (*Job,* 88), and Habel (*The Book of Job* [1985] 211) take God as the object of the colon. If, however, Eloah is read as the subject and *hēbî'* as "to lead," the meaning becomes clear (Michel, *Job in the Light of Northwest Semitic,* 268–69). The implication of this verse is similar to 13:7–10, where Job accuses the friends of partiality toward God.

[191] Fohrer, *Das Buch Hiob,* 240–241.

[192] A. de Wilde (*Das Buch Hiob,* 165–66) classes vv 4–6 as a complaint.

This introduction consists of two major components: first, a dispute over who possesses wisdom; second, a complaint concerning how Job is treated by his friends supplemented by two indirect accusations against his friends. The structure of this introduction may be laid out as follows:

	Announcement of response: Job replies to Zophar	(12:1)
1	Disputation: Who has wisdom?	(2–3)
	(a) Ridicule of opponents: Do they alone have wisdom?	(2)
	(b) Defense of Job's intellect: He is as knowledgeable as his friends	(3)
2	Complaint:	(4–6)
	1 Job is an object of derision	(4)
	(a) His friends laugh at him	(4a)
	(b) Direct quotation of mockery	(4b)
	(c) He is treated as a "laughingstock"	(4ca)
	(d) Direct quotation of mockery	(4cb)
	2 Indirect accusations against friends	(5–6)
	(a) They treat the unfortunate with contempt	(5)
	(b) They are in league with God	(6)

Rhetorical Analysis

(1) The Connections between 12:2–6 and Previous Passages

Although in this introduction Job is given the second person plural pronoun *ʾattem* (v 2a) and the comparable suffix *-kem* (vv 2b, 3) in reference to the three friends, there are several connections with chap. 11 which suggest that Job replies especially to Zophar. This third friend exhibits a particularly patronizing attitude toward Job. He dismisses Job's speeches as mere babble (11:3a), is certain that God already views Job as a guilty party (11:6c), and severely criticizes Job's intelligence (11:12). Further, Zophar is portrayed as having an acquaintance with the "secrets of wisdom" (*taʿălumôt ḥokmâ,* 11:6a)[193] which God could teach Job. This

[193] For the occurrences of the root *ḥkm* in Job see n. 158. Two further references to wisdom (*ḥokmâ*) appear in chap. 12. The first (12:12) is best understood as a rhetorical question in which Job alludes to his friends' lack of wisdom in a stronger attack than in 12:2. The second (12:13) takes up once again the theme of the wisdom and power of

disclosure implies that Zophar is a student of this "wisdom" and "understanding."[194] After all, Zophar's knowledge is presented as surpassing that of Job's, as he is certain not only of Job's guilt but also of the fact that God treats Job leniently (11:6c). Job's biting remark, "with you wisdom (*ḥokmâ*) will die" (v 2b) should, therefore, be read as a rebuttal of Zophar's supposed intellectual superiority especially as hinted at in his inference that he has some knowledge of the "secrets of wisdom" (11:6a). In short, Job makes the point that Zophar is not as wise as he thinks.

Second, the reason for Job's defense of his intelligence becomes even clearer when one takes into account the relationship between 12:3 and 11:12. Both texts have in common the root *lbb*.[195] With the wisdom saying, "A hollow person will gain understanding (*lbb*) when a wild ass is born human" (11:12), Zophar invokes against Job the authority of the wisdom tradition. Job, as might be expected, is presented as reacting vigorously to this denigration of his intelligence. To this end the noun *lēbāb* ("mind, understanding") is put upon his lips in his defense: "I have a mind as well as you" (12:3a).[196] As Dhorme observes, Job has previously argued on the basis of his knowledge ("Truly I know that this is so" [9:2a]) in response to Bildad.[197] At the present point in the dispute, Zophar's approach leads to the defense of Job's intellectual capacity once again.

In view of these two examples of the manner in which Job responds to Zophar's speech of chap. 11, it is likely that the plural demonstrative pronoun *'ēlleh* ("these things," v 3c) has as its antecedent a passage from

---

God (cf. 9:4–12) in which God is seen as the superior power. The implication is that both Job's wisdom and that of the friends is inferior to God's.

[194] Habel (*The Book of Job* [1985] 207) says that this "wisdom" and "understanding" has "a depth dimension discernible only by God—and perhaps by those who, like Zophar, are initiated in the esoteric ways of wisdom."

[195] The denominative verb *lbb* occurs only in 11:12. The noun *lēbāb* makes eight appearances in Job, one in 12:3a, five of which follow chap. 12, and two of which precede it (1:5, 10:13). The cognate noun *lēb* occurs a total of sixteen times in Job. Twelve of these references follow chap. 12, two precede chaps. 11 and 12 (7:17, 8:10), and two occur in these chapters (11:13, 12:24). The ethical context of 11:13, as compared to the strictly intellectual reference of 11:12, suggests that 12:3 unlikely responds to 11:12. The occurrence in 12:24, however, does involve intelligence, but of the leaders of the people, not of Job. Thus it should probably not be understood as a further response to 11:12.

[196] Some scholars (e.g., Pope, *Job,* 90; Habel, *The Book of Job* [1985] 218; and Hartley, *The Book of Job,* 206) have already drawn attention to this relationship.

[197] Dhorme, *A Commentary on Job,* 168.

chap. 11. It is possible that Job could be saying that there is nothing new in the conditional advice Zophar offers in 11:13–20, but, since *'ēlleh* is used with reference to knowledge and Zophar is portrayed as knowing more than Job, the antecedent could well be the "secrets of wisdom." Further, the impossible questions of 11:7–8, with their partial answers in vv 8 and 9, might be considered illustrations of the quality of knowledge subsumed under the subject "secrets of wisdom." If so, Job maintains in 12:3c that he already knows his limits and that Zophar is teaching him nothing new.

In the complaint of v 4, Job laments that his friends see him as a "laughingstock" (*śĕḥōq*). To reinforce Job's ignominy, the word is repeated (although with *plene* spelling [*śĕḥôq*]) in the third component of the tricolon. That the root *śḥq* is occasionally used with the root *l'g* as a word pair (Pss 2:4; 59:9; Prov 1:26; and 2 Chron 30:10) gives weight to the argument that the occurrence of these two roots in successive speeches (12:4a, c, 11:3b, respectively) is not simply coincidental.[198] As Zophar accuses Job of mockery (*l'g*) in 11:3b, Job's description of himself as a laughingstock recalls this accusation. It appears that Job responds to this allegation with a countercharge—that the friends, in their treatment of him as a laughingstock, are the ones who are guilty of derision. To illustrate his countercharge, Job quotes the two taunts spoken by his friends in v 4b and cb.

The presence of the root *ṣdq* in both 11:2b of Zophar's introduction and in 12:4cb hints at a relationship between these two introductions in terms of Job's character.[199] Zophar casts doubt on Job's righteousness when he asks if such a man should be "justified" (11:2b). The second epithet quoted by Job, "the just (*ṣaddîq*) and blameless one" (12:4cb), should be understood as an ironic insult used by the friends through which they reveal further doubt concerning Job's integrity. Job's recall of how the others mock his reputation logically follows from Zophar's questioning

[198] Beyond the two incidences to the root *śḥq* in 12:4, this root occurs in ten other passages of Job, eight of which follow this speech. In two earlier passages (5:22, 8:21), both Eliphaz and Bildad assure Job that his day of restoration will come, and on that day he will laugh once more. Although these two references are rather distant from chap. 12, it is possible that Job also may be understood as reacting to these previous assurances as if to say, "You intend to console me with promises that I will someday laugh; yet you now laugh at me in my suffering." For the occurrences of the verb *lā'ag* see n. 157.

[199] For a note on the occurrences of *ṣdq* in chaps. 8–10 see n. 142.

of Job's character. To call Job, "the just (*ṣaddîq*) and blameless one (*tāmîm*)" clearly harks back to the fourfold attributes which characterize Job in the prologue. The adjectives *tāmîm* (12:4cb) and *tām* (1:1, 8; 2:3) match as they derive from the same root *tmm*. Further, the title "the just one" (*ṣaddîq*, 2:4cb) aptly summarizes the three remaining attributes: Job as "upright, one who feared God and turned away from evil" (1:1, 8; 2:3). In response to the uncertainties raised by Zophar concerning Job's integrity, these epithets should be understood as quoted by Job with approval, for they recall his reputation as the "ideal" man of the prologue even though for others their truth gives cause for derision.

(2) An Overview of 12:2–6 with Attention to the Proposed Connections

In this passage Job is presented as reacting to apparent insinuations made against his intelligence. His disagreement is registered through ridicule similar to that which Bildad (8:2) and Zophar (11:2–3) directed against him.[200] This ridicule of his friends (v 2), introduced with the emphatic adverb *'omnām* ("truly," v 2a), is ironic as Job implies that they do not in fact have an exclusive claim on wisdom. Further, as Job points out in v 3c and in vv 7–12 of the body of this poem, the wisdom of his friends is nothing more than common knowledge. Specifically, Job's sarcastic reference to his friends' wisdom (v 2b) recalls Zophar's superior intellectual air and his assumed acquaintance with the "secrets of wisdom" (11:6a).

Job turns to a defense of his intellect in v 3, which he argues is as developed as that of his friends. When this verse is read against the cruel insult Zophar hurled against Job in 11:12, the motivation for Job's defensive stance may be appreciated. Following this outburst, Job delivers a brief complaint in which he describes his friends' treatment of him. The reference to himself as a "laughingstock" (v 4a) ties in with Zophar's charge of mockery against Job (11:3b) and makes the point that it is the friends who are guilty of mockery. Job supports his complaint with two quotations of the epithets hurled against him (vv 4b, 4cb). Habel translates the first quotation as, "'The one who summons God for an answer'"[201] and suggests that it "echoes Job's earlier desire to 'summon God to court'

[200] Habel (*The Book of Job* [1985] 218), cognizant of this fact, comments that 12:2–3 "matches" both 8:2 and 11:2–3.

[201] Habel, *The Book of Job* (1985) 211.

and obtain an 'answer'" (9:16, 19).[202] This text (12:4b) parallels 9:16a fairly closely, but that *wayya'ănēhû* should be translated as a purpose clause is unlikely. Further, verses 4b and c seem more likely to refer to Job's earlier life as depicted in the prologue. If the root *'nh* is understood as *'nh* III ("to afflict") following Terrien and Guillaume,[203] then the cause of the derision becomes apparent. During Job's "golden years," he lived in a close relationship with God (cf. 29:2–5) and enjoyed a reputation similar to that described in v 4c (cf. 1:8; 2:3), but now he is the object of derision as he has fallen from favor and is afflicted by God. In this context the reference to Job as "just" (v 4c) is reminiscent of Zophar's query, "Should a verbose man be justified (11:2b)?" The implication of Job's quotation (12:4cb) is that he indeed considers himself righteous despite Zophar's questioning of his integrity.

Fohrer interprets v 5 as directed against the friends but believes the following verse is a critique of their teaching that God punishes evildoers.[204] With Fohrer's understanding of v 5, we concur, but, as will be argued below, with the qualification that it is aimed primarily at Zophar. Verse 6, however, is best understood as a continuation of the critique of the friends themselves. In this verse Job describes the robbers as at "peace" and El's agitators as "secure." Since the description of the friends as "comfortable" (v 5a) is consonant with these characteristics, then it is likely that Job has the friends in mind in both verses. In addition, the designation of the friends as "El's agitators" (v 6b) is consistent with the allegations made against them in v 5. Habel comes closest of any of the commentators to relating v 5 with v 6. He writes, "Like the complacent who enjoy mocking the unfortunate, robbers who revel in their 'security' (cf. 11:18) treat God with disdain."[205] Since Habel is not convinced, however, that the first category refers to the friends, he does not develop this idea.[206]

When vv 5 and 6 are understood as directed against the friends, they are best approached as two separate, indirect accusations: the first accuses

[202] Habel, *The Book of Job* (1985) 218.

[203] See n. 186.

[204] Fohrer, *Das Buch Hiob,* 244.

[205] Habel, *The Book of Job* (1985) 218–19. Note, however, Habel's different understanding of v 6b, c.

[206] Of the complacent, Habel (*The Book of Job* [1985] 218) writes, "The 'complacent' (cf. Amos 6:1) may refer to the friends who have mocked Job for seeking litigation (v 4)."

the friends of treating the victims of tragedy with contempt; and the second accuses them of acting as God's allies in their attack on Job. The complaint of v 4, in which Job describes the friends' unjust treatment of him, should perhaps be seen as preliminary evidence in support of the accusations of vv 5 and 6. The complaint suits this purpose well as it allows the victim to describe the extent of the abuse suffered at the hands of enemies.

The Introduction to Part II of Job's Reply to Zophar

13:1 Look, all this my eye has seen,
my ear has heard and understood.
2 As to your knowledge, I also know as much;
I do not fall short of you.
3 Rather would I speak to Shaddai,
I desire to argue my case with El.
4 But you are plasterers of lies,[207]
quack healers—all of you.[208]
5 If only you would keep completely silent,
it would be your wisdom.

Form

The first half of chap. 13 consists of disputation (vv 1–16) and the second half (vv 17–28) is a complaint addressed to God.[209] In the opening verses (1–2) Job defends his knowledge as equal to that of his friends. Job, then, expresses his desire to enter into litigation against God (v 3). In the following verse, Job accuses his friends of deceit and assesses their advice as worthless. In the closing verse of this unit, Job wishes that his friends would remain silent. This wish is best understood as ridicule, for the implication is that their arguments reveal them as fools. This introduction may be laid out as follows:

[207] Tur-Sinai (*The Book of Job,* 221) draws on the Aramaic *syqr'* ("red paint") for his translation "putting on red paint" with the understanding that the friends apply red, the color of health, to Job's face to make it appear he is well. This somewhat exotic derivation is not necessary, as *šeqer,* with its usual meaning of "deception, falsehood," makes perfectly good sense here.

[208] This translation follows that of Pope's (*Job,* 96).

[209] Cf. Murphy, *Wisdom Literature,* 29–30.

1	Defense of Job's intellect: He is as knowledgeable as his friends	(13:1–2)
2	Wish for audience with God: Job desires to present his case	(3)
3	Accusation: His friends are frauds	(4)
4	Ridicule: Wish for silence	(5)

Rhetorical Analysis

(1) The Connections between 13:1–5 and Previous Passages

The disputation of 13:1–5 contains several noteworthy parallels to the introduction to the first poem of this speech (12:2–6) as well as what appear to be elements of a response to Zophar's first speech. The similarities of this passage with 12:2–6 will first be explored.

The defense of Job's knowledge in 13:1–2 corresponds to 12:3. Although the vocabulary of 13:1–2a largely differs from 12:3ac, the shared topic of Job's knowledge is readily apparent. The adverb *gam* with the rhetorical force of I "too" or "in addition,"[210] is present in both 13:2a and 12:3a. It occurs here in statements which compare Job's intellect with that of his friends. The colon, "I do not fall short of you" (12:3b; 13:2b) is common to both these passages. Without text critical support, some scholars delete 12:3b as a gloss on the grounds that it occurs in the following chapter.[211] It forms, however, one connection among several in the overall pattern of correspondences between these two passages and is comparable to the parallel between 7:1b and 14:6b.[212] Further, the recurrence of the colon in question is integral to these two passages as they both develop the idea of Job's equality, if not superiority, as a sage. Next, in 12:4b, Job cites an epithet by which he has become known, "The one who called to Eloah and is afflicted." The boldness of Job in 13:3—that he would speak to God and argue his case with him—is rooted in this past relation-

[210] Williams, *Hebrew Syntax* §378.

[211] Michel (*Job in the Light of Northwest Semitic,* 264) retains this colon on the grounds that when dropped it "obscures the A:B:A pattern which seems quite obvious here." His observation may be countered, however, by the fact that without v 3b the remaining cola fall into place as parallel components.

[212] "His days are like those of a hireling" (7:1b) as compared to "so that he may enjoy his day like a hireling" (14:6b).

ship of one who habitually called upon God. In addition, the allusive criticisms of the friends in 12:5–6 correspond with 13:4 where Job directly and unequivocally denounces his friends as frauds. Finally, the reference to *ḥokmâ* (13:5b) builds on *12:2*b. In the earlier passage, Job condemns the friends for behaving as if wisdom was their exclusive domain, and now in 12:2b he moves on to a criticism of their speeches as a betrayal of their lack of wisdom.

These similarities between 12:1–6 and 13:1–5 have the effect of drawing the reader's attention to one particular issue of importance to the argument of the protagonist: Job believes his argument carries more weight than those of his friends. To convince the reader of his credibility, Job again defends his intelligence and continues with his attack on the supposed wisdom of his friends.

With the discussion of the parallels between 12:2–6 and 13:1–5 complete, 13:1–5 will now be dealt with as a response to Zophar's speech of chapter 11. It is our contention that in this introductory strophe of 13:1–5, Job responds to several elements in particular from Zophar's introduction of 11:2–6. First, the verb *ḥāraš* and the noun *ḥokmâ* of v 5 occur also in 11:3a and 6a, respectively. Zophar employs the verb *ḥāraš* in an allusion to the silencing of Eliphaz and Bildad by Job's arguments. To Zophar this result is unfortunate, as he desires that Job be silenced and even shamed by the speeches of his friends (11:3b). Job, in turn, is given this verb in an emphatic clause (v 5a)[213] in which he approves of the result of his arguments, and with this verb he expresses his wish for the complete silence of his friends.[214] The connection between these two passages suggests that in response to Zophar's statement, "Your babbling may

[213] The infinite absolute of the verb *ḥāraš* (*Hiph'il* theme) precedes the conjugated form of the verb for emphasis (Williams, *Hebrew Syntax,* §205).

[214] The verb *ḥāraš* appears eight times in Job. Four occurrences fall well outside Zophar's first speech and Job's fourth speech (6:24; 33:31,33; 41:4). Two further appearances of *ḥāraš* which occur in 13:13a and 19b warrant comment. In the former, Job requests silence so that he might speak. This reference continues with the request for silence in 13:5 and should be understood along the same lines, i.e., as a further response to Zophar's observation of 11:3a. Job, in the latter text, speaks of the possibility of God testifying against him in court. Under such conditions Job maintains that he will be silent and listen. This statement could be understood as a continuation of the theme of silence in which Job now describes the conditions under which he would willingly be silent—before God, whom Job admits is wiser than he (9:4; cf., 12:13).

silence men" (11:3a), Job maintains that the first two friends should not only continue their silence but that Zophar should be silent as well.

Coupled with this wish is the message that Zophar and his friends show themselves to be fools through their speeches. As previously mentioned, Zophar is presented as having an awareness of the "secrets of wisdom" (*taʿălumôt ḥokmâ,* 11:6a). The noun *ḥokmâ* is again put on Job's lips to make the point that Zophar (and the others) have only exposed their ignorance through their speeches (v 5b).[215] If they desire to appear wise, Job suggests they would do best to keep silent and allow him to speak.

In addition to the ramifications proposed for the two words shared by these two passages,[216] two texts seem to build upon Zophar's comments of 11:2–6. The first involves the name calling of v 4 ("plasterers of lies" and "quack healers"). These epithets mark this verse as the sharpest denunciation of the friends thus far in the dispute (cf. 6:14–27). This reaction might well respond to Zophar's contention that Job engages in mockery and should be properly humiliated (11:3). It appears as if the poet decides to let Job unleash some real mockery. As a result, Job derides and humiliates his friends as frauds.

True to the discipline of the wisdom tradition, Job stresses, in the second text, that he has drawn knowledge from his senses of sight and hearing (13:1).[217] The antecedent of *kol,* in this verse, is the hymn on the dis-

[215] For a note on the two occurrences of *ḥokmâ* in the body of the poem of chap. 12 see n. 193.

[216] The verbs *yādaʿ, dābar* (*Piʿel* theme) and the expression *mî-yittēn* also appear in both 11:2–6; 13:5. The verb *yādaʿ,* occurs a total of fifty-two times in Job. In Job's fourth speech, the verb is used four times (12:9; 13:2, 18; 14:21), and in Zophar's speech it occurs three times (11:6,8,11). Due to the different contexts in which this verb is used in these two speeches and in view of the frequent use of this verb in the book as a whole, one must acknowledge that the appearance of *yādaʿ* in 13:5 is probably not significant as a specific response to Zophar. The same is true for the verb *dābar.* It occurs a total of thirty-seven times in Job: once in Zophar's first speech (11:5) and four times in Job's fourth speech (13:3, 7, 13, 22). The expression *mî-yittēn* does not occur as frequently (ten times) as do these two verbs in Job. One might be tempted to read Job's wish for silence (13:5) as a counterwish to Zophar's desire that God would speak to Job (11:5), yet Job's request that God reply to him in 13:22b rules out this approach.

[217] That the wisdom tradition stressed the value of lessons drawn from observations of everyday life is clear from the example stories of Prov 7:6–23; 24:30–34; Qoh 4:13–16; and the reflections of Qoheleth (e.g., 2:1–11, 12–17, 18–26).

ruptive power of God's wisdom (12:13–15).[218] With this pronoun Job brings forward observations concerning God's rule of the world which Zophar and the friends have not taken into account in their arguments. As Zophar derides Job as a "man of lips" (11:2b) skilled in disseminating "babble" (11:3a), Job's explicit reference to his eyes and ears as receptive organs of knowledge should be seen as a defense of his arguments. Job, rejects Zophar's assessment of his speeches and implies, in response, that since his eyes have witnessed God's destructive workings and his ears understood the significance of these actions, his tongue, which is dependent on their input, must utter more than mere babble.

(2) An Overview of 13:1–5 with Attention to the Proposed Connections

As evident from the foregoing argument, 13:1–5 relates to both 12:2–6 and Zophar's introduction of 11:2–6. Job defends his knowledge in both 13:1–2 and 12:3; he desires to have an audience with God (13:3) which relates to his reputation as "the one who called to Eloah" (12:4b); and he criticizes his friends in 13:4–5 as he did in 12:2 and 5–6.

Moreover, the namecalling of his friends (13:4) likely issues from Zophar's charge that Job engages in mockery (11:3b). This criticism should be understood as an attack on both Zophar's and the other two friends' integrity in an attempt to intimidate them. The pairing of silence and wisdom in 13:5 parallels Prov 17:28, Sir 20:5–8 and the Egyptian Instruction Literature.[219] The authority of the wisdom tradition is thus invoked to reveal the friends as fools in an effort to silence them. When the verb *ḥārаš* ("to silence," 13:5a) and the noun *ḥokmâ* ("wisdom," 13:5b) is read against the occurrence of these words in Zophar's introduction (11:3a, 6a, respectively) one can see that Job is portrayed as focusing on this friend in particular.

As with the preceding introduction to this speech, it appears that Job defends himself on two fronts: against Zophar, the last speaker, as indicated by the interrelationships between 11:2–6 and 13:1–5; and against the remaining friends as indicated by the plural forms of reference (13:2,

[218] Cf. Dhorme, *A Commentary on Job,* 182; and Habel, *The Book of Job* (1985) 222.

[219] E.g., chap. 4 of the *Instruction of Amenemope* in *The Ancient Near East: An Anthology of Texts and Pictures* (ed. J. B. Pritchard; Princeton: Princeton University, 1958) 1. 238.

4–5). Further, the correspondences with Zophar's introduction suggest that Job engages in debate with Zophar in particular; and Eliphaz and Bildad are involved simply by way of general reference.

The Introduction to Part III of Job's Reply to Zophar

14:1 A human, born of a woman,
short of days and full of turmoil.
2 Like a flower he blossoms and withers
and flees like a shadow and does not stay.
3 Even[220] on such a one you open your eyes;
and him,[221] you bring into judgment with you.
4 O that a clean person could come from an unclean person.
Not one can.[222]
5 His days are indeed[223] determined,
the number of his months is with you,

[220] For *'ap* as an emphatic adverb see Williams, *Hebrew Syntax,* §385.

[221] Several scholars (Dhorme, *A Commentary on Job,* 196; Driver and Gray, *A Critical and Exegetical Commentary on Job,* 127; Tur-Sinai, *The Book of Job,* 233; Fohrer, *Das Buch Hiob,* 239; Horst, *Hiob 1–19,* 182; Gordis, *The Book of Job,* 147; de Wilde, *Das Buch Hiob,* 163; and Hartley, *The Book of Job,* 229) follow the LXX, Vg. and Syriac and read "him." Terrien (*Job* [1963] 120), Pope (*Job,* 104), Habel (*The Book of Job* [1985] 233), and Michel (*Job in the Light of Northwest Semitic,* 317), however, read "me." Job alternates between first person descriptions of his fate and third person observations on the life-conditions of humanity in general, but as this first person reference exists, on its own, in the context of third person statements, it is likely a scribal error where the *yodh* was written for a *waw.*

[222] The sense of v 4 is particularly obscure. Pope (*Job,* 106) brackets this verse as misplaced if not a later interpolation (cf. Horst, *Hiob 1–19,* 207). De Wilde (*Das Buch Hiob,* 173) deletes v 4 as a gloss. Blommerde (*Northwest Semitic Grammar,* 69) builds on the Vg. ("Is it not you alone?" i.e., God) and Targum ("except God") and translates: "Who can make the impure clean? The Mighty One alone." Michel (*Job in the Light of Northwest Semitic,* 318–20) takes into account the proposals of Dahood ("Hebrew-Ugaritic Lexicography VIII," *Bib* 51 [1970] 428), Ceresko (*Job 29–31,* 129), and others that *'eḥad* may mean "unique" and translates: "O that He would declare 'clean' the unclean, O Victor Unique!" With the revocalization of *lō'* to *lē'* ("Mighty One, Victor"), Blommerde's and Michel's translations are plausible. Yet the unusually short colon of the MT stands out as a cry of futility and compliments the complaint of life as short and troubled. Cf. our translation with that of Guillaume (*Studies in Job,* 34): "Oh that a clean thing could come out of an unclean thing! Not one can."

[223] Taking *'im* as an emphatic adverb along with Gordis (*The Book of Job,* 148) and Pope (*Job,* 104).

you have set his limit and he cannot exceed it.
6 Look away from him! Let him be
so that he may enjoy his day like a hireling.

Form

This passage is a complaint as is chap. 14 as a whole.[224] Its components may be divided into two parts each consisting of three subsections. The subsections of part A correspond to part B, as demonstrated below. This passage opens with an observation concerning the human generative process (v 1a) which ties in with the wish of v 4.[225] The motif of the transient and troubled life of humanity (vv 1b–2) is elaborated in v 5 with its emphasis on humankind's unalterable, predetermined lifespan. The accusation made against God in v 3—that he conducts himself as an antagonist—is continued in v 6 where Job requests that God cease from such activities. The structure of this piece may be outlined as follows:

A1	The generative process: Humans are born of women	(14:1a)
2	The life of a human: Transient and troubled	(1b–2)
3	Accusation: God is the antagonist	(3ab)
	(a) He is a spy	(3a)
	(b) He enters into litigation against Job	(3b)
B1^{1}	On the possibility of cleanness	(4ab)
	(a) Wish: That a human could be clean	(4a)
	(b) Futility of wish: It is impossible	(4b)
2^{1}	Development of the transient life motif	(5)
3^{1}	Request: That God may cease his surveillance of humans	(6)

[224] Cf. Murphy, *Wisdom Literature,* 30.

[225] Cf. Dhorme, *A Commentary on Job,* 196; and Rowley, *Job,* 103. Of this relationship, Dhorme writes:

> Sometimes *ṭāhôr* is applied to physical purity (28:19), sometimes to moral purity 17:9). Here, of course, it is used in the latter sense, although *ṭāmē* "impure" is an allusion to the impurities incurred by woman in childbirth (v. 1a). Man is unable to attain purity, i.e., righteousness. . . He is sullied in his very origins (196).

Habel (*The Book of Job* [1985] 240) comments that such an interpretation is "gratuitous." A careful study of the structure of this passage, however, lends support to Dhorme's proposal, for it demonstrates that v 1a corresponds with v 4 as vv 1b–2 relates to v 5 and v 3 with v 6.

Rhetorical Analysis

(1) The Connections between 14:1–6 and Previous Passages

The introduction to Job's poem of chap. 14 appears to react to several elements of Zophar's speech mostly by way of allusion. The play on the word *'ayin* is the one exception to this observation.[226] Previously, Zophar, in words faithful to Job's stance, quotes Job as claiming that he is clean in God's "eyes" (11:4b). Job addresses the human condition in general in 14:1–6, but when it is understood Job has himself in mind, one can see that he indirectly maintains that God watches him solely to charge him with wrong. Job, in essence, sees himself as innocent, as Zophar indicates, but as he complains in response to Zophar, God's "eyes" do not see him in this light (14:3a).

Further, the description of Job's teaching as "pure" (*zak,* 11:4a)[227] and his character as "clean" (*bar,* 11:4b)[228] appears to form the basis of Job's futile wish of 14:4, in which he speaks of the impossibility of a "clean person" (*ṭāhôr*)[229] arising from an "unclean person." In response to this characterization of Job by Zophar in 11:4, Job claims that his integrity is not recognized by God. In his first speech, Zophar also argued that God convicts only "deceitful men" (11:11a). Job's wish of 14:4 should be understood in relation to this position as well. When read as a response, Job, in 14:4, disagrees with Zophar for, in his view, God sees the entire human race as unclean and is therefore antagonistic to all. Thus Job contends that he is not deceitful, but is attacked by God simply because he is a member of the human race. In his view, God considers humankind as born permanently unclean. Consequently, Job rejects Zophar's conditional advice of 11:13–20 which is rooted in the premise that humanity is able to put away impurity before God.

Finally, Job's observation that God brings mortals into "judgment"

[226] The word *'ayin* occurs forty-two times in Job, eight of which precede chap. 11. These earlier references are distant and are not likely relevant to Job's response to Zophar. Beyond the two references to "eyes" in Zophar's first speech and Job's fourth speech (11:4, 13:1), Zophar mentions "the eyes of the wicked" in 11:20. As this text does not refer to God's eyes, it will not form part of this discussion.

[227] The adjective *zak* is used also in 8:6 and in the later texts of 16:17; 33:9.

[228] The adjective *bar* occurs in Job only in 11:4b.

[229] The adjective *ṭāhôr* occurs elsewhere in Job in 17:9; 28:19.

(*mišpāṭ*, 14:3b)[230] appears to respond to 11:2b. In this text, Zophar expresses the concern that Job might be considered righteous (*ṣādaq*) if his speeches are not successfully countered. In reply, Job implies that God will not allow him to be vindicated regardless of whether the friends are able to stop his speeches.

(2) An Overview of 14:1–6 with Attention to the Proposed Connections

Job attests to the helplessness of humankind in the first verse of chap. 14: human beings are born into the world to a brief and troubled life. This theme of transitoriness is furthered with comparisons to a short-lived flower and a fleeting shadow in v 2. The accusation made against God—that he spies on and judges human beings (v 3) serves to reinforce the helpless aspect of their situation. That God's "eyes" (v 3) are portrayed in this manner is significant from the standpoint of Zophar's understanding of Job's position. Job may consider himself clean in God's "eyes" (11:4b) but, in allusion to himself in 14:3, he takes the position that God does not share this point of view. Similarly, Job complains, with an oblique reference to 11:2b, that God has "judged" (14:3b) him and therefore he has no chance of vindication even if he is able to proceed with his speeches.

The helplessness of the human condition is emphasized with the wish of v 4a which is immediately answered with a negative statement indicating the futility of such a wish. Again, the hopelessness of Job's situation becomes all the more evident from the perspective of Zophar's speech. The reference to Job's assessment of himself as "pure" and "clean" (11:4) is all the more tragic because, even so, no human being has a hope to appear "clean" before God (14:4). So distorted is God's sense of justice that, according to Job, God convicts all mortals and not just the "deceitful men" (11:11a) of Zophar's speech. Finally, 14:5, with its description of the limited life span of humanity, and 14:6, with the request that God let his creature be, continue with the theme of helplessness as introduced in their matching verses (vv 1b–2, 3, respectively).

[230] The noun *mišpāṭ* is used nineteen times in Job, three of which precede 14:3b (8:3; 9:19, 32).

CHAPTER 3

The Second Cycle

The Second Speech of Eliphaz (chap. 15)
His Response to Job

With thirty-four lines Eliphaz's second speech is the longest of the friends' contributions within the second cycle.[1] In subject matter this speech consists of two distinct sections: vv 2–16, which constitute a harsh rebuke of Job for his arrogance, and vv 17–35 which portray the punishment of the wicked. In Skehan's opinion, "alphabetic structures are no longer a factor" from the second cycle onwards.[2] As the alphabetic structure is the criterion Skehan uses to divide the discourses into separate poems, he treats chap. 15 as a single speech. Murphy distinguishes vv 2–16 (entitled "Reprimand") from vv 17–35 (entitled "A warning lesson from the wisdom tradition") as two subsections of the speech but stops short of dividing it into two separate poems.[3]

Conversely, Terrien and Webster approach vv 2–16 and 17–35 as two distinct poems.[4] In support of these two scholars, the call for attention and announcement that Eliphaz will divulge wisdom gleaned from his

[1] Zophar's speech ranks second with twenty-eight lines. Bildad's is the shortest speech with only twenty lines.

[2] Skehan, "Strophic Patterns," 108.

[3] Murphy, *Wisdom Literature,* 31. Cf. Fohrer, *Das Buch Hiob,* 265; Horst, *Hiob 1–19,* 220; Habel, *The Book of Job* (1985) 248; Hartley, *The Book of Job,* 242; and Clines, *Job 1–20,* 344.

[4] Terrien, *Job* (1963) 125; and Webster, "Strophic Patterns in Job 3–28," 44–45.

ancestors (vv 17–19) appears to function as an introduction to the piece on the wicked (vv 20–35).[5] Nevertheless, it should be noted that Eliphaz's previous introductions (4:2–6; 5:1–7) open with rhetorical questions. The same is true of the opening verses to his second and third speeches (15:2; 22:2). Yet, 15:17–19 begins with the indicative and not the interrogative as might be expected if this unit does, in fact, serve as an introduction to one of Eliphaz's speeches. Moreover, the *inclusio* formed with the noun *beṭen* ("belly") in vv 2b and 35b serves to bind the two units of this speech (vv 2–16, 17–35) into a unified speech. Verses 17–19, therefore, do not constitute an opening to a second poem and will not be studied as a response.

With regard to the opening strophe of chap. 15, Fohrer and others[6] select vv 2–6. Habel, however, takes vv 2–16 as a "section" which consists of four pairs of corresponding units. Each unit, according to Habel, is linked with a "pivotal thematic term." The first pair is composed on the topic, "the ground and form of knowledge" (vv 2–3, 9–10) and is governed by the root *ydʿ* ("know"); the second two units feature the name *ʾēl* and address the concern of Job's "undermining of traditional religion" (vv 4, 11); the third pair of units (vv 5–6, 12–13) have in common the noun *peh* ("mouth") and point to the "inner impulses that dictate speech"; and the last corresponding verses are linked by the topic "the nature of the human condition" (vv 7–8, 14–16) and the root *yld* ("to be born").[7]

The basic problem with Habel's understanding of vv 2–16 is that he imposes an orderly and unnatural structure on this passage. The major

[5] Note that Fohrer (*Das Buch Hiob,* 272) and Horst (*Hiob 1–19,* 217) refer to vv 17–19 as an *Einleitung*. Habel (*The Book of Job* [1985] 250) describes this passage as an "Introductory validation of Eliphaz' vision." As indicated above, these scholars, however, do not speak of vv 17–35 as a separate poem. Skehan ("Strophic Patterns," 108; cf. Murphy, *Wisdom Literature,* 31) and Webster ("Strophic Patterns in Job 3–28," 45) categorize vv 17–19 as a strophe but do not designate its function. Terrien (*Job* [1963] 128) takes vv 17–21 as a strophe.

[6] Fohrer, *Das Buch Hiob,* 265. Cf. Terrien, *Job* (1963) 125; Horst, *Hiob 1–19,* 217; Skehan, "Strophic Patterns," 108; Murphy, *Wisdom Literature,* 31; and Webster, "Strophic Patterns in Job 3–28," 45. Clines (*Job 1–20,* 345) separates vv 2–3 as the first strophe but then states, "The initial two-line strophe, vv 2–3 can perhaps be paralleled at the beginning of other speeches (8:2–3; 6:2–3; 4:2–3; 20:2–3), though it might be better to recognize initial five-line strophes here and elsewhere."

[7] For Habel's discussion on the structure of vv 2–16 see his commentary, *The Book of Job* (1985) 249–50.

objection is with his pairing of vv 7–8 with 14–16. The verb of the root *yld* occurs in both units, as Habel points out, but in very different contexts. In vv 7–8 Eliphaz accuses Job of behaving as though he was "born" the Primal Man[8] who was reputed to be especially wise, whereas in vv 14–16 the focus is on the "birth" of sinful humanity in general. Rather than tying vv 7–8 and 14–16 together under the topic "the nature of the human condition," which does not reflect the allegation brought against Job in vv 7–8, the text on the Primal Man should be linked with vv 9–10 on the grounds that these verses expand on the idea that Job conducts himself as though he possesses superior wisdom.[9] With the rejection of Habel's structure, vv 2–6 emerge as the introductory strophe of chap. 15 in agreement with Fohrer *et al.* (see n. 6 above). In support of this decision, vv 7–10, in which Eliphaz rebukes Job's presumption of superior wisdom, have a different focus and belong to a different strophe than vv 2–6 which address the negative qualities of Job's arguments (indirectly in vv 2–3).

The Introduction to the Second Speech of Eliphaz (with the Narrator's Opening Statement)

15:1 Then Eliphaz the Temanite answered and said:
2 Should a wise man answer with windy knowledge
and fill his belly with the east wind?
3 Should he argue with worthless words
or with meaningless speech?
4 You even[10] undermine[11] the fear (of God);
you diminish devotion to El.

[8] It appears from vv 7–8 that the mythical Primal Man was born prior to the completion of creation and attained wisdom by eavesdropping on the council of God. Cf. Fohrer, *Das Buch Hiob,* 268; Terrien, *Job* (1963) 126; Horst, *Hiob 1–19,* 223; Rowley, *Job,* 108; Pope, *Job,* 115; Habel, *The Book of Job* (1985) 253; and Hartley, *The Book of Job,* 245–46.

[9] In addition, one could criticize the pairing of vv 5–6 and 12–13 on the grounds that the "pivotal thematic term," *peh* ("mouth") can hardly be considered as such as it only occurs once (v 13b) in vv 12–13 and is used alongside of such diverse terms as "mind" (v 12a), "eyes" (v 12b) and "spirit" (v 13a). Further, the adjective *ḥākām* ("wise"), used substantively in v 2a, relates to Eliphaz's defense of his and his friends' "wisdom" (*ḥokmâ,* v 8b). This connection does not fit the pattern as proposed by Habel and is further evidence that his units do not correspond as neatly as he suggests. Yet, one does not dispute the fact that there are some links between the verses of the first part of chap. 15.

[10] For *'ap* as emphatic adverb see Williams, *Hebrew Syntax,* §385.

[11] G. R. Driver ("Problems in the Hebrew Text of Job," 77) derives the meaning of *pārar,*

5 Your iniquity surely[12] teaches[13] your mouth;
you choose the tongue of the crafty.
6 Your own mouth condemns you, not I;
your own lips testify against you.

Form

The two sections of this chapter (vv 2–16, 17–35) are employed as subgenres of the disputation speech.[14] The first section is a rebuke or reprimand, and the second section is an instruction on the fate of the wicked.[15] The introductory strophe of vv 2–6 opens with a series of rhetorical questions (vv 2–3) which lead to a direct accusation (v 4). Verses 5–6 serve to substantiate the accusation of v 4. The structure of vv 2–6 may be seen below:

	Announcement of response: Eliphaz replies to Job	(15:1)
1	Sarcastic critique of Job's speeches	(2–3)
	(a) Job's contributions are destructive (rhetorical question)	(2)
	(b) His words are ineffective (rhetorical question)	(3)
2	Direct accusation with proof	(4–6)
	(a) Accusation: Job rejects the fear of God	(4)
	(b) Proof: His speech testifies to his guilt	(5–6)

usually understood as "to break, destroy, annul, frustrate," from a second root *prr* with Syriac and Arabic equivalents meaning "to depart, flee." Thus he translates, "thou puttest fear to flight." His suggestion is plausible but adds little to the standard translation of this text.

12 For the conjunction *kî* as asseverative see Williams, *Hebrew Syntax* §449.

13 Dahood ("Hebrew Ugaritic Lexicography I," *Bib* 44 [1963] 294) reads the verb *yĕʾallēp* as denominative, derived from the numeral *ʾelep,* "thousand." Blommerde (*Northwest Semitic Grammar,* 73) follows Dahood and translates, "For your mouth increases your guilt a thousandfold." The meaning "teach" (cf. 33:33; 35:11), however, seems more appropriate as Eliphaz presents himself as a sage with the task of instructing Job in the ways of wisdom (e.g., 15:2–3; cf. Pope, *Job,* 114–15; and Habel, *The Book of Job* [1985] 246).

14 Cf. Murphy, *Wisdom Literature,* 31.

15 Cf. Fohrer, *Das Buch Hiob,* 265; Horst, *Hiob 1–19,* 220; Murphy, *Wisdom Literature,* 31; and Habel, *The Book of Job* (1985) 248.

Rhetorical Analysis

(1) The Connections between 15:2–6 and Previous Passages

In the light of the previous speech, several possibilities arise in 15:2–6 which indicate a purposeful response by Eliphaz to Job. First, that Eliphaz describes himself as a "wise man" (*ḥākām,* v 2a) appears to be significant in the context of Job's fourth speech. Previously, Job questioned whether or not his friends even possessed "wisdom" (*ḥokmâ,* 12:2b, 12a). He even went so far as to imply that the friends' speeches reveal them as fools (13:5). In Job's opinion any "wisdom" (*ḥokmâ,* 13:5b) which they might have should manifest itself in silence.[16] As a defense against Job's viewpoint, Eliphaz asserts his position as a sage. Furthermore, Eliphaz's indirect description of Job's arguments as "windy knowledge" (v 2a), "east wind" (v 2b), "worthless words" (v 3a), and "meaningless speech" (v 3b) should be seen as a rebuttal through which Eliphaz contends that the content of Job's speeches reveal that he is certainly not a sage.[17]

The word *ʿāwōn* ("iniquity") also figures in Job's fourth speech and Eliphaz's introductory strophe of 15:2–6. Job, in his previous speech, speaks of his supposed "iniquities" on three occasions. In 13:23 he inquires as to the quantity of his iniquities. Here the emphasis is on Job's ignorance of his wrongdoing. He wishes to know the extent of his sinfulness as he suspects that his apparent punishment outweighs his crimes. Since Job is not aware of any wrongdoing in his adult life worthy of such treatment, he proceeds to accuse God of holding the "iniquities" of his youth (13:26b) against him. The implication of such a charge is that if God insists on punishing Job for the indiscretions committed in his early life, then God oversteps the bounds of justice. Next, in 14:17, Job entertains the idea of being hidden in Sheol and having his "iniquity" covered up.

[16] A fourth occurrence of the noun *ḥokmâ* in 12:13a refers to God's "wisdom," which is of a different order and superior to human wisdom. Since Eliphaz reacts to Job's critique of the friends' wisdom, this reference is not directly relevant to this discussion.

[17] Two further references to the root *ḥkm* are made in chap. 15. The adjective *ḥākām* occurs in v 18a and the noun *ḥokmâ* is used in v 8b. In these two texts Eliphaz continues with his attempt to convince Job of his wisdom. His aim is to win Job over in order that he might heed the warning of 15:20–35. (For a note on the occurrences of the root *ḥkm* in passages preceding chap. 12 see p. 66 n. 158.) The noun *ḥokmâ* occurs eleven times in texts succeeding chap. 15, whereas the adjective *ḥākām* occurs only four times (17:10; 34:2, 34; 37:24) in this portion of the book.

This image suggests that Job's iniquities are relatively minor transgressions. Eliphaz, however, challenges this view and argues that Job's immorality is understated. Consequently, he clearly and unequivocally states that Job's "iniquity" surely teaches his mouth (15:5a).[18] With the statements concerning the testimony of Job's own mouth, Eliphaz specifies the consequence of Job's words as hinted at in 15:2 and 3—they substantiate Job's guilt. Further, Eliphaz's argument that Job's own "lips" (*śāpâ,* 15:6b) testify against him should be read as his reaction to Job's request that his friends listen to the pleading of his "lips" (13:6).[19] Thus, Eliphaz maintains that listening to Job's lips works against him as they only affirm his guilt.

The indirect allegation that Job speaks from the "belly" (*beṭen,* v 2b) is most interesting from the perspective of Job's defense of his "intellect" (*lēbāb*) in 12:3a especially since he, in this context, severely criticizes his friends' wisdom (12:2) and suggests that their presumed knowledge is nothing more than common sense (v 3c). It is understood that Job believes his mind is the source of his words (12:3), but Eliphaz argues otherwise and suggests that Job's words originate from the belly which, as he states in v 35b, is a source of deception.[20] Since these verses are linked not with shared words or synonyms but with the theme of the source of Job's words, the relationship between 12:3a and 15:2b is simply thematic.

(2) An Overview of 15:2–6 with Attention to the Proposed Connections

With the rhetorical questions of vv 2–3, Eliphaz maintains that he will not answer in the same manner as Job. Eliphaz's ascription of wisdom to himself reveals that he should be understood as defensive about his

[18] Beyond these references to *ʿāwon,* this noun occurs four times in earlier passages (6:21; 10:6, 14; 11:6) and seven times in the latter portions of the book.

[19] A third reference to "lips" (*śāpâ*) occurs in Job's fourth speech (12:20a), but as it refers to a third party it is not pertinent to this discussion. The noun *śāpâ* is used three times in earlier passages (2:10; 8:21; 11:5) and five times in the chapters following Eliphaz's second speech (16:5; 23:12; 27:4; 32:20; 33:3).

[20] The word *beṭen* occurs again in a third party reference (15:35b) probably in an allusion to Job. If so, it continues with the criticism Eliphaz made of Job in 15:2b. The noun *beṭen* occurs in one earlier text (3:11) and in five later texts (20:15, 20, 23; 32:19; 40:16). For a note on the references to *lēb* and on the occurrences of the root *llb* see Chapter 2, n. 195. In addition, the cognate noun *lēb* occurs in 12:24a in a third party reference which is not applicable to the above comments.

sagacity and subtly suggests, in the context of his critique of Job's speeches, that the protagonist is the one who is lacking in wisdom. Then to accuse Job of filling his belly, the source of deceit, with the "east wind" amounts to an intensification of Eliphaz's criticism. Job's words not only betray an absence of wisdom, according to Eliphaz, but they demonstrate that they are also deceitful and even dangerous and destructive.[21] These questions invite Job to reflect on the nature of his speeches in the light of Eliphaz's critique with the hope that Job might be discouraged from such talk.

In the second part of this introduction, Eliphaz charges Job with the subversion of religious faith. The use of the independent pronoun *'attâ* ("you") prefaced with the emphatic conjunction *'ap* ("even") underlines the intensity of Eliphaz's disgust with his interpretation of Job's argument. In Eliphaz's opinion, Job has gone too far in his thoughts about God. The proof of this charge is presented in vv 5–6 with Eliphaz's reference to the words which proceed from Job's own mouth. Here the nouns "iniquity" and "lips" become significant as Eliphaz is given two terms which recall Job's words from his last speech; and Eliphaz uses them in such a way so as to affirm the extent of Job's guilt.

The Fifth Speech of Job (chaps. 16–17) His Response to Eliphaz

Scholarly opinion varies over the structure of Job's fifth speech. Terrien and Webster, for example, divide this speech into two poems but do not agree on their limits. Terrien entitles the passage he takes as the first poem (16:2–22), "The Heavenly Witness." His second poem, "Waiting for Death," consists of the whole of chap. 17.[22] It is Webster's view that the first poem ends at 16:17. In content, Webster writes that this piece incorporates a rebuke of Job's friends (16:2–5) followed by a graphic description of his sufferings (16:6–17). Webster categorizes the second poem (16:18–17:16) as a "lament."[23] According to Murphy the lament, or "complaint" as he

[21] As the "east wind" or "sirocco" (*qādîm,* v 2b) is known for its strength, to liken Job's arguments to it is to imply that his speeches are destructive (cf. 27:21; see also the discussion on 8:2b in relationship to 1:19 [pp. 70–71]) and not simply "vain and frivolous" (Dhorme, *A Commentary on Job,* 208). Cf. Terrien, *Job* (1963) 125.

[22] Terrien, *Job* (1963) 131, 135.

[23] Webster, "Strophic Patterns in Job 3–28," 45.

prefers to call it, encompasses the bulk of this speech (16:7–17:16) which is preceded by "the ridicule of the opponent" (vv 2–6).[24] These two distinct passages warrant, in Murphy's view, a division of chaps. 16 and 17 into two distinct parts: 16:2–6 and 16:7–17:16.[25]

Fohrer proposes that the speech is composed in three parts: the first (16:2–6) consists of Job's repudiation of his friends; the second (16:7–22) is a description of his conflict with God; and the third (17:1–16) he classes a complaint concerning Job's afflictions.[26] Rowley approaches this speech as a fourfold presentation which he arranges as follows:

> Dismissal of the "comforts" of his friends (verses 2–5); his abandonment by God and man (verses 6–17); his appeal to his Witness in heaven (16.18–17.9); his anticipation of death as the end of his troubles (verses 10–16).[27]

On form-critical grounds, Horst arrives at a fivefold division which is close to Rowley's thematic arrangement but with one exception: he separates Rowley's third section into two parts. Horst's form-critical units are as follows: opening (16:2–6); complaint against God (16:7–17); wish (16:18–22); complaint against the friends (17:1–10); and complaint about Job's lack of hope (17:11–16).[28] Habel's divisions are almost identical to those of Horst except that he ends the first unit at v 5 instead of v 6, and his third unit (16:18–17:1) extends one verse beyond Horst's unit of 16:18–22. His approach varies from Horst's, however, in that Habel shows how the broad subject matter of this speech (excluding the opening unit of 16:2–5) is structurally bound into a unity with the aid of two cries which frame the complaint of 17:2–10 as a pair of "balanced opposites."[29] Habel's outline indirectly builds on Horst's form-critical approach and makes the best sense of any of the above proposals:

[24] Murphy, *Wisdom Literature,* 32.

[25] Murphy (*Wisdom Literature,* 31–32) breaks down the complaint portion of this speech (16:17–17:16) into six sections (16:7–14, 15–17, 18–21, 22–17:2, 3–5, 7–16).

[26] Fohrer, *Das Buch Hiob,* 282.

[27] Rowley, *Job,* 116.

[28] Horst, *Hiob 1–19,* 243–44. Hartley's (*The Book of Job,* 256) arrangement agrees with Horst's with the exception of the complaint of 17:1–16, which Hartley does not divide into two sections.

[29] Habel, *The Book of Job* (1985) 269. For a discussion and table depicting the relationship between the components of the two cries (16:18–17:1; 17:11–16) see p. 269 of Habel's commentary.

	A	Exordium	16:1–5
B		Complaint Against God as the Enemy	16:6–17
	C	Cry of Hope Amid Despair	16:18–17:1
B1		Complaint Against the Friends	17:2–10
	C1	Cry of Despair About Hope	17:11–16[30]

With the aid of Habel's analysis, the unity of Job's fifth speech may be upheld. This conclusion leaves one with the task of establishing the limits of its opening strophe. Terrien, Horst, Murphy, Hartley, and Clines take the opening strophe as vv 2–6.[31] Conversely, Rowley, Webster and Habel view it as extending to only v 5.[32] In support of these latter scholars, it is observed that v 6, with its description of Job's "pain" (*kĕ'ēb*), marks a transition from the friends as the object of derision to a complaint about God's unjust treatment of Job which extends to v 17. Verse 6, therefore, belongs to the following complaint and not to vv 2–5.[33]

The Introduction to Job's Reply to Eliphaz (with the Narrator's Opening Statement)

16:1 Then Job answered and said:
2 I have heard many such things!

[30] Habel, *The Book of Job* (1985) 267. Since Habel's "exordiums" do not normally include the narrator's opening statement (e.g., 18:2–3, p. 282; 19:2–5, p. 294; 20:2–3, p. 313; 21:2–6, p. 324; 26:2–4, p. 377) that v 1 is included with vv 2–5 in the outline of chaps. 16–17 is an oversight. Clines (*Job 1–20,* 375) uses the direction of address in this speech as a clue to its structure and sets out one more unit than Habel. Apart from a disagreement over a verse or two, the major difference concerns Habel's fourth section (17:2–10), which Clines divides into two subsections. Clines structure is as follows: 16:2–6; 16:7–17; 16:18(?–22); 17:1–5; 17:6–10; and 17:11–16.

[31] Terrien, *Job* (1963) 131; Horst, *Hiob 1–19,* 243; Murphy, *Wisdom Literature,* 31; Hartley, *The Book of Job,* 256; and Clines, *Job 1–20,* 376.

[32] Rowley, *Job* 116; Webster, "Strophic Patterns in Job 3–28," 45; and Habel, *The Book of Job* (1985) 267.

[33] In vv 2–5 Job ridicules his friends over the contents of their arguments. Then in the following verses (6–8) Job focuses on his physical condition as he leads into a graphic portrayal of God's actions as his enemy (vv 9–17). Skehan ("Strophic Patterns in Job," 108) counts vv 2–4 as the first strophe. Fohrer (*Das Buch Hiob,* 292) believes this strophe extends to only v 4a. As a result their second strophes (vv 5–7, 4b–6, respectively) obscure the transition in theme which follows v 5.

Troublesome consolers,[34] all of you!
3 Is there an end to windy words?
What distresses you that you answer so?
4 Even I could speak like you,
If you were in my place.
I could string words together[35] against you
and shake my head against you.
5 I could strengthen you with my mouth
and the movement of my lips could relieve you.[36]

Form

Form critics usually class the introductory strophe as disputation.[37] Although the bulk of this speech consists of complaint,[38] the introductory

[34] D. W. Thomas ("A Note on the Hebrew root *nḥm*," *ET* 44 [1932–33] 192) reads the participle *mĕnaḥămê* against the Arabic root *naḥama* and translates "breathers out of trouble." His proposal has not won the support of other scholars and does not add anything significant to an otherwise clear text.

[35] The verb *ḥābar* is variously interpreted. J. J. Finkelstein ("Hebrew *ḥbr* and Semitic *ḪBR*," *JBL* [1956] 331) derives it from the Akkadian verb *ḫabārum*, "to make noise" and translates, "I could harangue you with words." O. Loretz ("*ḪBR* in Job 16,4," *CBQ* 23 [1961] 293–94) relates it to the same Akkadian root and translates, "I could be noisy with words against you." Tur-Sinai (*The Book of Job*, 262–263) derives the meaning "to heap up" from the Ugaritic root *ḥbr*, Dhorme (*A Commentary on Job*, 229) emends the *ḥeth* of *ḥābar* to a *kaph* (following the Hebrew commentary of Avronin and Rabinowitz) and cites 35:16 as support. He, then, translates v 4c as, "I would *multiply* [italics his] words at your expense." These suggestions are unnecessary as the common biblical verb *ḥābar* with the meaning "to join together" makes sense in this context (cf. Gordis, *The Book of Job*, 174).

[36] G. R. Driver ("Studies in the Vocabulary of the Old Testament VI," *JTS* 34 [1933] 380) takes the verb *ḥāśak* as intransitive. Fohrer (*Das Buch Hiob*, 280) adopts Driver's proposal but adds the negative particle *lō*' on the basis of the LXX and the Syriac translations. As Job clearly addresses the friends in vv 2–5a, the object "you" is implied and supplied in the translation.

[37] Cf. Horst, *Hiob 1–19*, 243; Fohrer, *Das Buch Hiob*, 282–83; and Murphy, *Wisdom Literature*, 32. Hartley's commentary on Job is not, strictly speaking, form-critical; yet he also classes 16:2–5 as disputation (*The Book of Job*, 256). The second strophe, he writes, probably consists of wisdom disputation, but he allows for the possibility that it might have its provenance in legal argumentation. Murphy labels vv 2–6 as "ridicule of the opponent" and, in keeping with his position (and ours) that the placement of subgenres into their various presumed settings should be avoided, says that it is "characteristic of any dispute, whether at court or among the wise" (p. 32).

ridicule of the friends (vv 2–5) and Job's belittlement of his friends' wisdom (17:10), suggests that the speech as a whole is characteristic of a disputation speech.[39] It consists of two parts: in the first (vv 2–3), Job expresses his annoyance and impatience with his friends' speeches; and in the second (vv 4–5) Job states that if their positions were reversed, then he might present them with their own type of consolation. The details of this introduction emerge as follows:

	Announcement of Response: Job replies to Eliphaz	(16:1)
1	Impatience with the speeches of the friends	(2–3)
	(a) The friends have offered nothing new	(2a)
	(b) Condemnation of the friends	(2b)
	(c) Sarcastic critique of their speeches (rhetorical question)	(3a)
	(d) Sarcastic inquiry into the nature of their affliction (rhetorical question)	(3b)
2	Job's possible approach if roles were reversed	(4–5)
	(a) He might adopt their behavior	(4)
	(b) He might "strengthen" and "relieve" them in like manner	(5)

Rhetorical Analysis

(1) The Connections between 16:2–5 and Previous Passages

The first hint of a response to an earlier speech is provided with the verb *šāmaʿ* ("to hear"). Job uses it in the opening statement of this speech, "I have heard many such things." This verb is used on two occasions in Eliphaz's second speech: first, in the query through which it is asked if Job has ever "listened" (*šmʿ*) in on the council of God (15:8a); and second, in the request that Job "attend" (*šmʿ*, 15:17a) to Eliphaz's presentation on the fate of the wicked man (15:17–35).[40] As the possibility of Job over-

[38] Cf. Fohrer, *Das Buch Hiob,* 282–283; Horst, *Hiob 1–19,* 243–44; Westermann, *The Structure of Job,* 49–50, 55; and Murphy, *Wisdom Literature,* 32.

[39] Cf. Murphy, *Wisdom Literature,* 32.

[40] Beyond the three occurrences of *šāmaʿ* in chaps. 15–17, this verb is used seven times in the chapters preceding chap. 15 (2:11; 3:18; 4:16; 5:27; 13:1, 6, 17) and twenty-three times in the chapters following chap. 17.

hearing issues discussed at the divine council is mentioned merely for effect, and as his remark of 16:2a expresses an annoyance with what he has heard, it is likely that this remark refers to the lesson of 15:17–35. When understood in this manner, Job, in 16:2a, makes it clear that he is tired of listening to everything his friends have offered him, and as an example he indicates the lesson from the wisdom of the fathers (15:17–35).

Another term, *ʿāmāl* ("trouble"), occurs once in both speeches. Eliphaz uses it in the closing line of his speech (15:35a) when he says of the wicked, "conceiving trouble (*ʿāmāl*) gives birth to evil." Job employs the same noun, at the beginning of his speech when he calls his friends "troublesome consolers" (*mĕnăḥê ʿāmāl*).[41] In my view *ʿāmāl* is taken up from 15:35b to convey to his friends that they are in league with the wicked since they bring "trouble" to Job's life under the guise of consolation. The root *nḥm* of the epithet "troublesome consolers" occurs also in the prologue (2:11), where Job's friends were said to have come "to console" him. The use of the root in 16:2b is intended to remind the readers of the original purpose of the friends' visit and to make it clear that as far as Job is concerned, the friends have betrayed his trust.[42]

The expression "windy words" (*dibrê-rûaḥ,* 16:3a) plays directly on Eliphaz's designation of Job's argument as "windy knowledge" (*daʿat-rûaḥ,* 15:2a). As Job responds with a similar expression, it appears that it is directed against Eliphaz in particular and should be understood as a reaction to Eliphaz's criticism of his arguments. Eliphaz's phrase, *daʿat-rûaḥ* is not cited literally, as *dibrê* ("words") is substituted for *daʿat* ("knowledge").[43] Perhaps this substitution is made to avoid ascribing any

[41] The remaining occurrences of *ʿāmāl* are located in earlier chapters (3:10; 4:8; 5:6, 7; 7:3; 11:16).

[42] Cf. Habel, *The Book of Job* (1985) 271. In his article, "Only the Jackal is my Friend: On Friends and Redeemers in Job" (*Int* 31 [1977] 229), Habel says of Job's friends, "When Job needs a friend, he is confronted with theologians; when he calls for sympathy, he is given doctrine." For Job's reaction to this unexpected turnabout see Habel's section, "The Betrayal of Old Friends" (231–32).

[43] The noun *rûaḥ* as "wind" is used outside of chaps. 15–17 in 1:19; 6:26; 7:7; 8:2; 15:2; 21:18; 28:25; 30:15, 22; 37:21. This term occurs also in 15:13a, 30c. In the first reference it is used of Job and probably means "spirit." In the second, it refers to the wicked man and means "breath." As *dibrê-rûaḥ* (16:3a) relates fairly clearly to *daʿat-rûaḥ* (15:2a) both grammatically (each expression consists of a construct chain) and semantically (they are synonymous in meaning), it is unlikely that *rûaḥ* of 16:3a plays on 15:13a and/or 15:30c in any way.

semblance of knowledge to Eliphaz's speech because even "windy knowledge" might be considered too complimentary a description. The noun *dābār* is a more neutral term and would express Job's judgment of Eliphaz's speech more accurately.

The verb *'ānâ* ("to answer") occurs in the same colon as "windy knowledge" (15:2a) and in the same verse as "windy words" (16:3b). Although this verb is used frequently in Job (forty-eight times) and occurs consistently in the narrator's opening statements, as in 15:1 and 16:1, its presence in 16:3b appears to be significant from the standpoint of a response to 15:2a. Eliphaz employs the verb *'ānâ* when he asks if he should "answer" with windy knowledge which amounts to an indirect criticism of Job's speeches. When Job, in turn, asks, "What distresses you that you answer (*ta'ăneh*) so?" the verb *māraṣ* ("to be afflicted, sickened, distressed") suggests that the emphasis is on the manner in which Eliphaz responds (note the singular form of the verb *'ānâ*). Job, therefore, says to Eliphaz that his reply reveals that he is distressed. Verse 3b should be understood as extending the thought of v 3a. Thus Job's query concerning the manner of Eliphaz's response alludes to his view that Eliphaz speaks continuously with "windy words." The connection between the verb *'ānâ* and its object "windy knowledge" is obvious in 15:2a. With the link proposed between the verb *'ānâ* (16:3b) and the "windy words" of 16:3a, it seems likely that *'ānâ* was selectively placed in these two texts to help insure that the play on "windy knowledge" with "windy words" would be noted and appreciated by the reader. That Job criticizes Eliphaz for answering in a specific manner is ironic on two counts. First, Job maintains that, in his opinion, Eliphaz replies in the very way he wishes to avoid i.e., with "windy words" (cf. 15:2a). Second, if anyone should be distressed it is Job, and yet he is the one who asks why Eliphaz is distressed.

The second person plural suffixes of v 4 indicate that Job addresses the friends collectively. Yet there are clues in the root *dbr* ("to speak") and the noun *millâ* ("word, speech") which suggest that Job, at a deeper level, thrusts barbs at Eliphaz. Previously, in 15:3, Eliphaz asked if he should reply with "worthless words" (*dābār*) and "meaningless speech" (*millâ*) with the implication that Job's arguments consisted of such talk. The root *dbr* and the noun *millâ* occur also in the same sequence in 16:4.[44]

[44] The verb *dābar* occurs thirteen times in texts preceding chap. 15 (1:16, 17, 28; 2:10 [twice], 7:11; 9:35; 10:1; 11:5; 13:3, 7, 13, 22) and twenty-one times in texts following chap.

The fact that these two terms are found together in the same respective verses and in the identical order appears intentional and serves to indicate a response to 15:3. When read as a response, Job, in 16:4, assumes Eliphaz answers precisely in the manner in which he says he is capable. Further Job reveals what he has in mind when he states that he could speak like his friends. Thus, with the adoption of the root *dbr* from 15:3a, Job means that he is quite capable of using worthless words to "comfort" his friends if their roles were reversed. Similarly, the connection with the noun *millâ* suggests that the type of words which Job would be tempted to use would be those which Eliphaz referred to as "meaningless speech."

The play on "windy knowledge" (15:2a) with "windy words" (16:3a), supported with the shared verb "to answer" (15:2a; 16:3b), followed by the connections created by the root *dbr* (15:3a and 16:4a) and the noun *millâ* (15:3b and 16:4c), reveal that these verses from two successive introductions relate sequentially (i.e., 15:2 relates to 16:3, and 15:3 relates to 16:4). This pattern continues in the following proposal in that two words from 15:5 and 6 relate to the same two words in 16:5.

In 15:5 and 6 of Eliphaz's introduction, Job's organs of speech are brought into focus for their role in the promulgation of evil arguments. Eliphaz first speaks of Job's "mouth" (*peh*), then his "tongue" (*lāšôn*), after which he returns to the "mouth" (*peh*), before he concludes with a reference to Job's "lips" (*śāpâ*). The words "mouth" and "lips" frame Eliphaz's fourfold accusation. The incorporation of these two words (in the same order) into the statement of 16:5 transfers the full weight of this accusation into Job's reply.[45] When the context of Job's retort is taken

17. Job uses this verb also in 16:6a. As it falls outside of the pattern elaborated on below, it does not relate to 15:3a. The noun *dābār* occurs four times before chap. 15 (2:13; 6:3; 9:14; 11:2) and seven times in the chapters following chap. 17. This term is used a second time in chap. 15 (v 11b) but, as it also falls outside of the pattern of correspondences which link 15:2–6; 16:2–5, it unlikely is related to 16:4a. The same is true for the second occurrence of *millâ* (15:13b). Further references to *millâ* occur in 4:4; 6:26; 8:10; 12:11. In the chapters following chap. 17, this noun is used thirteen times.

[45] In texts preceding chap. 15, the word *peh* occurs in 3:1; 3:15, 16; 7:11; 8:2, 21; 9:20. Following chap. 17, this word occurs seventeen times. In Eliphaz's second speech, *peh* is also used in vv 13, 20, and in chap. 16 it occurs a further time in v 10. As with the words mentioned in the previous footnote, these additional occurrences of *peh* fall outside of the pattern of correspondences which tie 15:2–6 and 16:2–5 together and therefore do not play a part in Job's response.

The word *śāpâ* occurs four times in the chapters preceding chap. 15 (2:10; 8:21; 11:5;

into consideration (i.e., how he would speak if his situation and that of his friends were reversed [v 4ab]), the implication is that if he is able to convey the friends' argument with his mouth (which Eliphaz says is taught by iniquity in 15:5–6), then Job's arguments cannot be any more evil or deserving of condemnation than their contributions.

(2) An Overview of 16:2–5 with Attention to the Proposed Connections

As a response to Eliphaz's speech of chap. 15, it should not be surprising that Job openly disputes with his friend in this passage. After all, Eliphaz severely critiques Job's argument in 15:2–6, attacks his presumption of wisdom in vv 7–9, has the nerve to ask why Job reacts to his situation with such intensity in vv 12–13, and insinuates that Job drinks iniquity like water in v 16. From the opening of this speech, it is clear that Job is portrayed as exasperated—no doubt with Eliphaz but also with the friends as a whole. Indeed, Job should be understood as having heard enough, for as suggested, he is no longer receptive to the lessons handed down from the fathers (15:17–35) nor to the arguments of the friends in general. The friends have reneged on their original commitment (2:11) and turned against Job. Consequently, he calls them "troublesome consolers," a name through which he subtly associates them with the wicked man of Eliphaz's second speech.

The second person singular references in v 3b suggest that, in this colon, Job is addressing Eliphaz, the previous speaker. As such references are not present in v 3a, it is not immediately clear to whom Job directs this query. But, as argued above, the expression "windy words" (v 3a) takes up a similar criticism made by Eliphaz in 15:2a. Thus this question is aimed at Eliphaz as well.[46] The intent is to suggest that Eliphaz remain silent (cf. 13:5) given his disposition for counter-productive advice. The second rhetorical question is also directed against Eliphaz's reaction to Job's speeches. Job suggests, through this question, that Eliphaz should reconsider his view as his emotional zeal has clouded his objectivity.

13:6) and four times in the material following chap. 17. There are no additional occurrences of this word in chaps. 15–17.

[46] Dhorme (*A Commentary on Job*, 228) also takes the whole of v 3 as directed to Eliphaz.

The second part of this introductory strophe (vv 4–5) continues with the issue of Job's adverse treatment by his friends and returns to the second person plural form of address. Here Job announces a plan of action which he could conceivably implement if their roles were reversed and he were the counsellor. Scholars are divided over the interpretation of Job's approach. Does he mean that he could be of assistance to his friends if circumstances permitted? Or, does he mean that he could act vindictively and be as unsupportive as his friends? Tur-Sinai, Gordis, Habel, Janzen and Hartley advocate the former position,[47] whereas Driver and Gray, Powers, Fohrer, Horst, Rowley, de Wilde, Whedbee, and Clines support the latter.[48] In the light of this study, which has examined the connections between 16:2–5 and the preceding passages, the evidence supports the latter position. The play on *šāmaʿ* ("to hear," 15:17a; 16:2a), the association of "troublesome consolers" (16:2b) with "trouble" of 15:35a and the original intent of the friends' visit ("to console," 2:11), the relationship between "windy knowledge" (15:2a) and "windy words" (16:3a) and the connection between *ʿānâ* ("to answer," 15:2a; 16:3b) all support the idea that Job holds a negative view of the friends' speeches. Further, the adoption of the root *dbr* ("to speak," 16:4a) and the noun *millâ* ("word, speech," 16:4c) from statements of Eliphaz which are critical of Job's words (15:3a, 3b, respectively) suggests that when Job says he could speak in the same manner (16:4a), he must mean in an abrasive and accusatory fashion. Finally, the action of shaking one's head against another, as described in 16:4d is likely indicative of scorn.[49]

The Second Speech of Bildad (chap. 18)
His Response to Job

This speech consists of a single poem which falls into two parts. The direct address of Job in an outburst of anger distinguishes vv 2–4 from the more impersonal presentation of the *topos* on the fate of the wicked in vv 5–21. On this basis vv 2–4 may be considered the introductory

[47] Tur-Sinai, *The Book of Job,* 262–263; Gordis, *The Book of Job,* 175; Habel, *The Book of Job* (1985) 271; Janzen, 122; and Hartley, *The Book of Job,* 257.

[48] Driver and Gray, *A Commentary on the Book of Job,* 142; Powers, *A Study of Irony in the Book of Job,* 94; Fohrer, *Das Buch Hiob,* 284–85; Horst, *Hiob 1–19,* 246; Rowley, *Job,* 117; de Wilde, *Das Buch Hiob,* 191; W. Whedbee, "The Comedy of Job," *Semeia* 7 (1977) 12; and Clines, *Job 1–20,* 379.

[49] See Ps 22:8; cf. Ps 44:16; Jer 18:16; Sir 12:18; 13:7.

strophe to Bildad's second speech.[50] As the overall structure of chap. 18 is not in dispute amongst biblical scholars, no further discussion of its strophic division is necessary.[51]

The Introduction of Bildad's Reply to Job (Including the Narrator's Opening Statement)

18:1 Then Bildad the Shuhite answered and said:
2 How long will it be before you blow[52] an end[53] of words?

[50] Cf. Weiser, *Das Buch Hiob,* 135; Fohrer, *Das Buch Hiob,* 299; Gordis, *The Book of Job,* 190; Horst, *Hiob 1–19,* 267; Rowley, *Job,* 127; Westermann, *The Structure of Job,* 22–23; Habel, *The Book of Job* (1985) 282; Hartley, *The Book of Job,* 272; and Clines, *Job 1–20,* 407.

[51] Skehan ("Strophic Patterns in Job," 108) and Webster ("Strophic Patterns in Job 3–28," 47) consider vv 2–4 as the opening strophe of chap. 18 but do not deal with the overall structure of this speech. Terrien (*Job* [1963] 138–40) stands alone with his first strophe of vv 2–6. His division of chap. 18 into four strophes of equal length violates the natural division at v 4 and combines the beginning of the *topos* on the fate of the wicked with the variant subject matter of vv 2–4.

[52] The root of this verb is read as *nšm* ("to breathe, blow, pant" as in Isa 42:14). Moreover, Job is addressed with two plural verbs in v 2 and with a plural form of the possessive suffix in v 3b. Yet in v 4 he is referred to with singular forms. The LXX uses singular verbs in v 2 and, as a less difficult reading, does not likely reflect a different Hebrew text. Delitzsch (*Biblical Commentary on Job,* 316–17) is of the opinion that Bildad addresses Job in the plural as a representative of the "righteous," the class with whom Job identifies himself. Driver and Gray (*A Critical and Exegetical Commentary on Job,* 157) hold a similar point of view but do not specify those with whom Job is identified. Dhorme (*A Commentary on Job,* 257) suggests that Bildad addresses the audience. De Wilde (*Das Buch Hiob,* 201) insists that the plural forms indicate that Job is the speaker and inserts v 2 after 19:1 of Job's subsequent speech. Guillaume (*Studies in Job,* 99) suggests that the plural forms are a mark of "politeness." The impatience reflected in v 2 and the anger of v 3, however, indicate that his suggestion is improbable. Habel (*The Book of Job* [1985] 280) is probably closer to the truth with his proposal that the plural forms of 18:2–3 echo the plural language used by Job in 12:2 and 19:2 as a means of emphasizing sarcasm. Yet, in view of Bildad's inference—that Job is longwinded (18:2a, see following note)—it is possible that the plural forms are intended to convey the view that Job speaks voluminously, as much as two or more people.

[53] The plural construct *qinṣê* is a *hapax legomenon.* Dhorme (*A Commentary on Job,* 257) derives this noun from the Akkadian word *qinṣu,* "fetters, bonds, shackles" (cf. Terrien, *Job* [1963] 139, n. 1; and de Wilde, *Das Buch Hiob,* 208). Similarly, Pope (*Job,* 133) draws on the Akkadian *qinṣu,* which he translates as "trap," but also the Arabic *qanaṣa,* "hunt" (cf. Gordis, *The Book of Job,* 190) for his translation "snares." Driver (*Problems in Job,*

Be sensible and then we can speak.
3 Why are we counted as cattle,
considered stupid[54] in your eyes?
4 You who tear yourself in anger—
shall the earth be rearranged[55] for you
or the rock moved from its place?

79, n. 1) insists that the Akkadian word *qinṣu* does not exist and is a misreading for *kurṣu,* "bond," a point supported by von Soden's later lexicon (Wolfram von Soden, *Akkadisches Handworterbuch* [Wiesbaden: Otto Harrassowitz, 1965] 1. 512). Driver, therefore, proposes to rearrange the consonants and read *ṣinoq,* "bridle" with the support of the Syriac *ṣanqa,* "band, bridle," the Akkadian *z/s/šanāqu,* "to bind," and the Arabic *zanaqa,* "bound." Tur-Sinai (*The Book of Job,* 285), however, draws on the Akkadian *qinnazu,* "whip" for his translation, but this word fits poorly in the context of 18:2.

The LXX translates 18:2a rather loosely but it appears that *qēṣ* ("end") may have been read. Fohrer (*Das Buch Hiob,* 297) takes *qinṣê* as a derivative of the plural construct *qiṣê* from the noun *qēṣ*. Horst (*Hiob 1–19,* 268) reads *qinṣê* as an Aramaic plural form of *qēṣ*. Rignell ("Cruces Interpretum in Job," 115) posits that it is an "extended form" of *qēṣ*. Hartley (*The Book of Job,* 273) suggests that *qēṣ* is likely the correct reading because v 2b implies that "Job is speaking too much." Interestingly enough 8:2, particularly the first half of this verse, also makes this point. It is quite possible that Bildad opens both speeches in a similar manner (cf. *ʿad-ʾān,* "how long" of 8:2a and *ʿad-ʾānâ,* "how long" of 18:2a). In view of this possibility and with the support of the LXX, *qēṣ,* or at least a rare form of this noun, may be understood as a reasonable reading.

[54] The verb *niṭmînû* is also a *hapax legomenon.* Blommerde (*Northwest Semitic Grammar and Job,* 83) proposes that the root *ṭmn,* "to hide," lies behind this verb form. Fohrer (*Das Buch Hiob,* 297) suggests the root *ṭmʾ,* "to be clean." Dhorme (*A Commentary on Job,* 258), based on his conjecture of the Hebrew text relied on by the translators of the LXX, posits a form of *dāmâ* "to be compared with, likened." Moreover, he adds *kabaʿar* ("like cattle") to this colon which, in his view, was dropped from the text due to haplography (cf. de Wilde, *Das Buch Hiob,* 201). Guillaume (*Studies in Job,* 99) notes that cattle are associated with ignorance (Ps 73:22) rather than uncleanness and on the basis of three MSS, which read *nĕtammōnû,* he draws on the Arabic *tamtama,* "to speak unclearly" and translates, "Why are we regarded as stupid in your sight?" Gordis (*The Book of Job,* 190) regards the verb as a variant form of *ṭāman,* which occurs in Aramaic and in rabbinic Hebrew with the meaning "to stop up." In this context Gordis proposes the verb means "to consider stupid." In view of Job's comparison of the wisdom of the friends with the knowledge of "cattle" (*bĕhēmâ,* 12:7a) and the recurrence of the wisdom/folly motif in 12:2, 13:2 and 15:2, the meaning of stupidity is most appropriate for this verb (Habel, *The Book of Job* [1985] 281). Hence Gordis' proposal that the root of *niṭmînû* is a metaplastic form of *ṭmm* makes the most sense of any of the above suggestions.

[55] Following Dahood's proposal ("The Root *ʿzb* II in Job," *JBL* 78 [1959] 306) of reading the verb as *ʿzb* II, "to arrange, rearrange." This suggestion seems more logical than reading *ʿzb* I, "to abandon." Cf. the *JPSV,* "Will earth's order be disrupted for your sake?"

Form

The content of chap. 18 clearly suggests that it is a disputation speech. The request for an opportunity to speak (v 2), the defense of the friends' intelligence (v 3), the direct and indirect accusations (v 4a, 4bc, respectively), and the *topos* on the fate of the wicked (vv 5–21) directed against Job all reinforce the disputational character of the chapter. The structure of vv 2–4 may be laid out as follows:

	Announcement of Response: Bildad replies to Job	(18:1)
1	Job is longwinded	(2)
	(a) When will Job stop speaking? (rhetorical question)	(2a)
	(b) Request for an opportunity to speak	(2b)
2	Defense of the friends' intelligence (twofold rhetorical question)	(3)
3	Accusations against Job	(4)
	(a) He injures himself	(4a)
	(b) Job is self-centered (twofold rhetorical question)	(4bc)

Rhetorical Analysis

(1) The Connections between 18:2–4 and Previous Passages

When this introduction is examined for evidence of a response, the possibilities which arise link this strophe not only to Job's immediately preceding speech[56] but also to two of his earlier speeches. The clearest indication of a response to Job's last speech is provided with the verb *ṭārap* ("to tear") which occurs only in 16:9a and 18:4a of Job, and is used in both texts in conjunction with the noun *'ap* ("anger"). In 16:9a Job accuses God of "tearing" (*ṭrp*) him in "anger" (*'ap*). In response, Bildad accuses Job of "tearing" (*ṭrp*) himself in "anger" (*'ap*).[57] It is Bildad's

[56] The noun *nepeš* is also present in both 18:4a and 16:4b but coincidentally.

[57] In the chapters preceding chap. 16, the noun *'ap* is used in 9:5, 13; 14:13. Beyond chap. 18 this word is used twelve times. The fact that *ṭārap* and *'ap* occur together only in 16:9a and 18:4a is a good indication that 18:4a is Bildad's response to Job's accusation of 16:9a.

contention that Job is his own worst enemy, not God and by implication, not his friends.[58]

The second proposal involves the noun *qēṣ* but, as one cannot be entirely sure that it should be read in 18:2a,[59] this suggestion could be considered somewhat tenuous. If, however, one takes *qinṣê* as either a rare form of *qēṣ* or a scribal error for this noun, then it is noted that in 16:3a and 18:2a this term is used in reference to the desired "end" of one's opponent's speech. Also, a further connection may be established if the verb *tĕśîmûm* is repointed so as to derive from the root *nšm* ("to blow, breathe, pant") as opposed to *śîm* ("to set, make"). First, Job asks, "Is there an end to your windy words (*dābār,* 16:3a)?" If 18:2a is an intentional response to 16:3a, then Bildad should be understood as taking exception to this remark, and as a result counters with the point that he too finds Job's "words" (*millâ*) windy and hopes that he will soon "blow" himself out like a depleted windstorm.[60]

Bildad's defense of his own intelligence and that of his friends' (18:3) should be seen as a partial reaction to Job's statements that God has closed their minds to reason (17:4a) and that a wise man cannot be found among them (17:10b). Yet Bildad's objection that he and his friends are treated as "cattle" (18:3a) appears to refer back specifically to Job's earlier criticism that the "cattle" (*bĕhēmâ,* 12:7a) are more knowledgeable than the friends.[61] In his fourth speech (chaps. 12–14), Job demeans the wisdom of his friends (12:2–3) and insists that even the creatures of the earth know more than they (12:7–9). In view of these earlier remarks, the reader is given the impression that Bildad has had enough of such criticism and singles out the comment concerning the cattle because these animals are traditionally considered particularly unintelligent (e.g., Ps 73:22). This reaction underscores the degree of Bildad's disgust with Job's superior attitude. Bildad, therefore, attacks Job in an attempt to convince him that he is in fact the one who behaves as a fool.

[58] That Bildad indirectly defends the trio of friends is not surprising in the light of Job's name-calling (16:4b) and implied criticism of their assistance (16:4–5).

[59] See n. 53 above. The noun *qēṣ* occurs once in an earlier text (6:11) and twice in texts beyond chap. 18 (22:5 and 28:3).

[60] The synonyms *dābār* and *millâ* also help to tie these two texts together. The noun *millâ* occurs also in 16:4c but 18:2a unlikely responds to this text as well. Similarly, the verb *dābār* of 18:2b is not likely intended as a specific response to the use of the noun *dābār* in 16:3a, nor to the presence of the same verb in 16:4a and 6a.

[61] The noun *bĕhēmâ* occurs in Job only for a third time in 35:11.

Except for a small variation in word order the rhetorical question of v 4c is identical to 14:18b, a text also from Job's fourth speech.[62] In chap. 14, it forms part of a complaint (14:7–22) in which Job laments the fact that mortals, unlike a tree that rejuvenates itself when cut down, do not rise from the dead. The colon in mind, "and the rock is removed from its place" (14:18b), makes the point, in conjunction with 14:18a, that mortals are more like the rocks or mountains which erode continuously until they are gone forever. Job's observations on the long-term effects of erosion are made for comparative purposes: God takes away a mortal's hope for resurrection just as he destroys the mountains. When the same statement of 14:18b is heard from Bildad's lips in 18:14b, it gives the impression that he directly seizes upon Job's admitted vain hope in the resurrection in order to use it against him. In Job's description, the wearing away of rock is a process which may be understood as ultimately attributed to God, but which is indifferent to the hopes of humanity. Yet Bildad proceeds on the premise that the physical and moral aspects of creation are inextricably linked. His snide comment on the reordering of the rocks and of the earth is primarily concerned with the effects such an action would have on the moral order. As Job, in Bildad's opinion, is guilty, then his demands for vindication can only come to fruition if the world is restructured in such a way that the wicked are rewarded and the faithful punished. Hence the lengthy discourse concerning the punishment of the wicked (vv 5–21) is a defense of the status quo. As one might expect in a disputation, the simple statement from Job's complaint, in which he bemoans the fact that there is no hope for resurrection and consequent vindication, is taken up by Bildad and turned against him. Bildad argues that this eschatological dream is quite ludicrous, for it would necessitate the reversal of the doctrine of retribution.

Habel, however, links 18:4 to 9:5–6 and maintains that Bildad uses "Job's phraseology" of 9:5–6 to accuse Job of desiring to play God.[63] As this scholar observes, four words (*'ap*, "anger"; *'ātak*, "to move"; *'ereṣ*, "earth"; and *māqôm*, "place") are shared by 9:5–6 and 18:4. At the outset one reservation may be raised concerning Habel's proposal: a link established with a direct citation (as with 14:18b) is much stronger than one proposed

[62] In 14:18b the subject precedes the verb, whereas in 18:4c this order is inverted. Rowley (*Job*, 128) and Hartley (*The Book of Job*, 274) also link these two texts together.

[63] Habel, *The Book of Job* (1985) 285–86.

simply on the basis of a shared vocabulary. Yet, the possibility remains that the reader is expected to recall (on a secondary level) Job's previous allegations against God in 9:5–6. The *niphal* theme of *'zb* II (18:4b, "to rearrange"), however, suggests not that Job wishes to take over these activities of God, as Habel contends,[64] but that, in Bildad's estimation, Job desires that God would perform these actions on his behalf. Originally, Job alleged that God was engaged in the process of deliberately reducing creation to chaos (9:5–6). It appears from this complaint that the physical and moral elements of creation are to some degree intertwined, as Job insists that under such conditions it is impossible for a human being to appear just before God (9:2b). If this text does lie in the background of 18:4, then the intent is the same as that implicit in the adoption of 14:18b but with the addition of a reminder that Job has previously presumed a link to exist between the physical and moral aspects of the world. The implication is that Job may complain that God is destroying the order inherent in creation, but in reality Job desires that creation be reordered in such a way that he may find himself vindicated—an order which Bildad would interpret as chaos.

(2) An Overview of 18:2–4 with Attention to the Proposed Connections

Bildad opens this speech with one of the several rhetorical questions prevalent in this passage which reveal an impatience similar to Job's (16:3b). With this question (v 2a) Bildad indirectly requests that Job cease speaking. If, however, *qinṣê* refers back to *qēṣ* ("end") and *nāšam* ("to blow") is read in 18:2a, then it appears that Bildad replies to Job's earlier comment, "Is there an end to windy words (16:3a)?" The intent of Bildad's query is to suggest Job's words are like a windstorm which he hopes will soon be depleted. Next, Bildad asks that Job consider his request and allow his friends the opportunity to express themselves (v 2b). The queries of v 3 might sound at first like a request for an explanation of the reasons why Job discounts the intelligence of his friends, but the full impact of these questions must be appreciated from the perspective of the accusations of v 4. Job has accused God of tearing him in anger (16:9a), but as Bildad sees it Job's anger inflicts harm upon himself. Moreover, with

[64] Habel, *The Book of Job* (1985) 285–86.

the knowledge that 14:18b and perhaps 9:5–6 lies behind 18:4c, the reader is able to perceive that Job's position is distorted by Bildad in order to accuse Job of behaving as though God should order creation around his life. To Bildad such self-destructive behavior and self-centered thinking betrays Job's lack of intelligence. Bildad, then, is saying, "Why do you believe we are dim-witted when your speeches reveal your stupidity?" In the light of Job's judgment that the friends' intelligence ranks beneath that of "cattle" (12:7a), it is understandable that the poet would frame a rebuttal for Bildad (and the friends) along such lines so as to call Job's intelligence into question. The overall purpose of this attack, however, is to convince Job of his need to attend to the advice and warnings of his friends. The rhetorical questions of vv 3 and 4bc are most appropriate for this purpose as they direct Job to compare the wisdom of his own behavior to the insight offered in the speeches of his friends.

The Sixth Speech of Job (chap. 19)
His Response to Bildad

Scholarly opinion varies on the limits to the introductory strophe of this speech. Skehan proposes the shortest unit consisting of vv 2 and 3.[65] Fohrer and Janzen disagree and extend the first strophe to v 4.[66] Weiser and Habel, however, include v 5 in their division.[67] Terrien and others, however, maintain that the introductory strophe ends with v 6.[68]

An examination of vv 3 and 4 reveals a thematic link which suggests that Skehan cuts this strophe short. The clue to the connection between these verses is provided with the adversative conjunction *waw* of v 4. Here Job continues with the thought of v 3 to express his opposition to the friends' unjust treatment of him. Even if Job committed some indiscretion, he takes the position in v 4 that he is not deserving of the humiliation his friends have caused him (v 3).

Further, vv 4 and 5 also belong together as they both deal with the idea of Job's indiscretion. Job admits only to the possibility of an

[65] Skehan, "Strophic Patterns in Job," 109.

[66] Fohrer, *Das Buch Hiob,* 310; and Janzen, *Job,* 132.

[67] Weiser, *Das Buch Hiob,* 143; and Habel, *The Book of Job* (1985) 294.

[68] Terrien, *Job* (1963) 143; Horst, *Hiob 1–19,* 277; Anderson, *Job,* 190; Rowley, *Job,* 133; Webster, "Strophic Patterns in Job 3–28," 47; Hartley, *The Book of Job,* 282; and Clines, *Job 1–20,* 436.

inadvertent error[69] but, evident from v 5, his friends exploit his present condition as proof that he is guilty of some undisclosed, major offense. Also, except for the initial *waw* of v 4, vv 4 and 5 begin in a similar manner, i.e., with a monosyllabic particle followed with the adverb *'omnām* ("indeed"). Although v 4 is best understood as a conditional clause and v 5 as a concessive clause, the shared opening structure of these two verses links them together in the same strophe.

In addition, because v 6 functions as the main clause to the concessive clause of v 5, it too likely belongs to the introductory strophe of chap. 19. When vv 2–6 are treated as a single strophe, the basic theme becomes apparent: Job's friends have misunderstood the reason for his suffering. Consequently, Job makes the point in v 6, the climax of this strophe, that God is guilty of wrongdoing and not himself. This strophe should then be understood as Job's defense of his innocence before his friends who behave more like accusers than supporters. The following verses (vv 7–12) focus on God's brutal treatment of Job.[70] This transition from Job's defense of himself before his friends (vv 2–6) to the detailed description of God's warlike attack on him (vv 7–12) warrant a division of these verses into two strophes.[71] In sum, those scholars who take vv 2–6 as the introductory strophe of Job's sixth speech are likely correct.

[69] The verb *šāgâ,* "to err" (v 3a), refers to more of a moral error than a deliberate sin (cf. Lev 14:13; Num 15:22; and Job 6:24). The same is likely true for the word *měšûgâ,* "error" (v 3b), which appears to be a related noun.

[70] Cf. Murphy, *Wisdom Literature,* 33.

[71] Habel (*The Book of Job* [1985] 295) bases his division of vv 2–5 and 6–12 partly on the siege motif present in vv 6–12. In his outline of the second unit, he stresses the role of the preposition *'al* ("against") as typical of a siege motif. It occurs five times in vv 6–12 (Habel counts six). His emphasis on *'al* as a unifying feature of this section is misleading, for it occurs twice in v 5, where it may also be understood in reference to the attack from his friends. As with v 6, however, these occurrences in v 5 only serve to prepare for the siege motif of vv 7–12 and should not be viewed as evidence that vv 5 and 6 belong to the second strophe of chap. 19. Further, Habel (p. 298) takes the verb *yāda'* ("to know") of vv 6a and 29c as an *inclusio.* Strictly speaking, an *inclusio* occurs only twice in a literary unit (cf. Watson, *Classical Hebrew Poetry,* 283). The verb *yāda',* however, occurs a third time in v 25a. Since the idea of knowledge plays a pivotal role in chap. 19, it is properly considered a catchword (cf. Watson, *Classical Hebrew Poetry,* 288).

The Introduction of Job's Reply to Bildad (with the Narrator's Opening Statement)

19:1 Then Job answered and said:
2 How long will you torment my soul
and crush me with words?
3 These ten times you have humiliated me;
you are not ashamed to abuse me.[72]
4 But, if indeed I have erred,
my error stays with me.[73]
5 Though[74] indeed you make yourselves superiors over me

[72] The verb *hākar* is a *hapax legomenon.* A few MSS read *taḥkĕrû* with a *ḥeth* instead of a *he.* Fohrer (*Das Buch Hiob,* 307) and de Wilde (*Das Buch Hiob,* 208) follow this alternate reading and draw on the Arabic cognate *ḥakara,* "to wrong, ill treat, insult" to establish the meaning of this verb. Dhorme (*A Commentary on Job,* 271) also refers to the Arabic *ḥakara* but accepts the MT as arising from a weakening of the *ḥeth.* Gordis (*The Book of Job,* 200) and Habel (*The Book of Job* [1985] 291) note the similarity with the Arabic *ḥaqara* but derive the meaning of the verb from the root *klm* ("to humiliate") of v 3a on the basis of parallelism. Alternatively, the root may simply be *nkr* ("to treat as foreign, strange"), parsed as a *hiphil* denominative with an unelided *he* (see *Gesenius' Hebrew Grammar,* §53 n and q). This reading avoids the need to draw on a cognate language or to make a guess based on context for a translation.

[73] Tur-Sinai (*The Book of Job,* 296), Horst (*Hiob 1–19,* 277), Gordis (*The Book of Job,* 200), and de Wilde (*Das Buch Hiob,* 208) approach v 4 as a question. Delitzsch (*Biblical Commentary on Job,* 337), Fohrer (*Das Buch Hiob,* 306), Terrien (*Job* [1963] 143), Guillaume (*Studies in Job,* 41), Habel (*The Book of Job* [1985] 289), and Hartley (*The Book of Job,* 282) translate this verse as a conditional statement. Pope (*Job,* 138, 140) takes an intermediate position and renders v 4 as a conditional question. This verse is capable of any of the above translations. Yet, in view of the friends' misunderstanding of the cause of Job's demise (vv 2, 3, 5), it is more likely that Job informs the friends that any possible "error" he may have committed is not their business (cf. Dhorme, *A Commentary on Job,* 276; and Habel, *The Book of Job* [1985] 299). Verse 4 is thus translated as a conditional sentence.

[74] Scholars are divided over whether to translate v 5 as a question (Dhorme, *A Commentary on Job,* 272; Tur-Sinai, *The Book of Job,* 296; Fohrer, *Das Buch Hiob,* 312; Horst, *Hiob 1–19,* 77; and de Wilde, *Das Buch Hiob,* 208–9); as a conditional sentence with v 6 as the apodosis (Delitzsch, *Biblical Commentary on Job,* 337; Driver and Gray, *A Commentary on Job,* 165; Guillaume, *Studies in Job,* 41; Gordis, *The Book of Job,* 200; and Hartley, *The Book of Job,* 282); or as a declarative (Pope, *Job,* 138; and Habel, *The Book of Job* [1985] 289). The presence of the particle *'ēpô* ("then," v 6a) following *'im* (v 5a) suggests that v 5 is not simply an interrogative or a declarative sentence (cf. 9:24c and 24:25a). In the light of the friends' vehement attacks on Job in past speeches, v 5 as the protasis of a conditional statement allows for too hypothetical a meaning for v 5a.

and argue my disgrace against me,
6 know then that Eloah has wronged me;
he has thrown up his siegeworks[75] against me.

Form

In Fohrer's view, vv 2–4 are drawn from a legal background and vv 5–6, which he believes belong to vv 7–12 as an accusation against God, have their provenance in the complaints concerning one's enemies in the Psalms.[76] Murphy concludes that vv 2–6 are based on legal practice as they are "characteristic of a defendant replying to his accusers and affirming his innocence (v 6)."[77] In this case these verses do seem to show a relatively obvious legal background. One example of legal terminology present in this passage is the verb *'āwat* ("to wrong," v 6) which is sometimes used in reference to the unjust treatment of an innocent person (cf. Ps 119:78; Job 8:3; and Lam 3:36). The speech, on the whole, consists of elements similar to legal practice and the complaints of the Psalms.[78] As Job's purpose is to convince his friends, who are certain of his guilt, that he is innocent, chap. 19 is a disputation speech. Verses 2–6, with their reproof of the friends and Job's defense of his integrity, also should be considered as disputation. The structure of this introductory strophe may be laid out as follows:

	Announcement of Response: Job replies to Bildad	(19:1)
I	Reproof of the Friends	(2–3)
	(a) When will the friends stop speaking? (twofold rhetorical question)	(2)
	(b) Accusation: The friends debase Job	(3)

The conjunction *'im* is therefore best understood as the concessive particle "though" (cf. *JPSV*).

[75] Most scholars derive *mĕṣûdô* from *māṣôd,* "net" (Qoh 7:26). As the object of the verb *nāqap,* "to go around" and in the context of the military imagery of vv 7–12, Gordis' suggestion (*The Book of Job,* 201) that *mĕṣûdô* should be derived from *mĕṣûdâ,* "fortress, stronghold, seigeworks" with the pronominal suffix is preferable (note the LXX has *ochyrōma,* "fortress;" cf., Habel, *The Book of Job* [1985] 291 and the *JPSV*), although the word is best understood as *māṣôd* as in Qoh 9:14. "Siegeworks" understood as a type of fortified tower or protected ramp from which an assault against a walled-in city may be launched is a more appropriate translation than "fortress" or "stronghold."

[76] Fohrer, *Das Buch Hiob,* 310.

[77] Murphy, *Wisdom Literature,* 33.

[78] Cf. Fohrer, *Das Buch Hiob,* 310; and Murphy, *Wisdom Literature,* 33.

2 Job's Defense (4–6)
  (i) The possibility of an indiscretion (4)
    (a) Hypothetical admission of error (4a)
    (b) Any such error is of no concern to the friends (4b)
  (ii) Assertion of Innocence (5–6)
  (a) The friends belittle Job without just cause (5)
  (b) God—not Job—is in the wrong (6)

Rhetorical Analysis

(1) The Connections between 19:2–6 and Previous Passages

The plural verb forms of this introduction reveal that Job addresses all three friends, but there are several connections between 19:2–6 and 18:2–4 which suggest that Job responds especially to Bildad. The opening verses of these two passages exhibit the strongest links. The most obvious connection involves the shared expression *ʿad-ʾānâ,* "how long" which occurs only in 18:2a and 19:2a of the Book of Job. The noun *millâ* ("word"), used in reference to one another's speeches, is also present in both verses. Third, the *nun paragogicum*[79] of the verb *śîm* (here "to make," 18:2a) and of the verbs *yāgâ* ("to torment," 19:2a) and *dākāʾ* ("to crush," 19:2b) provides a further link between these verses.[80] In 18:2 Bildad emphatically expresses, as the *nun paragogicum* of the verb *śîm* indicates, his impatience with Job's persistent arguments. In reply to Bildad's criticism the three elements of 18:2 (listed above) are incorporated into the opening rhetorical questions of 19:2. Thus Job mocks and counters Bildad's query of how much longer the friends must listen to his speeches with a similar question but with the addition of a new dimension: the turmoil which his friends have caused him. The twofold use of the *nun paragogicum* in 19:2 serves to stress the degree of suffering that his supposed friends have added to his already troubled life. In sum, the idea of Bildad's fatigue expressed in the line, "How long will it be before you make an end of

[79] Although some scholars refer to this device as the "*nun energicum*" (Delitzsch, *Biblical Commentary on Job,* I, 334) or "*nun energicus*" (Gordis, *The Book of Job,* 200), the term "*nun paragogicum*" (GKB §47m) is preferred (cf. Hartley, *The Book of Job,* 282) to differentiate from the "*nun energicum*" as defined in §58i–l of GKB.

[80] There are no further occurrences of the *nun paragogicum* in chap. 18, although in chap. 19 there are three other places where this device is present (vv 23a, 24b and 29c).

words" (18:2a) is effectively answered with Job's expression of his impatience with his friends' hurtful speeches in 19:2.

The noun *nepeš* ("soul") also occurs in both of these passages.[81] Bildad uses this term in his accusation that Job injures himself with his anger (18:4a). With the adoption of this word in 19:2a, "How long will you torment my soul" (*nepeš*), this accusation is rejected and countered with the charge that, in fact, it is the friends who attack him. This connection serves to emphasize further Job's alienation from his so-called friends.

Of the verb *dākā'* (19:2b), Habel remarks, "The verb 'crush' (*dk'*) recalls Job's earlier 'hope' that Eloah would crush him to death and so relieve him of his intolerable misery" (6:9).[82] Habel's rationale for a reference to this relatively distant text is not at all clear. Job's complaint that his friends are crushing him with words does not have any bearing on his earlier request that God would crush him. The presence of this verb in both of these texts is probably not of any significance for the interpretation of 19:2b.

A stronger case for a reference to a distant text can be made with regard to the verb *'āwat* ("to wrong") of v 6 in relation to the twofold occurrence of this verb in 8:3 of Bildad's first speech.[83] In the only earlier usage of the verb *'āwat,* the belief of conventional theology is conveyed that God never subverts justice. As Job is firmly convinced that he has committed no sin deserving of such punishment, his only recourse is to assume that God treats him unjustly. Previously, in his response to Bildad's question concerning the integrity of the justice of God (9:2), Job implicitly insisted that God does pervert justice. The reader is given the impression that Job has not forgotten his earlier exchange with Bildad and therefore proceeds not only to restate his position that God deals with him unjustly but also to provide detailed testimony as to how God actually treats him. Thus, the second half of the last verse of the introductory strophe (v 6b) tells of one way in which God has wronged Job. This seige motif is then elaborated upon in vv 7–12 where Job is presented as a king under attack by a fierce and formidable enemy. Further Job also informs

[81] Beyond the two references to *nepeš* in chaps. 18 and 19, this word occurs sixteen times in the preceding chapters and seventeen times in the chapters following chap. 19.

[82] Habel, *The Book of Job* (1985) 299. The verb *dākā'* also occurs in 4:19; 5:4; 22:9; 34:25.

[83] Scholars such as Fohrer (*Das Buch Hiob,* 312), Terrien (*Job* [1963] 144), de Wilde (*Das Buch Hiob,* 206), Habel (*The Book of Job* [1985] 299–300), and Hartley (*The Book of Job,* 284) discuss the significance of this connection in their commentaries.

Bildad that God has wronged him by alienating him from his family, friends and servants (vv 13–22).

To liken God to a military commander is not new to this speech. In his last discourse, Job speaks of God as the one who set him up as a target for his archers (16:12c–13a), and then, with a transition in image, he images himself as a fortified city under attack by God (16:14). The lengthy presentation of the seige motif of 19:7–12, introduced in v 6b, should not be seen as simply a further development on the theme of 16:12c–14 but should be read as a response to Bildad's hunting imagery of 18:8–10. In this passage Bildad describes such devices as a "net" (*rešet*), "snare" (*paḥ*), "noose" (*ṣammîm*), "rope" (*ḥebel*) and "trap" (*malkōdet*) which are laid for the unsuspecting, wicked person. While Job clearly rejects any insinuation of wickedness, his choice of the word *māṣôd* ("seigeworks") alludes to the trapping metaphor of Bildad.[84] Job, however, rejects Bildad's assertion (18:7b) that his tragedy is a consequence of his own schemes and casts the blame on God who for no just cause actively searches him out to destroy him. Further, Job's allusion to 18:8–10 is intended to create a contrast between Bildad's portrayal of God as the hunter of the wicked and Job's experience of God. In Job's view God is more accurately portrayed as a merciless and unjust military commander who leads his troops to destroy one solitary, undeserving and defenseless individual.

Finally, if the anomalous *tahkĕrû* of 19:3b were read as the Hiphil denominative of the verb *nākar,* a connection with the prologue becomes apparent. So disfigured did Job appear to his friends that "when they raised their eyes from afar, they did not recognize (*nkr*) him" (2:12).[85] Although this root is conventually classified as *nākar* I ("to recognize") and II ("to treat as foreign"), one can readily see the basis for this interplay as created by the poet. Job stresses in 19:2–6 how his so-called friends

[84] Hartley (*The Book of Job,* 284 n. 11) allows this allusion to influence his translation of *mĕṣûdô*. Thus he renders this term as "his net" and in his discussion of the connection of 19:6b with 18:8–10 (p. 284) misses the distinction which Job draws between his experience of God and the image which Bildad portrays.

[85] The verb *nākar* II would appear only in 19:3 of Job, whereas *nākar* I occurs also in 4:16; 7:10; 21:29; 34:19, 25. A further connection with 4:16 is unlikely as here the verb is used in reference to Eliphaz' inability to recognize or discern the appearance of his vision. The idea that the dead are forgotten or no longer known in 7:10 sounds a familiar chord to 19:3, but as this text is also attributed to Job, 19:3 cannot be read as a response to 7:10.

have betrayed him. With the use of the root *nkr* his friends are reminded how they originally came to console Job and how they entered into his suffering with him (2:11–13). Their initial response is, then, contrasted with their present approach in which they "torment," "crush," "humiliate," and "treat Job like a stranger."

(2) An Overview of 19:2–6 with Attention to the Proposed Connections

Job opens this speech with a twofold rhetorical question which, with its emphasis on his suffering, is intended to win the friends' sympathy. As he has done in the past, Job informs his friends that he has grown weary of their arguments and indirectly requests that they put an end to them (cf. 12:3, 13:2, 5; 16:2–3). A recognition of the relationship between 19:2 and 18:2a, however, demonstrates that one should understand Job as replying to his friends through Bildad. The use of *nepeš* ("soul," 19:2a) in the context of discomfort recalls Bildad's charge that Job is the cause of his own pain ("You who tear yourself," [*nepeš*, 18:4a]). With this play Job insists that he is not responsible for his agony, but that it is attributable, in part, to the speeches of Bildad and the others.

In v 3 Job makes reference to the number of abusive speeches which he has already heard. Most scholars consider "ten times" (v 3a) as a "round number" (cf. Gen 31:7,41; Lev 26:26; and Num 14:22).[86] But Janzen is probably more accurate with his assessment that "ten times" functions as a hyperbole[87] as the friends have actually spoken only five times so far in the course of the dispute. At this point the verb *nākar* comes into view as it forms a connection with the prologue. With this play the reader is reminded how the friends have radically changed their stance toward Job. Initially, they came in support of their friend, but now they stand against him as his accusers.

After this reproof Job shifts to a defense of his innocence in vv 4–6. Pope suggests that v 4 might be directed to God and is comparable to 7:20 where Job inquires as to what harm a hypothetical sin might have on God.[88] This suggestion is rejected on the grounds that the remaining verses of the introductory strophe are addressed to the friends and there

[86] Fohrer, *Das Buch Hiob,* 311; de Wilde, *Das Buch Hiob,* 208; and Pope, *Job,* 140, etc.
[87] Janzen, *Job,* 132.
[88] Pope, *Job,* 140.

is no reason why v 4 should be viewed differently. As Job maintains his innocence throughout the book (cf. 9:21; 10:7; 16:17; 19:6; 27:5–6), here he states that any unintentional minor transgressions which he may have committed are not relevant to his present situation and should be of no concern to this friends.

Verse 5 consists of two concessive clauses which lead into the main clauses of v 6. In the first half of this statement, Job makes it clear that he will not give in to their intimidation. Then, with the aid of the imperative *dĕʿû* ("know!"), Job forcefully states that Eloah is the guilty party who has wronged him. As we have seen, Job's insistence that justice was breached recalls an earlier exchange between Bildad (8:3) and Job (9:2) in which Job insists that God does, in fact, pervert justice. Obviously, Job has not changed his opinion in the course of this debate. Finally, the comparison implicit in the allusion to the trapping imagery of 18:8–10 via the military metaphor of 19:6b builds on the allegation of God's injustice as it creates an image of a hostile deity who leads his troops on an all-out assault against an innocent individual.

The Second Speech of Zophar (chap. 20)
His Response to Job

There is a considerable consensus among scholars that chap. 20 consists of an introductory unit (vv 2–3) followed by a poem on the fall of the wicked (vv 4–29).[89] Terrien, however, differs from this position in that he takes vv 2–5 as the first strophe of this speech.[90] But, as Habel observes, the nouns *ʾādām* ("man, human") and *rĕšāʿîm* ("wicked") of vv 4b and 5a (respectively) form an *inclusio* with the expression *ʾādām rāšāʿ* "wicked man" of v 29a.[91] Moreover, it is noteworthy that the reference to the *rĕšāʿîm* (v 5a) functions as the antecedent for the subject of the poem of vv 4–29 and, therefore, cannot be separated from v 6. Hence this *inclusio* binds the contents of vv 4–29 together in a unified piece. On the basis of the aforesaid *inclusio,* Terrien's view is ruled out and vv 2–3 are understood as the introductory strophe of chap. 20.

[89] Weiser, *Das Buch Hiob,* 157; Fohrer, *Das Buch Hiob,* 327; Rowley, *Job,* 141; Murphy, *Wisdom Literature,* 33; Habel, *The Book of Job* (1985) 313; Hartley, *The Book of Job,* 299; and Clines, *Job 1–20,* 480.

[90] Terrien, *Job* (1963) 156–57.

[91] Habel, *The Book of Job* (1985) 313.

The Introduction to the Second Speech of Zophar (with the Narrator's Opening Statement)

20:1 Then Zophar the Naamathite answered and said:
2 In truth, my anxious thoughts make me reply,
because of my feelings[92] within me.
3 I hear reproof that humiliates me,
and with wind he answers me
without understanding me.[93]

[92] Fohrer (*Das Buch Hiob,* 325) reads *rāḥaš libbî,* "my heart is agitated." As this reading requires the insertion of an object, Fohrer adds the demonstrative *zōʾt* ("this"). Driver and Gray (*A Critical and Exegetical Commentary on Job,* 134–35 of the appendix) take *ḥûšî* as the infinitive construct of the verb *ḥûš,* "to hurry, rush" with the first person pronominal suffix. Similar to Fohrer they also insert *zōʾt* to this colon. Dhorme (*A Commentary on Job,* 289–90) appeals to the modern Hebrew word *ḥûš,* "sense," which derives from the verb *ḥûš,* "to feel" (cf. Delitzsch, *Biblical Commentary on Job,* 374; Gordis, *The Book of Job,* 214; and Hartley, *The Book of Job,* 300, etc.) and reads *ḥûšî* as "my sensation." The derivation of this term from the verb *ḥûš* II as in Qoh 2:5 (KB [Leiden: E. J. Brill, 1958] 287) avoids unnecessary emendations and makes good sense in this context.

[93] The ambiguity of this colon has led to various translations. The major problem concerns the phrase *wĕrûaḥ mibbînātî.* Does *rûaḥ* mean "wind" or "spirit?" And does the second term derive from *bînâ,* "discernment" or from some other word? If the second issue is tacked first, it is noted that Dahood ("Northwest Semitic Philology and Job," in *The Bible in Current Catholic Thought* [ed. J. McKenzie; New York: Herder and Herder, 1962] 53–64) first proposed the vocalization of *mabnîtî,* "my frame" for *mibbînātî.* Beyond Pope (*Job,* 151) this suggestion seems not to have attracted any following because the more common term *bînâ* is perfectly suited to this context.

With regard to the first issue, the *JPSV* translates "a spirit out of my understanding," reading the *min* of *bînâ* as a preposition of source (cf. Williams, *Hebrew Syntax,* §322). Habel takes a similar approach with his translation "my discerning spirit" (*The Book of Job* [1985] 310). Those scholars who translate *rûaḥ* as "wind" have difficulty with the first person suffix on *bînâ.* Terrien (*Job* [1963] 156), for example, omits this suffix in his translation without explanation. Driver and Gray (*A Critical and Exegetical Commentary on Job,* 176) translate *rûaḥ* as "wind," but drop the suffix and prefix the *taw* of *bînâ* to the verb to form the second person singular which reads as, "And with wind void of understanding thou answerest me." Alternatively, following the suggestion of William Irwin (St. Michael's College, Toronto in his written critique of this work in November, 1990), the suffix of *bînātî* may be parsed as objective genitive, "the understanding of me" as with *kĕlimmātî,* "the humiliation of me" (20:3a). The prefixed *min* of *bînātî* would then be parsed as privative and *rûaḥ* as accusative of means. As *rûaḥ* is more commonly feminine, the masculine verb *yaʿănēnî* would more naturally refer to a male speaker.

Form

The bulk of Zophar's speech consists of a wisdom lesson on the fall of the wicked (vv 4–29) which opens with an appeal to an ancient tradition (v 4) cited in v 5, developed in vv 6–28 and summed up in v 29.[94] As Job is implicitly identified with the "wicked man" of this wisdom lesson, this piece functions as disputation.[95] The opening two verses of Zophar's speech, in which he speaks of his compulsion to reply (vv 2a, 3b; cf. 4:2b) and of his reaction to Job's arguments, may also be considered typical of a disputation speech (cf. 8:2; 11:2–3; 15:2–3).[96] The structure of this brief passage is outlined below:

	Announcement of Response:	
	Zophar replies to Bildad	(19:1)
1	Compulsion to speak	(2)
2	Admission of humiliation	(3a)
3	Critique of Job's Response	(3b)

Rhetorical Analysis

(1) The Connections between 20:2–3 and Previous Passages

Although this introduction is relatively short, it presents the reader with three possibilities of a response to Job. The first involves the root *klm* ("to humiliate") in what we shall see is a clear and specific retort to a previous statement made by Job. The second involves the word *rûaḥ* ("wind"), which refers to Job's introductory remarks of 16:3. The third is of a more general, thematic nature and recalls Job's earlier criticisms of his friends' wisdom. With regard to the first proposal, the root *klm* occurs only three times in the book of Job (11:3b; 19:3a; 20:3a). Of the latter two occurrences which are of interest here, Job employs this verb first in an accusation directed against the three friends who have repeatedly humiliated him. Zophar takes exception to this charge and adopts the noun *kĕlimmâ* ("humiliation") which derives from the root *klm,* in what amounts to a countercharge. Thus he, in turn, replies that Job's speech "humiliates" him.

[94] Murphy, *Wisdom Literature,* 33, and Habel, *The Book of Job* (1985) 313.
[95] Cf. Murphy, *Wisdom Literature,* 33; and Hartley, *The Book of Job,* 299.
[96] Cf. Fohrer, *Das Buch Hiob,* 327.

This "reproof" of which Zophar speaks (20:3a) is considered by him as nothing more than "wind." The choice of the word *rûaḥ* ("wind") is significant in 20:3b as it ties in with Job's earlier critique of his friends' speeches, "Is there an end to windy words (16:3a)?" The intent of the play is to suggest that Job's, not Zophar's words are in fact "wind." This assessment is supported by the charge that Job's replies reveal he lacks understanding of Zophar's previous speech.

The response of v 3b, in conjunction with Zophar's obvious fervor, raises the question as to what the reader should perceive Job has said to receive such a reaction. Some scholars believe that Zophar should be understood as responding to specific passages of chap. 19. Anderson, for example, suggests that vv 2–3 should be read as a retort to Job's concluding warning of 19:28–29.[97] Habel agrees with Anderson on this point but adds v 22 as a second source for Zophar's strong response.[98] These scholars overlook the profound shock and disgust that Job's indictment of God (19:6) and subsequent description of God's unjust attack (vv 7–12) would create in an orthodox believer. In addition, the jibe against the friends' presumption of superiority (v 5) and the allegations that they have turned against Job (vv 14a, 19a) should also be considered as contributing to Zophar's reaction. When Job's complaint of his alienation from his family (vv 13a, 14a, 17), servants (vv 15, 16) and other acquaintances (vv 14b, 18), through no fault of his own, is taken into account along with his accusations against God and his friends, it becomes obvious that Job's stance is that everyone else but he is in the wrong. As Zophar indicts Job as one of the wicked in 20:4–29, Job's alienation from God and others should be interpreted, in his view, as a sign of his guilt. That Job presumes himself innocent in the face of such contradictory evidence should be understood as too much for Zophar to withstand. Consequently, he is portrayed as reacting with extreme agitation which gives rise to a strong desire to have his say. In sum, it is more accurate to view Zophar's emotional reaction of vv 2–3 as a response to chap. 19 as a whole.

[97] Anderson, *Job,* 195.

[98] Habel, *The Book of Job* (1985) 315.

(2) An Overview of 20:2–3 with Attention to the Proposed Connections

Zophar opens his second speech with the disclosure of his compulsion to respond to Job which serves as an indication of the degree of this character's exasperation. He states that he has "anxious thoughts" (v 2a) and "feelings" (v 2b) which, no doubt, stem from Job's rebuke (v 3a) and give rise to his need to speak. Further, Zophar's admission of humiliation (v 3a) should be seen as a response to Job's complaint that his friends humiliate him with their speeches (19:3a). It may also be understood as a further reason for his urgent need to respond to Job. Finally Zophar's description of Job's speeches as "wind" should be understood as a response to Job's earlier criticism of his friends' speeches as "wind" (16:3a).

The Seventh Speech of Job (chap. 21) His Response to Zophar

The consensus of opinion is that this speech consists of two main sections: an introductory passage in which Job demands that his friends hear him out (vv 2–6) and a poem on the prosperity of the wicked (vv 7–34).[99] Fohrer differs from this consensus as he takes vv 2–5 as the introductory strophe and links v 6 to the subsequent statement on the wicked.[100] Verses 5 and 6, however, should not be divided into separate strophes, as they both describe the shock registered by persons of integrity at the unsettling contradictions between theory and reality.

Webster divides vv 2–6 into two units (vv 2–3, 4–6).[101] Verse 5, in which Job requests that his friends attend to him in order that they might be shocked into silence, however, clearly belongs with Job's appeal for a hearing (vv 2–3). Webster's twofold division of vv 2–6 is, therefore, ruled out as well. Consequently, those scholars who take vv 2–6 as the introductory unit of this speech are probably correct.

[99] Driver and Gray, *A Critical and Exegetical Commentary on Job,* 182; Weiser, *Das Buch Hiob,* 164; Terrien, *Job* (1963) 161; Skehan, "Strophic Patterns in Job," 108; Rowley, *Job,* 146; Murphy, *Wisdom Literature,* 34; de Wilde, *Das Buch Hiob,* 226; Habel, *The Book of Job* (1985) 324; and Hartley, *The Book of Job,* 311.

[100] Fohrer, *Das Buch Hiob,* 339.

[101] Webster, "Strophic Patterns in Job 3–28," 48.

The Introduction to the Seventh Speech of Job (with the Narrator's Opening Statement)

21:1 Then Job answered and said:
2 Listen carefully to my words
and let this be your consolation.
3 Bear with me while I speak;
and after I have spoken, you may mock.[102]
4 Is my complaint against a human being?
Why should my spirit not be impatient?
5 Look at me and be appalled,[103]
and put your hands over your mouths.
6 When I think of it, I am horrified
and my flesh is seized with shuddering.[104]

Form

Job's presentation on the prosperous life lived by the wicked is a disputation which is designed to refute the friends' beliefs that the wicked meet a disasterous and premature end (Eliphaz in 15:20–35; Bildad in 18:5–21, and Zophar in 20:4–29).[105]

With regard to the introductory strophe, it is noted that the imperative mood abounds (five times), due particularly to the three demands for the friends' attention (vv 2a, 3a, 5aa). The call for attention dominates vv 2 and 3. Then, with two rhetorical questions, Job requests that the friends reconsider their treatment of him (v 4). In the two closing verses

102 The imperfect aspect of the verb is used here to express a "permissive" sense (see Williams, *Hebrew Syntax,* §170).

103 The verb *šāmēm* ("to appall") is currently pointed as a *hiphil* imperative but reads best as a *niphal* imperative (*hiššammû*). Cf. Fohrer, *Das Buch Hiob,* 337 and the editor's note in the *BHS.*

104 As Fohrer (*Das Buch Hiob,* 337) observes *bĕśārî* ("my flesh") is the subject of the colon. To express this fact the verb *'āḥaz* ("to seize") is translated as a passive (cf. *JPSV*).

105 Cf. Fohrer, *Das Buch Hiob,* 339; Habel, *The Book of Job* (1985) 323; and Murphy, *Wisdom Literature,* 34. Job also argues against Bildad's insistence that the "light of the wicked is extinguished" (18:5a; cf. 21:17). Despite these connections with earlier speeches of the friends, Job takes up several themes from Zophar's last speech (e.g., the reference to the offspring of the wicked [21:11; cf. 20:10a]; the rejoicing of the wicked [21:12; cf. 20:5]; the eating metaphor [21:23–26; cf. 20:12–18]; and "the day of wrath" [21:30; cf. 20:28b]) which indicates that he responds primarily to Zophar and to the remaining friends only in a secondary fashion.

of this strophe Job, after renewing his demand for his friends to hear him (v 5aa), speaks of their forthcoming shock at what he is about to relate and conveys his own anxiety over his observations on the life of the wicked.[106] The structure of vv 2–6 may be laid out as follows:

	Announcement of response: Job replies to Zophar	(21:1)
1	The call for attention	(2–3)
	(a) Demand for attention	(2a)
	(b) Ironic reference to this speech as a source of comfort	(2b)
	(c) Renewed demand for attention	(3a)
	(d) Permission granted to mock after the speech	(3b)
2	Request that the friends reconsider their treatment of Job	(4)
	(a) Job's complaint is not lodged against the friends (rhetorical question)	(4a)
	(b) Request that Job's cause be refuted (rhetorical question)	(4b)
3	Call for attention with reaction of Job and his friends to his speech	(5–6)
	(a) Further demand for attention	(5aa)
	(b) The friends will be shocked	(5ab–5b)
	(c) Job's reaction of shock	(6)

Rhetorical Analysis

(1) The Connections between 21:2–6 and Previous Passages

An examination of 21:2–6 for clues of connections to earlier texts reveals

[106] Cf. Driver and Gray, *A Critical and Exegetical Commentary on Job,* 183; and Rowley, *Job,* 147. Habel (*The Book of Job* [1985] 326) and Hartley (*The Book of Job,* 311), however, maintain that Job has in mind his recent experiences, and that he asks in v 5 that his friends respond accordingly, i.e., in a sympathetic fashion. The former position is taken because (a) the focus of vv 2 and 3 is on Job's forthcoming argument, and (b) it is more likely that the friends would be shocked into silence (cf. 29:9 and 40:4) by Job's provocative theory than by an allusion to his tragic experience of which they are well aware.

two possibilities.[107] The first involves the verb *šām'a* ("to hear, listen").[108] Zophar employed this verb in the statement, "I hear reproof that humiliates me" (20:3a), which registers his disturbance over what Job has said in his previous speech.

It is one thing, however, to argue that God has treated a single individual unjustly (19:6), but it is quite another for Job to insist in chap. 21 that God imposes no punishment whatsoever on the wicked. When Job attacks the belief that the wicked are always inevitably punished he threatens the very foundations of social order. For this reason he informs his friends that they will be shocked into silence by his speech (21:5). Job, too, has an investment in this doctrine as his case rests on the teaching that God punishes the wicked and rewards the righteous. Thus the argument of his speech is distressing for him also (21:6).

When the provocative nature of Job's argument is understood, one can see that the twofold use of the root *šm'* in the emphatic clause of 21:2a is intended to form a link with 20:3a. The implication is that if Zophar is disturbed by Job's previous speech, then he should "listen carefully" to what Job is now about to unfold which promises to be all the more disturbing. An appreciation of the significance of the play on the verb *šāma'* draws out the inherent sarcasm of this colon which complements the sarcasm implicit in Job's description of his speech as a source of "consolation" to Zophar and his other two friends.

The second term which ties 21:2–6 to chap. 20 is *rûaḥ* (here "spirit").[109] In 20:3b Zophar speaks of (literally) "the spirit out of my understanding," by which is meant his inner insight or discernment. Job uses *rûaḥ* in an idiomatic expression, "my spirit is short," which conveys a sense of impatience. As God has not yet appeared to hear Job's case, a degree of impatience with God's tardiness might be expected. But in the context

[107] Four other words (*'ādām*, "human being," 20:4b; *śîm*, "to put, place," 20:4b and 21:5b; *yad*, "hand," 20:22b and 21:5b; and *peh*, "mouth," 20:13a and 21:5b) occur in both 21:2–6 and chap. 20, but the words from the former passage do not appear to give any indication of a response to those of chap. 20.

[108] Apart from 20:3a and 21:2a the verb *šām'a* ("to hear, listen") occurs ten times in earlier texts and fourteen times in the chapters following chap. 21.

[109] The noun *rûaḥ* may mean either "wind" or "spirit." It is used with the former meaning in 21:18a in an unrelated reference. The noun used for "wind" occurs four times in passages after chap. 21 and six times (1:19; 6:26; 7:7; 8:2; 15:2; 16:3) in the chapters preceding chap. 20. This word is used for "spirit" in 4:15; 6:4; 7:11; 10:12; 15:13 and six further times in the material following chap. 21.

of the rhetorical question of 20:4a, which is directed against the friends' lack of support, it is more probable that Job is expressing his impatience with his friends. The connection created between 20:3b and 21:4b with the noun *rûaḥ* suggests that Job's description of himself as an "impatient spirit" is a deliberate foil to Zophar's smug designation of himself as a "discerning spirit." With this play Job expresses his impatience with the conventional wisdom of Zophar which also implicates the arguments of Eliphaz and Bildad as well.

(2) An Overview of 21:2–6 with attention to the Proposed Connections

The plural imperative *šim'û* ("listen," v 2a) followed by the infinitive absolute of the same root stresses Job's desire for his friends to listen to his speech.[110] At another level this verb relates to Zophar's use of it in his remark that he "hears" humiliating reproof from Job's lips (20:3a). With this link the point is indirectly made that Zophar should prepare himself, for Job is about to say something more provocative. To designate his forthcoming presentation as a source of "consolation" (*tanḥûm,* v 2b) can only be understood as intense sarcasm as Zophar and the others would predictably find Job's viewpoint revolting.

In the following verse, Job employs the personal pronoun *'ānōkî* ("I") to lay further emphasis on his position. His friends do not wish to hear such thoughts, but Job insists that they continue to attend to him. The verbs of this passage, inflected in the second person form are all plural except for *lā'ag* ("to mock," v 3b). Hartley is of the opinion that this verb probably refers to the last speaker, although he admits to the possibility that it might address Eliphaz who is due to speak next.[111] As Job responds primarily to the last speaker (see n. 105 above), it is likely that the verb *lā'ag* is addressed to Zophar. It is contended, therefore, that Job does not expect Zophar to be receptive to his ideas and requests that he remain silent until the speech is completed.

Verse 4 consists of two rhetorical questions. With the first question Job leads the friends to consider the motives for their attack on him. The friends take his suit against God personally due to their investment in

[110] Williams, *Hebrew Syntax,* §205.

[111] Hartley, *The Book of Job,* 311, n. 4.

conventional theology. Yet, Job wishes to clarify the fact that, in essence, his complaint is directed not against them but against God. The first question expects a negative response accompanied with some reflection on the friends' behavior, but the second is worded in such a way so as to give the effect that the friends are expected to formulate the reasons why Job does not have just cause for his "impatience." The expectation would be that the friends will come to the conclusion that there are no valid reasons why Job should behave otherwise. These two questions put upon the mouth of Job direct the friends to re-evaluate their lack of support for his case. Their purpose is to lead the friends to recognize their lack of objectivity in order that they might become more receptive to the observations of this speech. At the same time, the reference to Job's "impatient spirit" in the second question (v 4b) recalls Zophar's description of himself as a "discerning spirit" (20:3b) in such a way that doubt is cast upon Zophar's discriminating powers. Finally, as previously stated, v 5 tells of the friends' probable reaction to Job's forthcoming speech, and v 6 relates Job's own shock at what he has discovered.

CHAPTER 4

Chapters 22–24 of the Third Cycle

As is commonly observed, the latter part of the third cycle is in disarray. Bildad's speech is unexpectedly brief, Zophar's is missing, and Job appears to argue against himself in 24:18–24 and 27:7–23. To restructure this portion of the book in such a way so as to reclaim what could possibly be the missing sections of Bildad's speech and to relegate to Zophar what might originally have belonged to his third speech could conceivably be done along the lines proposed by various scholars.[1] But then to attempt to identify the introductory portions of these proposed speeches would be extremely conjectural, especially as one cannot be certain if the complete speeches were recovered. If, however, chaps. 25–27 are studied in their existing form, one would find that Bildad's speech of chap. 25 does not seem to respond to Job's previous speech in any significant way through shared words, themes or by allusion and that the passages which might be argued as the introductions to Job's following speeches (26:2–4; 27:2–7) do not appear to respond to Bildad's speech of chap. 25. Consequently, only Eliphaz's third speech and Job's speech of chaps. 23–24 will be studied in this chapter as they provide some evidence of a response to the speeches which they follow, and one can be reasonably sure that their introductory units are intact.

[1] See for example Rowley (*Job,* 169–70, 172, 175–76), Pope (*Job,* 180, 187–89) and Habel (*The Book of Job* [1985] 366–68, 376–78, 384–85).

The Third Speech of Eliphaz (chap. 22)
His Response to Job

Three scholars, Anderson, Habel and Hartley,[2] divide Eliphaz's last speech into three broad sections: vv 2–11, 12–20, and 21–30. This division does partial justice to chap. 22 as one can readily see that the second unit, with its indirect accusation issued against Job for his assumption that God is unaware of humanity's activity on earth (vv 12–14) and the subsequent warning concerning the lifestyle of the wicked (vv 15–20), may be distinguished from the list of Job's offenses and their result (vv 6–11) and the concluding call to repentance and assurance of restoration (vv 21–30).

A second group of scholars divide this speech into either six, (Fohrer, Skehan, Murphy, and Webster[3]) or eight (Delitzsch[4]) strophes or units of which vv 2–5 is one. Of these scholars, Skehan justifies the separation of v 5 from vv 6–11 on the basis that the opening verses all begin with the letter *he.*[5] Three further scholars, Terrien, de Wilde, and Rowley,[6] treat chap. 22 as a four-part speech with vv 2–5 as the opening unit. Apart from a difference of opinion over the first four verses, de Wilde and Rowley's arrangement agrees with the first group of scholars. Verse 11 as the opening of Terrien's third strophe is indefensible, however, and should be seen as the conclusion to the second strophe with de Wilde and Rowley.

In agreement with the majority of the scholars, vv 2–5 are best seen as introduction to this speech. As in Murphy's schema, the balance of the chapter is considered the body of Eliphaz's speech.[7] Building on Skehan's observation with regard to the letter *he,* which introduces each verse of the opening strophe, it is pertinent to note that this letter marks the interrogative particle *hă-* in all four verses. Rather than appealing

[2] Anderson, *Job,* 202; Habel, *The Book of Job* (1985) 334; and Hartley, *The Book of Job,* 323.

[3] Fohrer, *Das Buch Hiob,* 353; Skehan, "Strophic Patterns in Job," 110 (note that Skehan inserts 21:22 after 22:2); Murphy, *Wisdom Literature,* 34; and Webster, "Strophic Patterns in Job 3–28," 50.

[4] Delitzsch, *Biblical Commentary on Job,* 1. 427.

[5] Skehan, "Strophic Patterns in Job," 110. Cf. Webster, "Strophic Patterns in Job 3–28," 50.

[6] Terrien, *Job* (1963) 166; de Wilde, *Das Buch Hiob,* 233; and Rowley, *Job,* 153.

[7] Murphy, *Wisdom Literature,* 34.

to an alphabetical arrangement as does Skehan in his article, "Strophic Patterns in the Book of Job,"[8] one may then justify this division on the grounds that the rhetorical questions which govern Eliphaz's opening statement distinguish this section from the list of Job's sins in vv 6–9.

The Introductory Strophe of the Third Speech of Eliphaz (with the Narrator's Opening Statement)

22:1 Then Eliphaz the Temanite answered and said:
2 Can a strong man[9] be of use[10] to El,
a sage be really useful to him?
3 Does it please Shaddai if you are righteous?
Or is it his gain if you are perfect in your ways?
4 Is it because of your fear (of God) that he arraigns you
and enters into judgment with you?
5 Is not your wickedness great?
Are not your iniquities boundless?

Form

Eliphaz's final contribution to the debate is clearly a disputation speech. His accusation of gross sin (v 5) and list of specific charges against Job (vv 6–9) must be seen as a strong reaction against a person who maintains his innocence (9:15, 20; 10:7) and yet argues that God allows the wicked to prosper (chap. 21). Indeed Eliphaz, in his argument against Job's thesis of chap. 21, directly cites from 21:14a and 16b in 22:17a and 18b to refute this claim.

[8] Skehan, "Strophic Patterns in the Book of Job," 96–113.

[9] As the noun *geber* derives from the root *gbr,* "to be strong, mighty," the emphasis lies on the prowess of subject (cf. Blommerde, *Northwest Semitic Grammar and Job,* 97).

[10] BDB (p. 698) lists three distinct roots for *sākan:* (I) "to be of use, service or benefit"; (II) "to incur danger"; and (III) "to be poor." Most translators favor "I," although E. Lipiński ("*SKN* et *SGN* dans le Sémitique Occidental du Nord," *UF* 5 [1973] 191–92) argues for "II" on the basis of Talmudic and Aramaic usage. Habel (*The Book of Job* [1985] 331) adopts Lipiński's suggestion and translates *sākan* as "to endanger." This rendition makes sense in this context, but I believe that the verb *sākan* is related to 15:3a, where the same verb translates best as "to be useful." The verb *sākan* is, therefore, translated with a similar meaning. (Note that Habel [p. 245] does not follow Lipiński's translation [p. 191] of *sākan* as "s'exposer" [with danger implied] in 15:3a.)

Verses 2–5 of this speech are classed by Fohrer as a series of questions which correspond to wisdom disputation.[11] As stated earlier, whether or not a particular unit may have its origins in the wisdom or legal traditions is not only difficult to decide but is not of pertinence for this study.[12] What is important is to establish that vv 2–5 are a unit characteristic of disputation which derives from a larger disputation speech.

This passage may be divided into two subsections: a reprimand (vv 2–4) culminating in an accusation (v 5). Rhetorical questions are used only in the introductory strophe of this speech. In structure the first five verses of chap. 22 appear as follows:

	Announcement of response: Eliphaz replies to Job	(22:1)
1	Reprimand	(2–4)
	(a) The effect of Job's physical strength and wisdom on God is questioned (twofold rhetorical question)	(2)
	(b) The effect of Job's so-called righteousness and moral perfection is questioned (twofold rhetorical question)	(3)
	(c) That Job's piety is the cause of his suffering is questioned (twofold rhetorical question)	(4)
2	Accusation Job is guilty of great wickedness (twofold rhetorical question)	(5)

Rhetorical Analysis

(1) The Connections between 22:2–5 and Previous Passages

A scrutiny of the opening of Eliphaz's third speech reveals several connections with previous passages from the Book of Job.[13] First, a text from

[11] Fohrer, *Das Buch Hiob,* 353.

[12] In the present passage, for example, one could conceivably argue on the basis of legal language (*yākaḥ* and *mišpāṭ*) that v 4 derives from a legal provenance.

[13] In addition, the root *gbr* occurs in 21:7 and 22:2 in an unconnected manner. The related nouns *ra*ʿ (21:30) and *rāʿâ* (22:5) are also used in Job's speech and Eliphaz's response. Further, the synonym *ršʿ* is employed by Job in 21:7, 16, 17, 28. Eliphaz's reference to Job's "wickedness" (22:5) relates to Job's description of the wicked in only a very general way and consequently is not singled out for discussion.

Job's previous speech (21:14–15) appears to relate to 22:3 through the shared root *ḥpṣ*[14] ("to take pleasure in, delight in, care") and the repetition of the noun *derek* ("way").[15] Further, the verb *yāʿal* ("to gain, profit," 21:15b) appears to form a link with the noun *beṣaʿ* ("gain," 22:3b) as both words are synonymous in meaning.

In his radical presentation on the benefits enjoyed by the wicked, Job depicts the wicked as saying that they do not "desire" or "care" about understanding the "ways" of God (21:14b); and in a continuation of this quote, Job maintains that the wicked justify their behavior on the grounds that piety does not result in personal "profit" (21:15b). This disregard for God's will can only be viewed by the faithful as defiance of the worst kind which is deserving of swift retribution. Yet Job's thesis is that the wicked not only get away with such offenses but actually prosper in this life. The assumption implicit in Job's argument is that God does not intervene in human lives to punish them for their wickedness. Eliphaz obviously disagrees with the rationale of this argument, as he accuses Job of great "wickedness" (22:5), lists several crimes he believes Job committed (22:6–7, 9) and describes the punishment Job has received (22:10–11). Moreover, the links between 21:14–15 and 22:3 suggest to the reader that the poet has Eliphaz take his cue from the attitude of the wicked and its implications about God and adapts this idea to his argument on the detachment of God in 22:2–3. This development makes the point that God does not "care" (*ḥpṣ*) about Job's assumed righteousness any more than the wicked who do not care about the "ways" (*derek*) of God. Similarly, Eliphaz

[14] The noun *ḥēpeṣ* also occurs in 21:21; 31:16. The former reference is with regard to the attitude of the wicked, who are dead, toward the fate of their descendents and does not seem to relate to its use in 22:3a. In addition to 21:14b, the verb *ḥāpēṣ* occurs in 9:3, 13:3; 33:32.

[15] The noun *derek* is used on eight occasions in passages preceding chaps. 21 and 22, and nineteen times in later chapters. It occurs twice more in chap. 21 in vv 29 and 31. In the former reference it is used more concretely with the meaning of "road" as opposed to "way," in the abstract moral sense, as in 21:14, 31; 22:3 and is, therefore, not related to 22:3. The second time *derek* is used with the meaning of "way" in 21:31 is in the question, "Who will tell him of his way to his face?" In the light of the accusation of 22:5 and the list of sins in vv 6, 7, 9, it is possible that in a secondary manner Eliphaz might be understood as implying that he will take it upon himself to declare Job's "way" to his face which is, in his view, as evil as the wicked man of 21:27–33. The noun *derek* occurs for a second time in 22:28 where it is used with reference to 22:3 in continuation of the motif of "way."

reacts to the claim of the wicked that there is no "profit" (*yā'al*) from serving God with the argument that God does not "gain" (*beṣa'*) from human moral behavior.[16] But in questioning the idea that God somehow "cares" about or "gains" from human righteousness, Eliphaz unwittingly withdraws his support from the idea that God rewards piety.[17] A touch of realism is added to the debate through this lapse of logic, as the poet creates the impression that Eliphaz has briefly lost his composure and ends up arguing with himself.

The character of Eliphaz may be understood as assuming only a negative answer could be given to his question of 22:3. This view finds support in his presentation of God's detachment from personal righteousness (22:2, 12). Habel and Janzen draw out the ironic dimension of this question which becomes evident when it is approached from the perspective of the prologue.[18] Eliphaz speaks of the "perfection" of Job's ways with the verb *tāmam* ("to be perfect," 22:3b) but sarcastically, as it is clear he views Job as a sinner. Unknown to Eliphaz, however, God describes Job as a "perfect" (*tām,* 1:8) man in the prologue and, as indicated by his boasting, the deity derives a certain amount of pleasure from this fact. When this question is approached with the knowledge of the events of the prologue, it becomes clear that for the reader an affirmative answer would be given to the query of 22:3; for God does take pleasure in morality—especially if it is disinterested. The reader, therefore, finds himself or herself in disagreement with the insinuation of Eliphaz in 22:3.

Habel is of the opinion that the clause of 22:4b, formed with the verb *bw'* ("to enter") and the noun *mišpāṭ* ("judgment, lawsuit"), refers to the

[16] Cf. Janzen, *Job,* 161.

[17] Power (*A Study of Irony in Job,* 116–17) makes a similar observation and writes:

> And now Eliphaz is saying that Job is wasting his time, that God does not care one whit for his innocence, and in so saying he has given away the argument to Job. His own anger and frustration have driven him into Job's arms. His own blind intransigence has driven him to absurdity, for he now agrees with Job that God is simply the Mighty One, and that *ḥsd* is not necessary characteristic of his relationship with man.
>
> In the heat of his anger, however Eliphaz does not realize the consequences of his words. He forges ahead, blindly and angrily castigating Job for sins he has not committed, but which he must have committed if the old theory—no longer of any importance in any case in the light of what Eliphaz has just said—contains any truth. . .

[18] Habel, *The Book of Job* (1985) 338; Janzen, *Job,* 161.

similar expression of 9:32b and 14:3b.[19] He states that, "Eliphaz derides Job's sense of justice by quoting these very words of Job as evidence of Job's folly."[20] Habel's viewpoint makes sense but does not rule out a more immediate connection. The verb *šāpaṭ* ("to judge") occurs in 21:22b and appears to hold some bearing on the presence of the noun *mišpāṭ* in 22:4b.[21] In his argument that the wicked are spared from calamity (21:17–26), Job asks:

> Can El be taught knowledge,
> he who judges the exalted ones? (21:22)

In this query Job criticizes his friends for presuming to speak for God on how humanity should be governed. As God is the judge of the "exalted ones," Job maintains that he is far above the insights that could be offered him by humanity. Although Eliphaz cannot disagree with the theology of 21:22, the reader could reason that he would take exception to the insinuation that Eliphaz's powers of discernment are relatively useless. To register his displeasure with Job's comment, the verb *šāpaṭ* of 22:4b is, then, put upon the lips of Eliphaz in reference to 21:22. With the creation of this link the allegation of 21:22 is appropriately redirected against Job who has previously implicated God for treating him unjustly (9:15, 17, 20; 28–29). The implication is that God, "the judge of the exalted ones" also sees through what Eliphaz believes is Job's pretense of piety and innocence and enters into judgement with Job for just cause.[22]

[19] Habel, *The Book of Job* (1985) 338.

[20] Habel, *The Book of Job* (1985) 338.

[21] Beyond the reference to *šāpaṭ* in 21:22b, this verb occurs also in 9:24; 12:17; 22:13. The noun *mišpāṭ* occurs five times in earlier texts (8:3; 9:19, 32; 14:3; 19:7) and thirteen times in passages following chap. 22. The presence of the verb *šāpaṭ* in 22:13b could very well be intended as a further reaction to 21:22. If so, one is given the impression that Eliphaz deliberately misquotes 21:22 in a further effort to turn what Job has said about God against him.

[22] Driver and Gray (*A Critical and Exegetical Commentary on Job,* 187–188) regard 21:22 as a gloss. Skehan ("Strophic Patterns in Job," 110, n. 32) believes it properly follows 22:2 (cf. Pope, *Job,* 160). Dhorme (*A Commentary on Job,* 318) insists that this verse is integral to Job's speech of chap. 21. In his view (with which we concur) Job castigates the friends for imposing upon God their beliefs on how the world should be ruled. Gordis (*The Book of Job,* 231) and Webster ("Strophic Patterns in Job 3–28," 49) approach this verse as a quotation of the friends. This view is a reasonable alternative to that adopted here. If it is approached as a quotation it must be understood as originally directed against Job. (The second half of the verse is reminiscent of Eliphaz in 4:18 and might allude to

Finally, on the basis of the relationship established between 21:14b and 15b and 22:3, it appears that Eliphaz's presentation on the self-sufficiency of God stems from Job's comments on the self-reliant attitude of the wicked. One such remark attributed to the wicked, "What is Shaddai that we should serve him?" (21:15a) may well lie behind Eliphaz's opening questions of his third speech,

> Can a strong man be of use to El,
> a sage be really useful to him (v 2)?

Furthermore, in two descriptions of God's attacks on Job (16:9–14; 19:8–12), military imagery was used of God which could conceivably lend itself to the interpretation by a disputant that Job sees himself as a "strong man" or even as a warrior in his struggle against God. The same may be said for the other points where Job speaks as though he were a sage (12:2–3; 13:1–2). It appears that Eliphaz draws on these passages in which Job might be understood sometimes as a "strong man" and at other times as a "slave," in order to make a counterpoint to 21:15a. Thus, in effect, he says in v 2, "What are you to God? Even if you were a strong man or a slave, you are of no use to God." This point is continued in v 3 in which Eliphaz may be understood as saying, "Of what consequence is your so-called righteousness or purity to God?"

(2) An Overview of 22:2–5 with Attention to the Proposed Connections

The first set of rhetorical questions (v 2) indirectly refers to Job in the third person with reference to portions of previous speeches (12:2–3; 13:1–2; 16:9–14, 19:8–12) where his comments lend themselves to the interpretation that he sees himself as a "strong man" and a "sage." Eliphaz expects a negative answer to vv 2 and 3 which may be seen as a response to Job's presentation of the claim of the wicked (21:15b), that they realize no gain if they pray to God. He does not answer the claim directly but maintains that God does not benefit from what humanity might offer him either. Similarly, in v 3, Eliphaz contends that, like the wicked who

---

this previous reference.) The significance of 22:4b as a response to 21:22 remains much the same if the latter is viewed as a quotation—God, who is the judge of the "exalted ones," enters into judgment with Job.

have no use for the ways of God (21:14), the deity would take no special notice of Job even if he were "righteous." The intention of these two sets of questions is to impress upon Job his unimportance in the eyes of God. Job has argued as though his life is of prime concern to God and worthy of his immediate attention, but Eliphaz attempts to silence Job by convincing him otherwise. Ironically Eliphaz, without the benefit of the knowledge gained from the prologue, is not aware that Job is indeed special to God and worthy of his attention. If one reads v 3 from the perspective of the prologue the answer, to Eliphaz's surprise, would be in the affirmative.

The sarcasm of v 4 is obvious as Eliphaz clearly believes that Job is wicked (v 5) and deserving of his treatment. As with vv 2 and 3, the answer "no" is expected to this twofold question. Eliphaz prepares for the answer he expects from the questions of v 5 by asking Job to reflect upon the reason (as he sees it) for Job's suffering. Here Eliphaz takes up the idea of God's judgment from 21:22 in order to make the point that as God is above all human instruction and has the power and authority to judge the "exalted ones," he cannot be unjust or in error in his judgment of Job. In the last verse of this introduction, Eliphaz anticipates an affirmative answer to his pair of questions through which it is hoped that Job will admit to his "guilt."

The Eighth Speech of Job (chaps. 23–24) His Response to Eliphaz

In chap. 23, Job speaks of his search for God that he might enter into litigation with him. In contrast, chapter 24 consists of a discussion on the punishment of the wicked. On the basis of different subject matter, the introductory question of 24:1 is judged as the beginning of a second poem. The contents of chap. 23 are appropriate on Job's lips, but critical scholars question the placement of chap. 24, especially the latter portions, as part of Job's speech.[23] Considering the fact that Job has recently argued

[23] Hartley's commentary (*The Book of Job*), which belongs to the NICOT series, is an example of noncritical conservative scholarship. In this instance he ignores the difficulties associated with chap. 24 and interprets it as a legitimate portion of Job's eighth speech (see pp. 336 and 342–43 of his text). Gordis (*The Book of Job,* 269) adopts a somewhat less conservative position with his proposal that 24:18–24 be understood as a quotation indicative of the friends' position.

against the view that the wicked are punished for their sins (chap. 21), Dhorme, Pope, and Rowley[24] relegate the opposite point of view in 24:18–24 to Zophar, who in the present arrangement of the book, does not have a third speech.

Fohrer divides and reorganizes chap. 24 into four poems: (a) vv 1–4, 10–12, and 22–23; (b) vv 5–8; (c) 13–17; and (d) vv 18–21.[25] Only the first poem fits with Job's thought, according to Fohrer, and the rest correspond to the viewpoints of the friends.[26] Habel takes a different approach and argues for the unity of chap. 24 which he attributes to Zophar.[27] He presents a convincing argument that the chapter as a whole consists of a debate on the question of why the faithful do not witness God's judgment on the wicked as raised in the opening verse (24:1). Two opposing positions are discussed in this chapter: that exploitation freely occurs in a society where the perpetrators flourish (vv 2–17) and that these evildoers are punished for their offenses (vv 18–20). The question in dispute (v 1) is, then, resolved in favor of the latter position in vv 22–24. In further support of the unity of chap. 24, Habel cites several terminological links between vv 2–12 and 18–24 such as: the "treaders" (*drk*) of grapes (vv 11, 18), the verb *rāʿâ* ("to pasture, feed on," vv 2, 21), and the verb *gāzal* ("to carry off," vv 2, 9, 19) which, in Habel's opinion, function as key words in this chapter.[28]

As chap. 24 does not appear to belong to Job, his speech may be considered to end at the last verse of chap. 23. With respect to the limits of the opening strophe of chap. 23, several scholars take vv 2–7 as its introductory unit.[29] Fohrer, however, is of the opinion that the first strophe ends at v 6.[30] But v 7, which speaks of the possibility of Job reasoning with God and of being acquitted by his judge, does not fit with the theme of the inaccessibility of God in vv 8 and 9 as well as it does with the

[24] Dhorme, *The Book of Job,* xlix–l and Rowley, *Job,* 167. Pope (*Job,* see pp. xx and 174), however, retains v 21 as spoken by Job and inserts it into the position preceding v 4 of chap. 24.

[25] Fohrer, *Das Buch Hiob,* 368 and 370. Verses 9, 24, 25 are excised by Fohrer as glosses.

[26] Fohrer, *Das Buch Hiob,* 370.

[27] Habel, *The Book of Job* (1985), see pp. 355–58.

[28] Habel, *The Book of Job* (1985) 356–57.

[29] Terrien, *Job,* 171; Rowley, *Job,* 159; Murphy, *Wisdom Literature,* 35; and Hartley, *The Book of Job,* 337.

[30] Fohrer, *Das Buch Hiob,* 364.

theme of v 6. The thought that God would listen to Job (v 6b) logically leads to the idea that Job would, then, present his case to God and find himself acquitted. Verse 6, therefore, should not be separated from v 7.

Conversely, Irwin, Skehan, and Webster treat vv 2–7 as two distinct strophes (vv 2–4, 5–7).[31] This decision overlooks the relationship between vv 3–4, 5–7. In vv 3–4 Job verbalizes his desire to find God to present his case which Job expects will result in an intelligible response (v 5). As the theme of Job's anticipated court case dominates the opening verses of this chapter, vv 2–7 should be treated as the introductory unit to Job's eighth speech in agreement with Terrien *et al.*

The Introductory Strophe of the Eighth Speech of Job (with the Narrator's Opening Statement)

23:1 Then Job answered and said:
2 Today again my complaint is defiant;
his hand[32] is heavy despite[33] my groaning.
3 O that I knew where to find him,
that I might enter his dwelling.
4 I would set out my case before him
and fill my mouth with arguments.

[31] Irwin, "Poetic Structure in the Book of Job," 37; Skehan, "Strophic Patterns in Job," 112; and Webster, "Strophic Patterns in Job 3–28," 52.

[32] The MT reads "my hand" and is retained by Dhorme (*A Commentary on Job,* 343–344) and Hartley (*The Book of Job,* 337, n. 1). On the basis of the perceived awkwardness of the text and the fact that the root *kbd* is sometimes used to describe the dysfunction of other bodily organs (cf. Gen 48:10; Exod 4:10; 17:12), de Wilde proposes to read "his ear" for "my hand." He freely translates v 2b as "er ist meinem Seufzen taub" (de Wilde, *Das Buch Hiob,* 241–242. (This idea was first presented by de Wilde in "Eine Alte Crux Interpretum: Hiob XXIII 2," *VT* 22 [1972] 368–74.) Scholars have not adopted de Wilde's suggestion. Most follow the LXX and Syriac translations and read "his hand" (e.g., Driver and Gray, *A Critical and Exegetical Commentary on Job,* 200; Fohrer, *Das Buch Hiob,* 362; and Gordis, *The Book of Job,* 260). Blommerde (*Northwest Semitic Grammar and Job,* 99) assumes, with the support of a Ugaritic text (54:11–13), that the final *yodh* was used also as an alternative third masc. sing. suffix (cf. Anderson, *Job,* 208). Lastly, Guillaume (*Studies in Job,* 107) and Pope (*Job,* 171) observe that the *waw* and *yodh* were often indistinguishable in MSS. This observation provides the simplest explanation for the present text.

[33] The preposition *'al* as adversative, expressing disadvantage (Williams, *Hebrew Syntax,* §288).

5 I would know the words with which he would answer me
and discern what he said to me.
6 Would he contend with me with great force[34]?
No! Surely he would heed[35] me.
7 Then an upright man could reason with him,
and I could escape forever from my judge.[36]

Form

Chapter 23 is a disputation speech cast in the form of a complaint[37] which, as Fohrer observes, contains elements common to both the Psalms and legal proceedings.[38] This introduction opens with Job's complaint of God's oppression (v 2) and, then, moves to a description of his anticipated court case (vv 3–7). It may be outlined as follows:

	Announcement of response: Job replies to Eliphaz	(23:1)
I	Opening Lament: Job continues his complaint against God	(2)

[34] Pope (*Job,* 171) is persuaded by Tur-Sinai's argument (*The Book of Job,* 353) that *kōaḥ* has the meaning of "legal power" in this context. But, in agreement with Habel (*The Book of Job* [1985] 345), the meaning "great force" makes sense here especially in view of the fact that Job has previously expressed his fear that God might victimize him with his overwhelming power (9:4, 17–19) in a lawcourt.

[35] The verb *śîm* is an elliptical expression for *śîm lēb* (Gordis, *The Book of Job,* 260; cf. Rowley, *Job,* 159 and Habel, *The Book of Job* [1985] 345).

[36] Some scholars (e.g., Blommerde, *Northwest Semitic Grammar and Job,* 100; Fohrer, *Das Buch Hiob,* 363; Pope, *Job,* 172; de Wilde, *Das Buch Hiob,* 242; and Habel, *The Book of Job* [1985] 345) revocalize *miššopṭî* as *mišpāṭî* ("my case") whereas others read the text as it stands (e.g. Driver and Gray, *A Critical and Exegetical Commentary on Job,* 202; Dhorme, *The Book of Job,* 346; Rowley, *Job,* 160; Gordis, *The Book of Job,* 260; and Hartley, *The Book of Job,* 337). Habel, a representative of the former position, justifies his decision on the grounds that God plays the role of Job's adversary at law in this passage (v 2) rather than his judge. Rowley defends the MT on the grounds that the one who pronounces Job's acquittal (v 7b) would be considered Job's judge. Both arguments have some validity as God could be viewed as playing either role in chap. 23 and indeed in the dialogue as a whole. In the absence of any compelling reason to choose one side over the other, the present vocalization of the MT is retained.

[37] Cf. Murphy, *Wisdom Literature,* 35. That chap. 23 is a disputation speech will become clear when vv 2–7 are studied for hints of a response to chap. 22.

[38] Fohrer, *Das Buch Hiob,* 364.

2	Wish: He would approach God if he knew where to look	(3)
3	Job imagines the court case	(4–7)
	(i) Job's approach	(4–5)
	(a) He would present his case	(4)
	(b) He would expect an intelligible response	(5)
	(ii) God's response:	(6)
	(a) Would he overcome Job? (rhetorical question)	(6a)
	(b) Answer—No, God would listen attentively	(6b)
	(iii) Result: Job would win his case	(7)

Rhetorical Analysis

(1) The Connections between 23:2–7 and Previous Passages

Hartley is of the opinion that Job ignores the friends in this speech,[39] but it is my contention that the introduction to this speech contains several examples of a response to chap. 22.[40] The clearest connection involves the roots *ykḥ* and *špṭ*, which occur in both vv 4 and 7 of chap. 23 and in v 4 of chap. 22.[41] In a particularly sarcastic remark, Eliphaz queried Job over the possibility that God "arraigns" (*yākaḥ*) him and enters into "judgment" (*mišpāṭ*) with him on account of his piety (22:4). If we were to look at Job's use of the term *mišpāṭ* in 23:4a, we would see that he employs this term in reference to his legal "case" directed against God. Eliphaz has previously implied that God has judged Job on the basis of his "wickedness" (22:5), but as Job steadfastly maintains his righteousness in 23:7, it is understood that he bases his lawsuit on his innocence. The term *mišpāṭ* is put on Job's lips (23:4a) to make the point that Eliphaz unjustly accuses Job of wrongdoing and to imply that Job in his "defiance"

[39] Hartley, *The Book of Job,* 336. Cf. Janzen, *Job,* 165.

[40] The verbs *yādaʿ* ("to know," 22:13; 23:3), *mālēʾ* ("to fill," 22:18; 23:4), and *ʾāmar* ("to say," 22:13, 17, 29, 23:5), however, occur in both speeches but do not appear to provide a specific response in Job's reply.

[41] Besides these occurrences of the verb *šāpaṭ*, it is also found in 9:15, 24; 12:17; 21:22. This verb is used of God in 22:13 but does not enter into the play on this root in 22:4 and 23:4, 7. The related noun *mišpāṭ* occurs in 8:3; 9:19,32; 14:3; 19:7 and in nine texts succeeding chap. 23. The verb *yākaḥ* is also used in 5:17; 6:25,26; 9:33; 11:5; 13:3,10,15; 15:3; 16:21; 32:12; 33:19; 40:2. The related noun *tôkaḥat,* derived from the same root, occurs also in 13:6.

(22:2a) plans to put God on the defensive by naming him as the defendant in a court case. The second time the root *špṭ* occurs in the passage (v 7b), it is used in a participial form with reference to God as "judge." When read against 22:4, Job's use of this title carries the admission that he is quite aware that God has entered into judgment against him, but as Job believes the judgment will eventually be repealed he speaks of his acquittal by this judge despite Eliphaz's allegations.

The adoption of the root *ykḥ* from 22:4a in vv 4b and 7a of chap. 23 makes the same point as the interplay featuring the root *špṭ*—Job rejects Eliphaz's interpretation of God's arraignment of him as proof of gross wickedness. To counter Eliphaz's viewpoint, Job speaks of the "arguments" (*tôkāḥôt,* 23:4b) he would use against God, and the effort he would make to "reason" (hiphil participle of the root *ykḥ,* 23:7a) with him to establish his innocence. Further, similar to the previous suggestion involving the play on *mišpāṭ,* Job's tactic of arguing with God is presented as mirroring God's "arraignment" of him.

The second proposal involves a reference to the depiction of Job as the ideal man in the prologue. In this portion of the book (1:1,8; 2:3), Job is described as "blameless" (*tām*), "upright" (*yāšār*), one who "fears" (*yārēʾ*) God and turns away from "evil" (*raʿ*). Eliphaz mentions three of these qualities: "perfection" (*tōmām,* 22:3b), "fear" (*yirʾâ,* 22:4a), and "wickedness" (*rāʿâ,* 22:5a) in the same order, preceded with the verb *ṣādēq* ("to be righteous," 22:3a), all with reference to Job's character. Eliphaz, however, takes none of these qualities seriously in this highly sarcastic passage and even turns the mention of evil into a direct allegation against Job. Curiously, the attribute which Eliphaz does not speak of, that of Job's "uprightness" (*yāšār,* 1:1, 8; 2:3), is used by Job of himself in 23:7a. As this word completes the characterization of Job in the prologue as the ideal man, it seems that the poet has intentionally recreated this image for the purpose of having Job claim for himself the virtues which Eliphaz has discredited in a subtle defense of his character.

Three further words, the verb *bôʾ* ("to come," 22:21b; 23:3b),[42] the noun *peh* ("mouth," 22:22a; 23:4b)[43], and the verb *śîm* ("to lay, set," 22:22b;

[42] The word *bôʾ* occurs often in Job. It is used twenty-eight times before chap. 22 and ten times in the chapters following chap. 23.

[43] In addition to these occurrences the noun *peh* occurs sixteen times in earlier texts and eleven times in texts following chap. 23.

23:6b)[44] occur within two verses of Eliphaz's speech (22:21b, 22) and are found in the same order within the introduction of Job's succeeding speech. Eliphaz uses the verb *bôʾ* to describe the benefits which will "come" to Job (22:21b) if he would only submit to God. Conversely, Job speaks of himself as "coming" to God in the sense of approaching him for an audience. Rather than passively making amends for something of which Job believes he is not guilty and thereby receiving good from God, the verb "to come" is put into Job's mouth to express his rejection of Eliphaz's advice and vocalizes his desire to take the initiative "to come" before God for redress. With the second connection involving the word "mouth," Eliphaz, in his advice for Job to return to God, recommends that he "accept instruction from his [God's] mouth" (22:22a). Job, however, speaks of the arguments with which he would fill his "mouth" (23:4b). This play on "mouth" communicates the idea that Job has no desire to receive instruction from God. What Job desires is for God to play the role of defendant and to listen attentively to his arguments. Similarly, Eliphaz, in his advice for Job to "lay up (*śîm*) his words in your heart," admonishes him to take God's message seriously. This same verb is given to Job in 23:6b, "surely he would heed (*śîm*) me." On Job's lips this verb carries a response to Eliphaz's advice that Job attend to God's words. For Job the time of listening to God is over. God must now listen to him.

The overall impression gained from an examination of these last three connections is that Job strongly rejects Eliphaz's advice of 22:21–30 and presents his own plan of action. This approach consists essentially of a planned, bold encounter with God in which Job hopes to argue his case successfully. Perhaps Job's tactic explains why he says he is defiant "today again" (23:2). Such a retort implies that he persists with his approach and will not allow his resolve to be shaken by Eliphaz's recommendation.

(2) An Overview of 23:2–7 with Attention to the Proposed Connections

Although his trauma at the hand of God continues unabated, Job speaks of his attitude of continued defiance in v 2. He shows no inclination of relenting under the pressure. Job desires to receive an audience with God

[44] The verb *śîm* is used fifteen times in texts prior to chap. 22 and on twenty occasions in texts following chap. 23.

for the purpose of presenting his case, but he does not know where he might find God's dwelling place (v 3). Here, in v 3b, the verb "come" is reminiscent of Eliphaz's use of it in 22:21b. With Job's use of this verb the point is made that he does not desire to have good things "come" to him by submitting to God when it is uncalled for. Rather his wish is that he might "come" to God in order that his case might be heard. That Job believes he has a legitimate "case" carries with it the assumption of his innocence. When this term is used in the light of Eliphaz's comment concerning God's "judgment" on Job (22:4b), the implication is made that God unjustly judges him, and that he desires to engage God in the same way that God treats him. Further, that Job would fill his "mouth" with "arguments" (*tôkāḥôt,* v 4) plays both on God's "mouth" in 22:22a and the fact that, as Eliphaz puts it, God "arraigns" (*yākaḥ*) Job (22:4a). The play on "mouth" makes the point that Job wants God to listen to his words and not vice-versa. Further, the play on the root *ykḥ* brings to light Job's claim of innocence as does the connection established with *mišpāṭ* (22:4b; 23:4a).

Assuming that God might listen and issue a response to him, Job reflects on the comfort he would experience on receiving a clear reply (v 5). Job, then, restates an earlier fear that God might overwhelm him (9:17–19, 34; 13:20–21; 14:21) in the form of a rhetorical question (v 6a). He immediately answers his query in the negative in the hope that God would listen to his case (v 6b). Here Job responds to Eliphaz's earlier recommendation that he attend to God's words (22:22b) and counters it with the idea that he would rather have God "heed" him.

In the last verse of this introduction (v 7), in which the desired result of Job's audience with God is stated (that he would win his case), Job plays on Eliphaz's condemnation of his virtues (22:3–5a) with the noun *yāšār* ("upright man") in such a way that he claims for himself his reputation as presented in the prologue. In v 7, as in v 4, Job responds to Eliphaz's statements that God "arraigns" (*yākaḥ*) him (22:4a) and "judges" him (22:4b) with the counterpoint that he, armed with his innocence, will "reason" (*yākaḥ*) his way out of his predicament by proving himself before his own "judge."

CHAPTER 5

Synthesis and Conclusion

Synthesis

(1) Various Types of Connections Uncovered between the Speeches

In a disputation one side seeks to win over the opposing party to a particular point of view. The fundamental strategy of any such debate is to counter the opponent's position so as to promote one's own argument. By far the majority of the interplays examined in this study consist of such interactions which may be called "disagreements." Most of the disagreements are composed in a manner which acknowledges a specific point made by a previous speaker through the employment of a related word, phrase, or theme. The idea is then pursued by the current speaker in such a way as to register a counterpoint. Job's description of his friends' arguments as "windy words" (*dibrê-rûaḥ,* 16:3a), for example, draws on Eliphaz's remark of 15:2a in which Job's position is indirectly dismissed as "windy knowledge" (*da'at-rûaḥ*). Through this interplay the reader is expected to understand that Job rejects this insinuation but not without making a similar criticism of his friend. At some points a speaker takes up an earlier text not only as a point of contention but also to issue some advice. An illustration of this type of interaction may be seen in a particular exchange between Job and Bildad. At the end of Job's second speech, the protagonist speaks of God as "seeking" (*šāḥar*) him (7:21d).

Bildad contests this point that God might possibly seek Job and recommends that Job take the initiative and seek God instead.

On other occasions a speaker takes up an earlier text not only as a point of contention but also to defend himself against a critical remark. As might be expected, Job is normally the one on the defense, but the friends sometimes take up defensive positions as well. One example of Job defending himself occurs with the interplay involving the noun *kaʿaś*. Job's admission of his "indignation" (*kaʿaś*, 6:2a) is clearly a rejection of the negative quality which Eliphaz attaches to *kaʿaś* in 5:2a. After he rejects Eliphaz's judgment, Job justifies his anger on the basis of the magnitude of his personal tragedy (6:2).

An example of Eliphaz on the defense may be seen in his reference to himself as a "wise man" (*ḥākām*) which should be understood as a reaction against the doubts Job casts upon the "wisdom" (*ḥokmâ*) of the friends in his earlier speech (12:2b, 12a; 13:5b). Eliphaz's defense of his sagacity signals to the reader that this character is in disagreement with Job's assessment of the quality of his wisdom.

On at least one occasion an accusation forms part of the disagreement. Job, in 9:23b, speaks of God as "mocking" (*lāʿag*) the tragedies of the innocent. In the following speech this verb, *lāʿag*, is given to Zophar, not only to indicate disagreement with Job's allegation against God, but also to put forward his accusation against Job that it is he who, in fact, stoops to mockery (11:3b).

Instances of agreement between Job and his friends in the passages studied are relatively few likely because the emphasis of the dispute is not on the common ground but on the differences of opinion which exist between the opponents. There are, however, two examples of a measure of agreement which are worth comment. The first involves the wisdom sayings cited by Eliphaz in 5:6–7 which speak of the inevitability of trouble in this life. In his following speech a similar saying is put on Job's lips (7:1–2) which also makes an observation concerning the preponderance of difficulties facing humans in this world. On the difficulties inherent in life both characters agree, although there is a difference of opinion about the "why" or cause of this suffering. Eliphaz holds the view that suffering is simply an unavoidable component of human life, whereas Job believes that God, who may be compared to an employer or slave-owner, is responsible for the suffering in life.

A further level of agreement may be seen in the exchange of ideas between Job and Bildad over the friends' perception of Job's speeches. First, in 6:26b, Job complains that the friends treat his words as "wind" (*rûaḥ*). Bildad is portrayed as in agreement with this assessment when he says that the words of Job's mouth are a "mighty wind" (*rûaḥ,* 8:2b).

The pursuit of the various connections between the introductions and the contents of the previous speeches, such as those just mentioned, allows the reader to enter more deeply into the dynamics of the dispute. This approach allows one to appreciate why any one speech begins as it does or why a certain detail is expressed in a specific way or even mentioned at all.

(2) The Pattern of Connections and the Implications for the Principle of "Delayed Reaction"

An overview of the pattern of connections established between introductions, between introductions and bodies of speeches, and between introductions and the prologue allows one to categorize the introductions into three general groupings based on the degree to which an introduction responds to its respective preceding introduction (or introductions if the previous speech consists of two or more poems).[1]

Beginning with those introductions which show the strongest relationship, nine out of sixteen introductions[2] were found to form links solely with the introduction(s) belonging to the immediately preceding speech or at most to have only one out of three or more connections which relates the introduction also to the body of that speech.[3] Of these introductions seven belong to the first cycle and one to the second cycle. Four intro-

[1] For a summary of these proposals, see the appendix.

[2] Two introductory passages (4:2–6; 5:1–7) are omitted from the present discussion as they form links to the complaint of chap. 3, the structure of which was not dealt with in this study.

[3] The introduction of 6:2–7 is bound exclusively to 5:1–7 as is 12:2–6 to 11:2–6, 13:1–5 to 11:2–6, and 21:2–6 to 20:2–3. The introduction of 7:1–8 has four links with the two introductions of the preceding speech (4:2–6; 5:1–7) with one of these connections relating also to a text from the body of the speech of chap. 5. Similarly, of the three connections between 14:1–6 and 11:2–6, one also ties in with the body of chap. 11. The introductions, 9:2–4 and 8:2–7 share two links. A third related connection also ties in with a text (4:17a) from the body of an earlier speech. There are three connections between 19:2–6 and 18:24 and one further connection in 19:2–6 which relates thematically to five words from the body of chap. 18 as well as to the prologue.

ductions belong to the second group, which exhibits a relatively even mix between connections to the immediately preceding introduction(s) of a speech and those which form a link with the body of that speech.[4] Of these four passages two belong to the second cycle, one to the first and one to the third. Finally, three introductions may be placed in the third group as they show few clear links with the introductions to their respective previous speeches.[5] One of these introductions belongs to the third cycle and the three remaining passages are from the second cycle of speeches.

When the evidence is viewed with attention to the three speech cycles, it becomes clear that the first cycle shows the strongest relationship of a response which links the introduction(s) of one speech to the introduction(s) of the speech belonging to the previous speaker. It appears that relatively systematic and careful attention was given to the composition of the introductions belonging to the first cycle in order to relate

[4] Of the seven connections between 16:2–5 and previous passages, four relate to 15:2–6, two relate to the body of chap. 15 and one relates to the prologue. Chaps. 11:2–6 and 9:2–4 are linked in two places. One of these connections also relates 11:2–6 with two further texts from the body of the speech spanning chaps. 9 and 10. Two additional connections relate 11:2–6 to the speech of chaps. 9 and 10. Similarly, 15:2–6 forms two links with the two introductions of Job's speech which runs from chaps. 12 to 14 (12:2–6; 13:1–5) of which one also extends to the body of the poem of chap. 12. In addition, there are two other connections which relate 15:2–6 to the bodies of the poems of chap. 13 and 14. Chaps. 23:2–7 and 22:2–5 link in two ways. Chap. 23:2–7 also forms three further connections with the body of the speech of chap. 22. The opening of Bildad's second speech (18:2–4) forms two links with 16:2–5, that is, if the verb *tĕšîmûn* is derived from *nāšam* ("to blow") and the noun *qēṣ* is read in 18:2a. Of the four remaining connections, two link 18:2–4 with the body of the previous speech and two relate this introduction to two different earlier speeches.

[5] Zophar's second introduction (20:2–3) shows one clear connection with 19:2–6. His admission of humiliation and desire to speak possibly results from two of Job's statements in 19:2–6 but also could be understood as following from several passages belonging to the body of chap. 19. Two further connections relate to Job's earlier introductory strophes. One forms a link with 16:2–5 and the other refers back to 12:2–6 and 13:1–5 as well as to a statement in the speech body of chap. 17. The second introduction of this group (22:2–5) forms one link with 21:2–6 which also draws in a text from the body of chap. 21. In addition to a second connection which involves a text from the body of chap. 21, there is a set of conditions which relates 22:2–5 to the prologue. The third introduction (8:2–7) does not link up with the two introductions of Job's second speech (6:2–7; 7:1–8), but it does share four connections with the body of this speech as well as one with the prologue.

one to another as a reply.[6] Yet, as the lack of relationship between 8:2–7 and the two introductions to Job's second speech (6:2–7; 7:1–8) demonstrates, the writer did not rigidly adhere to this arrangement. As the dispute developed it appears that less of an effort was expended to relate the introductions together in this manner as a greater incidence of connections between an introduction and the body of the preceding speech was uncovered in the latter two speech cycles.

In addition, several connections were noted which fall outside of the links between succeeding speeches. Ten of these connections recall texts from earlier speeches which suggests that on occasion the writer created a response to something that was said in the earlier stages of the dispute.[7] The first introduction which recalls a text from an earlier speech is 9:2–4. If the various connections proposed for chaps. 9 to 23 were tallied, according to this study, one would arrive at a figure of almost one hundred. Ten texts out of nearly one hundred demonstrates that the introductions do not respond to the contents of earlier speeches with any regularity. This evidence, although limited to the links established with those passages called introductions of chaps. 9 to 23, casts doubt on the principle of "delayed reaction" as presented by S. Terrien and W. Whedbee. Of this supposed feature, Terrien writes:

> He [the poet] was ignorant of the art of swift dialogue, but he cultivated the highly original method of "delayed reaction" by which Job or a friend answers the argument not of the immediately preceding, but of the penultimate speaker (as in 9:2ff. which replies to 4:17ff.).[8]

Similarly, Whedbee states:

> One notices that the poet has built into Job's responses to his friends the stylistic feature of delayed reaction: Job *often* [italics mine] seems to ignore the immediately preceding speech in order to deal with an earlier argument of one of the comforters (cf. 9:2 which is the answer

[6] As the bodies of the speeches were not studied for connections with preceding introductions, one must not make the assumption, however, that any one introduction is tied to another in an exclusive manner.

[7] Chap. 9:2b responds to 4:17a as does 18:3 to 12:2–3, and 7–9; 18:4c to 14:18b; 19:6a to 8:3ab, and 20:3b to 16:3 and 12:2; 13:5; and 17:10.

[8] S. Terrien, "The Book of Job: Introduction and Exegesis" (*IB* 3; Nashville: Abingdon, 1954) 892.

> to Eliphaz in 4:17). Thus a certain incongruity is present in the very structuring of the speeches. The various speakers are sometimes portrayed as talking past one another.[9]

Both Terrien and Whedbee describe what they call "delayed reaction" as though it were a common and sustained practice. In the light of our findings their supposition seems unfounded, as these infrequent connections to earlier speeches occur alongside other links which clearly tie the introduction in question to the contents of the speech of the last speaker.

At the same time sixteen links with the prologue occur in seven of the introductions (4:2–6; 8:2–7; 12:2–6; 16:2–5; 19:2–6; 22:2–5; 23:2–7). This relationship suggests that a significant effort was made to weave the folktale together with at least the introductions to the speeches studied. Almost all of these connections are associated with Job's reputation (ten refer to his character and three are reminiscent of his care for his children). As will be discussed below, Job's morality is obviously an important theme in this work.

(3) Genre

In terms of genre, the speeches dealt with in this study (chaps. 4–24) were identified as disputation speeches. Within the overall context of the disputation speech, elements of a complaint may be discerned in the opening lines of a speech or a poem attributed to Job (e.g., 6:2–7; 7:1–8; 12:2–6; 14:1–6; 23:2–7). As one might expect of the friends, who fail to identify with Job, the eight introductions attributed to them belong exclusively to disputation.

One subgenre of frequent use in the introductions is the rhetorical question. Fifteen out of eighteen introductory units (excluding 13:1–5; 14:1–6; 20:2–3) employ such questions. Further, all of the friends' introductions (except Zophar's introduction of 20:2–3) begin with rhetorical questions. These queries, which are often sarcastic in nature, express the friends' disapproval of Job's stance and create a somewhat hostile tone for the dispute. In comparison, only three of Job's ten introductions (7:1–8; 9:2–4; 19:2–6) open with a rhetorical question.

In two of Job's introductions, a particular type of rhetorical question known as the "impossible question" is used (6:5–6; 9:2b). As the answers

[9] W. Whedbee, "The Comedy of Job," *Semeia* 7 (1977) 14.

to such questions are obvious to the reader, the very posing of the question elicits surprise that it would even be asked. For this reason the impossible question allows Job to make his point rather forcefully and evokes from the reader a recognition of the extremity of Job's position.

Beyond the rhetorical question and its subtype, the impossible question, the accusation is the only other subgenre which occurs with any frequency in the introductions studied. It occurs in eight of the introductions mostly in the form of a declaration (6:4; 12:5–6; 13:4; 14:3; 15:4; 19:3) but occasionally as a rhetorical question (18:4; 22:5).[10] All but three of the accusations (6:4; 12:5–6; 18:4) are composed in direct language. In a direct accusation the speaker addresses the accused with either one or more of the second person forms of address (i.e., the independent personal pronoun, the pronominal suffix attached to a noun, preposition, or direct object marker, and/or the pronominal prefix or suffix added to a verb) and states the behavior in question of which the subject is accused. In an indirect accusation either the third person is used (e.g., "he who tears himself," 18:4a), or a name (e.g., "Shaddai," 6:4a), or a descriptive epithet such as "El's agitators" (12:6b). If both direct and indirect accusations are considered, Job directs three against his friends (12:5–6; 13:4; 19:3) and two against God (6:4; 14:3). As might be expected the three accusations issued by the friends (15:4; 18:4; 22:5) describe a wrong of which they believe Job is guilty.

The introductions studied do not share a common, predictable structure. They vary in length ranging from three to eight verses, although the majority (fourteen out of eighteen) consist of four to six verses. Beyond a rough correspondence in length, the most one can say of these introductions from a form-critical perspective is that they share, to a degree, the use of rhetorical questions and accusations. The quest for any further interrelationships which may exist between the introductions requires a different method such as that used by rhetorical critics. The significance these scholars attach to recurrent words, roots and themes is useful for the tracing of any further similarities between the introductions attributed to the same speaker and for the discernment of any additional patterns in the introductions as a whole.

[10] Cf. Westermann, *The Structure of the Book of Job,* 51.

(4) Rhetorical Features of the Introductions

(a) Characteristics Common to the Introductions of Each Speaker

A comparison of the four introductions belonging to Eliphaz (4:2–6; 5:1–7; 15:2–6; 22:2–5) reveals some interesting similarities. The threefold recurrence of the noun *yir'â* ("fear," 4:6a; 15:4a; 22:4a), used in reference to piety, in three of the four introductions is significant. In the first text, Eliphaz instructs Job to put his hope in his "fear of the Lord." By the time Eliphaz is given his second opportunity to speak, the reader meets a character who has lost his composure and hurls serious allegations against Job, one of which charges Job with destroying the basis for piety. Eliphaz, in his final introduction, is presented as resorting to sarcasm with his questioning of the quality of Job's piety. A review of the use of this word in Eliphaz's introductions not only provides one with a glimpse of the transition in this character's emotional state as created by the author, but also clarifies for the reader the importance piety plays in facing suffering for the orthodox believer as represented by Eliphaz. In the three speeches attributed to Eliphaz, this word *yir'â* occurs only in the introductory passages. The mention of piety at the outset of Eliphaz's speeches, therefore, signals the reader that this concept is critical for his character.

A second word, the verb *sākan,* occurs in two of Eliphaz's introductions. The first time this verb is used the point is indirectly made that Job's arguments are "worthless" (15:3a). Then in 22:2 Eliphaz argues, in an allusion to Job, that "warriors" and "sages" are of no use to God. Eliphaz, however, does not devalue the pursuit of wisdom completely, for he indirectly refers to himself as a wise man in 15:2a, the third of his introductions. When the idea of the "uselessness" of human effort and wisdom is viewed in conjunction with Eliphaz's regard for the reverence of God, the overall point seems to be that piety is of utmost importance. Mortals are unable to resolve their difficulties on their own, according to Eliphaz, therefore, they are to maintain their piety at all costs.

In addition to the recurrence of the words *yir'â* and *sākan,* which relate three of Eliphaz's four introductions, 4:2–7 and 5:1–7 exhibit a level of consistency, as previously demonstrated, from which it was concluded that the writer had the earlier introduction in mind when composing the latter. The concept of "fear," which plays a significant role in three of Eliphaz's introductions, is not mentioned in 5:1–7. This introductory passage, however, does not open a speech but only introduces the second installment of a speech. It seems likely, therefore, that it was not thought necessary to include a reference to "piety" in 5:1–7 as it functions as an introduction on a secondary level.

Bildad's two introductions (8:2–7; 18:2–4) open in a similar fashion. The first reads,

> How long will you say these things,
> and the words of your mouth be a great wind (8:2)?

The second is translated, "How long will it be before you blow an end of words?" (18:2a). Both of these opening lines begin with the adverbial phrase, "how long" (*ʿad-ʾān,* 8:2a; and *ʿad-ʾānâ,* 18:2a) through which Bildad's impatience with Job's arguments is expressed. The description of Job's words as a "great wind" (8:2b) is also carried forward in the opening line of Bildad's second speech if the verb *tĕśîmûn* is derived from the root *nšm* ("to blow"). It appears that the poet wished to reinforce the idea that Bildad should be understood as rejecting Job's arguments as nothing more than mere wind. Thus Bildad's impatience with Job is reinforced at the outset of both introductions attributed to him.

Similarly, two introductions were identified as Zophar's (11:2–6; 20:2–3). These passages critique Job's contributions to the debate. In the two opening verses of chap. 11, Zophar refers to Job's speeches as a "multitude of words," "babbling," and "mockery," in addition to describing him as a "verbose man." Then, in Zophar's opening to his second speech, this character is given the line, "with wind he answers me without understanding me" (20:3b). Zophar, it seems, is made to side with Bildad as is evident by his critique of Job's words as "wind." In addition, Zophar accuses Job of lacking the intellect to comprehend what was previously said. In both these introductions attributed to Zophar, a highly critical evaluation of Job's speeches is evident. This critique, placed at the outset of Zophar's speeches, makes it clear to the reader that this character is greatly displeased with Job's stance.

In any speech, ancient or modern, the introductory remarks play a pivotal role as they put forward significant points or issues that will be elaborated on or will clarify for the audience certain assumptions on which the speaker operates. As the theme of piety or "fear" recurs in three of Eliphaz's introductions, one may conclude that this concept should be viewed as significant for him. Further, in the two introductions which belong to Bildad, and in the two attributed to Zophar, a similar critical outlook emerges concerning the content of Job's speeches. As both introductions given to Bildad open with the phrase "how long" (8:2; 18:2), one is given the impression that this speaker should be understood as impatient and intolerant of Job's views. This perception is, then, reinforced with Bildad's treatment of Job's speeches as "wind" in both passages (8:2b; 18:2a).

The use of the word "wind" to describe Job's speeches in 20:3b suggests that Zophar should be understood as in agreement with Bildad's assessment of Job's speeches. As noted above, Zophar is given several other negative comments about Job's words which make him appear perhaps even more critical of the protagonist. As the debate unfolds, one is given the impression that the friends become increasingly irritated with Job's speeches. The fact that these criticisms are placed at the beginning of Bildad's and Zophar's speeches highlights for the reader the level of disagreement which exists between Job and these two friends.

On the basis of the similarities between the introductions of the friends, one would expect to find further parallels between the introductions attributed to Job (ten in all). Yet the parallels are not as extensive as might be expected. The general theme which dominates these passages is, not surprisingly, that of Job's suffering. Within this theme (in two introductions which share a common outlook on the troubles inherent in this life) the simile of the "hireling" (*śākîr,* 7:1b; 14:6b) is uttered by Job to depict the difficult life awaiting those who are born into this world. In the latter passage Job refers to the relative "enjoyment" of life for the hireling (14:6b) which, he argues, must be understood in comparison to one who experiences the judgment of God (14:3). Life for the hireling is difficult, Job maintains in both these texts, as God must be understood as the oppressive overseer. In Job's view, however, life is not nearly as difficult for the hireling as it is for one who has fallen under the judgment of God.

A second parallel shared by two introductions involves "name calling." The first incident occurs in 13:4b where Job refers to his friends as "quack healers." On the second occasion, Job describes his friends as "miserable comforters" (16:2b) in a syntactically similar statement which, like the first, also ends with the construction, *kullĕkem* ("all of you"). These two epithets, put upon Job's lips and hurled at the friends, express his disappointment and disgust with the friends' lack of support. Job's complaint against God as a cruel taskmaster, together with his expressed alienation from his friends, creates the image of one who is very much alone in his struggle. In sum, the significance of the references to the "hireling" (7:1b; 14:6b) and to the "namecalling" of 13:4b and 16:2b keep before the reader the tragedy of Job's position so as to create a sympathetic view for the protagonist.

Lastly, as with two of Eliphaz's introductions (4:2–7; 5:1–7), the discovery of several characteristics which relate two of Job's introductions (12:2–6; 13:1–5) suggests that the writer intended to open both poems in a similar manner so as to tie them together. This technique creates a certain consistency in the approach and argument of a speaker and allows for the reinforcement and/or development of specific points.

(b) Themes Shared by the Introductions

When the eighteen introductions are viewed collectively, four themes, which recur in several of the passages, emerge as significant. The most obvious is the critique of the quality of each other's speeches. As we have seen, Bildad is given the first retort when he calls Job's words a "great wind" (8:2b) which follows from an earlier statement where Job complains that his friends treat his words as "wind" (6:26b). Zophar joins this attack next with his criticism of the quality and type of Job's words ("multitude of words," 11:2a; "man full of talk," 11:2b; "babble," 11:3a; and "mockery," 11:3b). Then, in his introduction to his second speech, Eliphaz also makes several, albeit indirect, critical references to Job's arguments. The first two descriptions ("windy knowledge," 15:2a; and "east wind," 15:2b) remind the reader of Bildad's reference to a "great wind." Eliphaz's latter two criticisms ("unprofitable talk," 15:3a; and "words that can do no good," 15:3b) continue to sound this character's disgust with Job's words. Next Job, in direct response to Eliphaz, but in a comment addressed to the friends as a whole, calls their arguments "windy words" (16:3a). Then, in the second cycle of speeches, Bildad and Zophar continue with this "wind" motif. Bildad inquires of Job, "How long will it be before you 'blow' an end of words (18:2a)?" This query is later followed by Zophar's remark, "and with 'wind' he answers me without understanding me (20:3b)." Through this criticism, uttered initially by the friends and then adopted by Job, the disputants register their profound disagreement with one another and attempt to discredit each other's argument.

A second theme, which involves wisdom, is present in several of the introductions and is related to the critical comments directed against the quality of one another's arguments. First Job introduces this theme with his reference to the incomparable "wisdom" of God (9:4a). In the following introduction, Zophar responds to this remark with the wish that God might share the "secrets of wisdom" (11:6a) with Job. The implication of this wish is that Zophar knows something of this wisdom which he desires God would share with Job. This understanding explains Job's sarcastic retort in the next introduction where he criticizes Zophar and the others for their assumption of intellectual superiority and defends his own intelligence:

> Truly you are the intelligentsia
> and with you wisdom will die.
> I have a mind as well as you;
> I do not fall short of you.
> Who is not mindful of these things? (12:2–3)

To reinforce his point Job once again defends his knowledge as being at least on a par with that of his friends in his following introduction (13:2). Further, in what should be understood as complete exasperation with his friends, Job makes the sarcastic request that they demonstrate their so-called wisdom by keeping silent (13:5).

From this point onwards, it is the friends who continue with the theme of wisdom in their introductions usually in defense of their intelligence. Eliphaz, who speaks next, indirectly refers to himself as a "wise man" (15:2a). Bildad defends the wisdom of the friends next with two queries (18:3). The first asks why they are treated as "cattle" (i.e., dull-witted) and the second inquires as to why they are considered "stupid" by Job. In Eliphaz's last introduction, however, he goes on the attack and instead of defending his own wisdom or that of his friends, he downplays the value of wisdom as a means of gaining favor with God (22:2b). The point is that wisdom has its limitations, and they are such that Job cannot successfully twist the facts to secure his righteousness before God. Job, however, would not disagree with this point (cf. 9:4). Eliphaz's questioning of the value of wisdom, therefore, has little effect on Job.

As we have seen, alongside of the fairly consistent criticism of one another's speeches, is the denigration of each other's wisdom. Each participant at some point is put in the position of defending his wisdom. Also Job, Eliphaz and Zophar attack or delimit one another's wisdom at some point in their introductions. The attack of a rival's wisdom and the defense of one's own along with repeated criticisms of each other's speeches are techniques used by the writer to discredit what an opponent has said in an attempt to make the speaker's remarks appear more convincing. Such critical bantering at the outset of many of the speeches is a natural way to begin a speech within a dispute and consequently adds an element of realism to the argument.

The final two themes which recur in several introductions concern Job's personal character and reputation, on one hand, and the issue of justice on the other. With regard to Job's character, Eliphaz was the first to mention Job's past, which he does favorably as a means of encouragement (4:3–4). Next, Bildad refers to Job's "purity" and "uprightness" in a conditional statement which indicates that the quality of Job's former life is open to question (8:6a). Zophar is presented as even more skeptical of Job's reputation as he merely quotes Job's defense of his integrity (11:4) in the context of critical comments directed against the protagonist's arguments (11:2–3). In the following introduction, Job defends his character, questioned by Zophar and Bildad, with his description of himself as a "just and blameless man" (12:4c). Job's reputation is not mentioned again in the subsequent introductory passages until the introduction to Eliphaz's last speech. Here Eliphaz first questions whether Job's assumed "righteousness" and "blamelessness" (22:3) would have any effect on God before he accuses Job of "wickedness" and of committing seemingly endless "iniquities" (22:5). Lastly, in the following introduction, Job speaks of himself as an "upright man" (23:7), which must be seen as a defense against Eliphaz's questioning of the value of Job's so-called integrity and his allegation of gross wickedness on Job's part.

In sum, after Eliphaz's initial, positive assessment of Job's past (4:3–4), all three friends soon turn against him and question his integrity. Consequently, in two of his introductions, Job is given positive statements concerning his character in defense of his integrity. The remarks about Job's character are not restricted to the introductory passages but the fact that they occur in several introductions, where they would make the greatest impact, suggests that the writer intended to keep the issue of

Job's character—a central concept in the prologue—before the reader throughout the disputation.

The last theme, which occurs in several of the introductory passages, is that of God's justice. The first time this theme is mentioned in an introduction, it is with a rhetorical question posited by Bildad in which the speaker implies that God's justice is above question (8:3). In response, Job hints that God's justice might be perverted (9:2). Zophar responds next to this issue with a query which suggests that Job's arguments betray him as not deserving of vindication (11:2). Later, in the second cycle, Job implicates both God and his friends for "wronging" him (19:3 and 6). Then, in the last introduction studied, Job insists that, as he is "upright," he is hopeful that he will be acquitted by his judge (23:7).

Both Job and his friends base their arguments on the assumption that there is a direct relationship between human behavior and subsequent treatment by God. The friends defend God's justice and consequently defame Job's character, as they believe his suffering is indicative of guilt. Similar to the model of the penitential psalms of individual complaint (Pss 38:4–5, 18; 51:4–6; 69:6), they advise Job to confess his sin in order that he might find restoration. Nevertheless, Job clings unyieldingly to his integrity and protests his innocence as in the complaints commonly referred to as the "prayers of the falsely accused" (e.g., Pss 7:4–6; 17:3–5; 25:21; 31:7). In these psalms, the request for deliverance from personal enemies is a significant feature (7:2–3,7; 17:7–14; 25:2,19–20; 31:12–16). Yet, unlike the human enemies of the psalmist, Job clearly identifies his enemy as God. He believes he is wrongfully accused of sin and, as a result, questions the ethical quality of God's justice.

Due to the repeated references to Job's integrity as presented in the prologue, the reader is naturally sympathetic to his position. In the larger context of the individual complaint, Job is seen as one of the "falsely accused." The focus of the disputation, therefore, ultimately shifts to the question of God's integrity. In response to this development, the Yahweh speeches reveal a deity who is not Job's enemy, but one who challenges both Job and the friends for inaccurately speculating on the ways of God. As a result, the theophany leaves the reader with the impression that the nature and work of God as ruler over creation is largely beyond the comprehension of mortals. Consequently, in retrospect, the disputants' criticism of one another's speeches and the wisdom displayed in them is finally resolved in the Yahweh speeches as all the participants are shown to lack wisdom.

Conclusion

Based on the above discussion the following conclusions may be drawn:

(a) The pursuit of shared words, roots, allusions formed with synonyms, and themes uncovered in the introductions of the speeches (or poems) of chaps. 4–24 and earlier passages reveals a significant degree of response to the immediately preceding speech. Further, there is a general trend for the introductions to respond especially to the introduction(s) of the previous speaker particularly in the first cycle. On the strength of the overall pattern of connections established between the introductions and their respective preceding speeches, one may postulate that the whole of any one speech likely contains further evidence of a response to the speech of the previous speaker. Thus the speeches do not appear to be governed by the principle of "delayed reaction" as explained by Terrien and Whedbee.

(b) The links between speeches presented in this study are found in integral texts and are substantive in nature. Thus they do not appear to be the work of a later editor(s). An examination of the wisdom poem of chap. 28 and the Elihu speeches (chaps. 32–37), pieces commonly viewed as interpolations, with attention to the possibility that some of the details might be incorporated into these texts from preceding speeches could prove informative. If such a study reveals a number of connections with preceding speeches, it could conceivably be argued that a later writer(s) noted the dynamics of the disputation and adopted a similar approach in his contribution to the work. A simpler explanation, however, would be that these pieces are the work of the original author who merely followed through with his established approach.

In this study only those passages classed as "introductions" were examined with respect to how they might take up ideas from preceding speeches. Further work on the speeches as a whole is warranted as this research would surely uncover further responses. The implications for such study are far reaching for the exegete as, contrary to their usual treatment, no speech in the Book of Job is an isolated unit. An exacting interpretation of any speech from this work is not possible without addressing how it is related to preceding chapters.

(c) Although rhetorical questions and accusations are common to the introductions, a form-critical examination of these passages demonstrates that they do not share a common structure. The search for shared words, roots and themes, however, shows a level of consistency in the introductions of the individual speakers which reveals something of the approach and personality created for the participants of the dispute.

Moreover, an overview of the introductions uncovered key themes such as the integrity of Job, the justice of God, and the wisdom or lack of wisdom of the disputants which, in an otherwise complicated and often convoluted disputation, would be reinforced for the benefit of the reader each time they were presented at the beginning of a speech. In the end Job's integrity is preserved, God's justice is elevated above humanity's comprehension, and limitations are set for any human wisdom which would seek to understand the ways of God.

Appendix

Table of Proposed Connections[1]

	Passage	Speaker	Word and Text	Related Word/ Phrase/Theme and Text
(1)	4:2–6	Eliphaz	(a) *nāga'*, "to touch" (4:5b)	*nāga'* (1:11; 2:5)
			(b) *bāhal*, "to be horrified" (4:5b)	*pāḥad*, "fear" (3:25a)
			(c) *yir'â*, "fear" (4:6a)	*yārē'*, "to fear" (1:1, 8; 2:3)
			(d) *tōm*, "integrity" (4:6b)	*tām*, "blameless" (1:1, 8; 2:3)
				yāgōr, "to dread" (3:25b)
			(e) *tiqwâ*, "hope" (4:6b)	*qāwâ*, "to hope" (3:9b)
			(f) *derek*, "way" (4:6b)	*derek* (3:23a)

[1] The key to the abbreviations, which identify connections previously made by scholars, is as follows: (P) for Power, *A Study of Irony in the Book of Job;* (H) for Holbert, *The Function and Significance of "Klage" in the Book of Job;* (K) for Klaus "Between Job and His Friends" and "Joban Parallels to Job"; and (HL) for Habel, *The Book of Job* (1985).

(2)	5:1–7	Eliphaz	(H)	(a) *qābab,* "to curse" (5:3b)	*qābab* (3:8a)
			(K)	(b) *lāqaḥ,* "to take" (5:5b)	*lāqaḥ* (3:6a)
				(c) *ʿāmāl,* "trouble" (5:6b,7a)	*ʿāmāl* (3:10b, 20a)
				(d) *yālad,* "to bear" (5:7a)	*yālad* (3:3a)
				(e) *běnê-rešep,* "sons of Reshef" (5:7b)	*měrîrê yôm* "demons of the day" (3:5c)
(3)	6:2–7	Job	(P)(H)(K)(HL)	(a) *kaʿaś,* "indignation" (6:2a)	*kaʿaś* (5:2a)
				(b) *dābār,* "word" (6:3b)	*millâ,* "speech" (4:4a)
			(HL)	(c) *ḥēṣ,* "arrow" (6:4a)	*běnê-rešep,* "sons of Reshef" (5:7b)
			(HL)	(d) *biʿût,* "terror" (6:4c)	*bāhal,* "to be horrified" (4:5b)
				(e) *biʿûtê ʾĕlôah* "terrors of Eloah" (6:4c)	*běnê-rešep,* "sons of Reshef" (5:7b)
(4)	7:1–8	Job		(a) *ṣābāʾ,* "hard service" (7:1a)	*ʾewen,* "evil" (5:6a) *ʿāmāl,* "trouble" (5:6b)
				ʾĕnôš, "mortal" (7:1a)	*ʾādām,* "humanity" (5:7a)
				ʾereṣ, "earth" (7:1a)	*ʿāpār,* "dust" (5:6a) *ʾădāmâ,* "ground" (5:6b)
				(b) *šāʾap,* "to pant" (7:2a)	*šāʾap* (5:5c)
				(c) *qāwâ,* "to hope" (7:2b)	*tiqwâ* (4:6; 5:16a)

			(K)	(d) *ʿāpār,* "dust" (7:5a)	*ʿāpār* (5:6a)
(5)	8:2–7	Bildad	(K)(HL)	(a) *rûaḥ,* "wind" (8:2b)	*rûaḥ* (6:26b)
				(b) *rûaḥ kabbîr,* "mighty wind" (8:2b)	*rûaḥ gĕdôlâ,* "great wind" (1:19)
				(c) *ṣedeq,* "the right" (8:3b)	*ṣedeq* (6:29b)
			(HL)	(d) *bānîm,* "children" (8:4a)	*bānîm ûbānôt,* "sons and daughters" (1:18)
			(HL)	(e) *ḥāṭāʾ, "to sin"* (8:4a)	*ḥāṭāʾ* (1:5 and 7:20a)
			(HL)	(f) *šālaḥ,* "to send" (8:4b)	*šālaḥ* (1:5)
			(K)	(g) *pešaʿ,* "wickedness" (8:4b)	*pešaʿ* (7:21a)
			(P)(H)(K)(HL)	(h) *šāḥar,* "to go early" (8:5a)	*šāḥar,* "to seek" (7:21d) *šākam,* "to rise early" (1:5)
			(HL)	(i) *yāšār,* "upright" (8:6a)	*yāšār* (1:1,8; and 2:3)
(6)	9:2–4	Job		(a) *ṣādaq,* "to be just" (9:2b)	*ṣedeq,* "the right" (8:3b)
			(K)(HL)	(b) *ṣādaq ʾĕnôš,* "a mortal be just" (9:2b)	*ʾĕnôš ṣādaq,* (4:17a)
				(c) *šālēm,* "to emerge unharmed" (9:4b)	*šālēm,* "to restore" (8:6c)
(7)	11:2–6	Zophar	(HL)	(a) *ṣādaq,* "to justify" (11:2b)	*ṣādaq* (9:2b, 15a, 20a; 10:15b)

			(K)	(b) *lāʿag,* "to mock" (11:3b)	*lāʿag* (9:23b)
				(c) *ḥokmâ,* "wisdom" (11:6a)	*ḥăkam,* "wise" (9:4a)
				(d) *ʿāwon,* "iniquity" (11:6c)	*ʿāwon* (10:6a, 14b)
(8)	12:2–6	Job	(K)(HL)	(a) *ḥokmâ,* "wisdom" (12:2b)	*taʿălumôt ḥokmâ,* "secrets of wisdom" (11:6a)
			(K)(HL)	(b) *lēbāb,* "mind" (12:3a)	*lābab,* "to understand" (11:12a)
				(c) *śĕḥōq,* "laughingstock" (12:4a, 4c)	*lāʿag,* "to mock" (11:3b)
				(d) *ṣaddîq,* "just one" (12:4c)	*ṣādaq,* "to be justified" (11:2b)
				(e) *ṣaddîq* (12:4c)	*yāšār,* "upright"; *yārēʾ,* "to fear" (God) *sār mērāʿ,* "to turn away from evil" (1:1,8; and 2:3)
				(f) *tāmîm,* "blameless one" (12:4c)	*tām,* "blameless" (1:1,8; and 2:3)
(9)	13:1–5	Job		(a) *ḥāraš,* "to be silent" (13:5a)	*ḥāraš* (11:3a)
				(b) *ḥokmâ,* "wisdom" (13:5b)	*taʿălumôt ḥokmâ,* "secrets of wisdom" (11:6a)

(10)	14:1–6	Job		(a) *ʿayin,* "eye" (14:3a)	*ʿayin* (11:4b)
				(b) *mišpāṭ,* "judgment" (14:3b)	*ṣādaq,* "to be justified" (11:2b)
				(c) *ṭāhôr,* "clean person" (14:4a)	*zak,* "pure" (11:4a) *bar,* "clean" (11:4b) *mĕtê-šāwĕʾ,* "deceitful men" (11:11a)
(11)	15:2–6	Eliphaz		(a) *ḥākām,* "wise man" (15:2a)	*ḥokmâ,* "wisdom" (12:2b, 12a; 13:5b)
				(b) *beṭen,* "belly" (15:2b)	*lēbāb,* "mind" (12:3a)
				(c) *ʿāwon,* "iniquity" (15:5a)	*ʿāwon* (13:23a, 26b; 14:17b)
				(d) *śāpâ,* "lips" (15:6b)	*śāpâ* (13:6b)
(12)	16:2–5	Job		(a) *šāmaʿ,* "to hear" (16:2a)	*šāmaʿ* (15:17a)
			(HL)	(b) *mĕnaḥămîm,* "comforters" (16:2b)	*niḥam,* "to comfort" (2:11)
				(c) *ʿāmāl,* "troublesome" (16:2b)	*ʿāmāl,* "trouble" (15:35a)
			(HL)	(d) *dibrê-rûaḥ,* "windy words" (16:3a)	*daʿat-rûaḥ,* "windy knowledge" (15:2a)
				(e) *ʿānâ,* "to answer" (16:3b)	*ʿānâ* (15:2a)
				(f) *dābar,* "to speak" (16:4a)	*dābār,* "word" (15:3a)

					millâ, "word" (16:4c)	*millâ* (15:3b)
				(g)	*peh,* "mouth" (16:5a)	*peh* (15:5a)
						lāšôn, "tongue" (15:5b)
						peh (15:6a)
					śāpâ, "lips" (16:5b)	*śāpâ* (15:6b)
(13)	18:2–4	Bildad		(a)	*tĕšîmûn* from *nāšam,* "to blow" (18:2a)	*rûaḥ,* "windy" (16:3a)
				(b)	*qinṣê* from *qēṣ,* "end"? (18:2a)	*qēṣ* (16:3a)
				(c)	defense of friend's intelligence (18:3)	ignorance of friends (17:4a, 10b; 12:2–3, 7–9)
			(HL)	(d)	*bĕhēmâ,* "cattle" (18:3a)	*bĕhēmâ* (12:7a)
			(P)(HL)	(e)	*ṭōrēp napšô bĕʾappô,* "you who tear yourself in anger" (18:4a)	*ʾappô ṭārap,* "he has torn me in his anger" (16:9a)
				(f)	*wĕyeʿtaq-ṣûr mimmĕqomô,* "or the rock moved from its place" (18:14c)	*wĕṣûr yeʿtaq mimmĕqomô* (14:18b)
(14)	19:2–6	Job	(P)	(a)	*ʿad-ʾānâ,* "how long" (19:2a)	*ʿad-ʾānâ* (18:2a)
					millâ, "word" (19:2b)	*millâ* (18:2a)

				(b) *nepeš,* "soul" (19:2a)	*nepeš* (18:4a)
				(c) *nākar* II, "to treat as strange" (19:3b)	*nākar* I, "to recognize" (2:12)
				(d) *ʿāwat,* "to wrong" (19:6a)	*ʿāwat* (18:3ab)
				(e) *mĕṣûdâ,* "siegeworks" (19:6b)	*rešet,* "net" (18:8a)
					paḥ, "snare" (18:9a)
					ṣammîm, "net" (18:9b)
					ḥebel, "rope" (18:10a)
					malkōdet, "trap" (18:10b)
(15)	20:2–3	Zophar	(HL)	(a) *kĕlimmâ,* "humiliation" (20:3a)	*kālam,* "to humiliate" (19:3a)
				(b) *rûaḥ,* "wind" (20:3b) Zophar's humiliation and consequent need to speak stems from various passages within ch. 19	*rûaḥ,* (16:3a) Job's jibe against friends (19:5) Friends turned against Job (19:14a, 19a)
					Undeserved alienation from others (19:13a, 14, 15–16, 17, 18)

(16)	21:2–6	Job	(a) *šāmʿa,* "to listen" (21:2a)	*šāmʿa* (20:3a)
			(b) *rûaḥ,* "spirit" (21:4b)	*rûaḥ* (20:3b)
(17)	22:2–5	Eliphaz	(a) *ḥāpēṣ,* "to be pleased" (22:3a)	*ḥāpēṣ,* "to desire" (21:14b)
			(b) *derek,* "way" (22:3b)	*derek* (21:14b)
			(c) *beṣaʿ,* "gain" (22:3b)	*yāʿal,* "to gain, profit" (21:15b)
			(d) *tāmam,* "to be perfect" (22:3b)	*tām,* "perfect" (1:1, 8; 2:3)
			(e) *yirʾâ,* "fear" (22:4a)	*yārēʾ,* "to fear" (1:1, 8; 2:3)
			(f) *mišpāṭ,* "judgment" (22:4b)	*šāpaṭ,* "to judge" (21:22b)
			(g) *rāʿâ,* "wickedness" (22:5a)	*raʿ,* "evil, wickedness" (1:1, 8; 2:3)
(18)	23:2–7	Job	(a) *bôʾ,* "to enter" (23:3b)	*bôʾ* (22:21b)
			(b) *mišpāṭ,* "case" (23:4a)	*mišpāṭ,* "judgment" (22:4b)
			tôkaḥat, "argument" (23:4b)	*yākaḥ,* "to arraign" (22:4a)
			yākaḥ, "to reason" (23:7a)	
			mišpaṭ, "judge" (23:7b)	
			(c) *peh,* "mouth" (23:4b)	*peh* (22:22a)
			(d) *śîm,* "to heed" (23:6b)	*śîm* (22:22b)

(e) *yāšār,* "uprightness" (23:7a)	*ṣādēq,* "to be righteous" (22:3a) *yir'â,* "fear" (22:4a) *rā'â,* "wickedness" (22:5a) *tāmam,* "to be perfect" (22:3b) *yāšār,* "upright" (1:1, 8; 2:3)

Selected Bibliography

Anderson, Francis I. *Job: An Introduction and Commentary.* London: Intervarsity, 1976.

Baker, J. A. "The Book of Job: Unity and Meaning," *JSOT* 11 (1978) 17–26.

Blommerde, Anton, C.M. *Northwest Semitic Grammar and Job.* Rome: Pontifical Biblical Institute, 1969.

Blumenthal, David R. "Play on words in the nineteenth chapter of Job," *VT* 16 (1966) 497–501.

Ceresko, Anthony R. "The A:B B:A Word Pattern in Hebrew and Northwest Semitic with Special Reference to the Book of Job," *UF* 7 (1975) 73–88.

——. *Job 29–31 in the Light of Northwest Semitic.* Rome: Pontifical Biblical Institute, 1980.

Clines, J. J. A. "Job 5:1–8: A New Exegesis," *Bib* 62 (1981) 185–94.

——. "The Arguments of Job's Three Friends" in *Art and Meaning: Rhetoric in Biblical Literature.* Ed. D. J. A. Clines, et al. JSOTSup 19; Sheffield, England: JSOT, 1982, 199–214.

——. *Job 1–20.* WBC 17; Dallas: Word Books, 1989.

Cox, Dermot. "A Rational Inquiry into God: Chapters 4–27 of the Book of Job," *Greg* 67 (1986) 621–59.

Crenshaw, James L. "Wisdom" in *Old Testament Form Criticism.* Ed. John H. Hayes. San Antonio: Trinity University, 1974, 225–64.

——. "Impossible Questions, Sayings and Tasks," *Semeia* 17 (1980) 19–34.

——. *Old Testament Wisdom: An Introduction.* Atlanta: John Knox Press, 1981.

Dahood, Mitchell. "The Root ʿ*zb* II in Job," *JBL* 78 (1959) 303–9.

——. "Northwest Semitic Philology and Job" in *The Bible in Current Catholic Thought.* Ed. J. Mckenzie. Herder and Herder, 1962, 53–64.
——. "Hebrew-Ugaritic Lexicography I," *Bib* 44 (1963) 289–303.
——. *Psalms 1: 1–50,* AB 16; Garden City, NY: Doubleday, 1966.
——. "Hebrew-Ugaritic Lexicography V," *Bib* 48 (1967) 421–38.
——. "Ugaritic-Hebrew Syntax and Style," *UF* 1 (1968) 15–36.
——. "Hebrew-Ugaritic Lexicography VIII," *Bib* 51 (1970) 391–404.
——. "Hebrew-Ugaritic Lexicography XI," *Bib* 54 (1973) 351–66.
Delitzsch, F. *Biblical Commentary on the Book of Job.* 2 vols. Edinburgh: T. and T. Clark, 1866.
Dhorme, Edouard A. *A Commentary on the Book of Job.* Originally published 1926. Reprinted, London: Thomas Nelson and Sons, 1967.
Driver, Godfrey R. "Studies in the Vocabulary of the Old Testament VI," *JTS* 34 (1933) 33–44.
——. "Problems in the Hebrew Text of Job," VTSup 3 (1955) 73–93.
——. "On Job v. 5," *TZ* 12 (1956) 485–86.
Driver, Samuel R. and Gray, George B. *A Critical and Exegetical Commentary on the Book of Job.* ICC; Edinburgh: T. and T. Clark, 1921.
Finklestein, J. J. "Hebrew *HBR* and Semitic *HBR," *JBL* 75 (1956) 328–331.
Fohrer, Georg. *Das Buch Hiob.* KAT 16; Gütersloh: Gütersloher, 1963.
Fulco, W. J. *The Canaanite God Rešep.* New Haven, CT: American Oriental Society, 1976.
Fullerton, Kemper. "Double Entendre in the First Speech of Eliphaz," *JBL* 49 (1930) 320–74.
Gemser, Bruce. "The *rib-* or Controversy-pattern in Hebrew Mentality," VTSup 3 (1960) 120–37.
Glatzer, Nahum. "The Book of Job and Its Interpreters," in *Biblical Motifs, Origins and Transformations.* Ed. A. Altmann. Cambridge, MA: Harvard University, 1966, 197–220.
Good, Edwin M. "Job and the Literary Task: A Response," *Soundings* 56 (1973) 470–84.
Gordis, Robert. *The Book of God and Man: A Study of Job.* Chicago: University of Chicago, 1965.
——. *The Book of Job: Commentary, New Translation, and Special Notes.* New York: Jewish Theological Seminary of America, 1978.
——. "Virtual Quotations in Job, Sumer and Qumran," *VT* 31 (1981) 410–27.
Guillaume, A. *Studies in the Book of Job, with a New Translation.* Leiden: Brill, 1968.
Habel, Norman C. *The Book of Job.* Cambridge: Cambridge University, 1975.
——. "'Only the Jackal is my Friend': On Friends and Redeemers in Job," *Int* 31 (1977) 227–36.

——. "The Narrative Art of Job: Applying the Principles of Robert Alter," *JSOT* 27 (1983) 101–11.
——. "Of Things Beyond Me: Wisdom in the Book of Job," *CurTM* 10 (1983) 142–54.
——. *The Book of Job.* OTL; Philadelphia: Westminster, 1985.
Hartley, John E. *The Book of Job.* NICOT; Grand Rapids, MI: Eerdmans, 1988.
Hoffmann, Yair. "The Use of Equivocal Words in the First Speech of Eliphaz (Job 4–5)," *VT* 30 (1980) 114–19.
——. "The Relation between the Prologue and the Speech-Cycles in Job: A Reconsideration," *VT* 31 (1981) 160–70.
Holbert, John Charles. *The Function and Significance of the "Klage" in the Book of Job with Special Reference to the Incidence of Formal and Verbal Irony.* Ph.D. Dissertation, Southern Methodist University, 1975.
——. "The Skies will Uncover his Iniquity: Satire in the Second Speech of Zophar (Job 20)," *VT* 31 (1981) 171–79.
Hölscher, G. *Das Buch Hiob.* HAT 17; Tübingen: Mohr, 1937.
Horst, Friedrich. *Hiob 1–19.* BKAT 16; Neukirchen-Vluyn: Neukirchener, 1968.
Irwin, W. A. "An Examination of the Progress of Thought in the Dialogue of Job," *JR* 13 (1933) 150–64.
——. "The First Speech of Bildad," *ZAW* 51 (1933) 205–16.
——. "Poetic Structure in the Book of Job," *JNES* 5 (1946) 26–39.
Isbell, C. "Exodus 1–2 in the Context of Exodus 1–14; Story Lines and Key Words," in *Art and Meaning: Rhetoric in Biblical Literature.* Ed. D. J. A. Clines *et al.* JSOTSup 19; Sheffield, England: JSOT, 1982, 37–59.
Jackson, Jared J. and Kessler, Martin (eds.). *Rhetorical Criticism: Essays in Honor of James Muilenburg.* PTMS 1; Pittsburgh, PA: Pickwick, 1974.
Jansen, J. Gerald. *Job.* Interpretation Series. Atlanta: John Knox, 1985.
Kissane, Edward J. *The Book of Job.* Dublin: Browne and Nolan, 1939.
Klaus, Natan. "Between Job and His Friends," *Beth Mikra* 31 (1985–86) 152–68.
——. "Joban Parallels to Job," *Beth Mikra* 32 (1986–87) 45–56.
Lambert, W. *Babylonian Wisdom Literature.* Oxford: Oxford University, 1960.
Larue, Gerald A. "The Book of Job on the Futility of Theological Discussion," *The Personalist* 45 (1964) 72–79.
Laurin, Robert. "The Theological Structure of Job," *ZAW* 84 (1974) 86–89.
Lévêque, J. *Job et son Dieu.* 2 vols. Paris: J. Gabalda, 1970.
Lichtenstein, Aaron. "Toward a Literary Understanding of the Book of Job," *Hebrew Studies* 20/21 (1979–80) 34–35.
Lipiński, E. "*SKN* et *SGN* dans le Sémitique Occidental du Nord," *UF* 5 (1973) 191–207.
Loretz, Oswald. "ḤBR in Job 16:4," *CBQ* 23 (1961) 293–94.
MacKenzie, R. A. F. "The Transformation of Job," *BTB* 9 (1979) 51–57.

Michel, Walter L. "Death in Job," *Dialog* 11 (1972) 183–89.
——. *Job in the Light of Northwest Semitic.* Vol 1. Rome: Pontifical Biblical Institute, 1987.
Moore, Rick D. "The Integrity of Job," *CBQ* 45 (1983) 17–31.
Muilenburg, James. "A Study in Hebrew Rhetoric: Repetition and Style," VTSup 1; Leiden: Brill, 1953, 97–111.
——. "The Linguistic and Rhetorical Usages of the Particle in the Old Testament," *HUCA* 32 (1961) 135–60.
——. "Form Criticism and Beyond," *JBL* 88 (1969) 1–18.
Murphy, Roland E. "Job" in *Wisdom Literature.* FOTL 13; Grand Rapids, MI: Eerdmans, 1981, 14–45.
Patrick, Dale. "Job's Address of God," *ZAW* 91 (1979) 268–82.
Polzin, Robert. "Framework of the Book of Job," *Int* 28 (1974) 182–200.
Pope, Marvin H. *Job.* AB 15; 3d ed.; Garden City, NY: Doubleday, 1973.
Power, W. J. A. *A Study of Irony in the Book of Job.* Ph.D. Dissertation, University of Toronto, 1961.
Reddy, Mummadi P. "The Book of Job—A Reconstruction," *ZAW* 90 (1978) 49–94.
Richter, Helmut. *Studien zu Hiob.* Theologische Arbeiten 11; Berlin: Mohr, 1959.
Rignell, L. G. "Comments on some *cruces interpretum* in the Book of Job," *ASTI* 11 (1978) 111–18.
Roberts, J. J. M. "Job's Summons to Yahweh: The Exploitation of a Legal Metaphor," *ResQ* 16 (1973) 159–165.
Robertson, David A. "The Book of Job: A Literary Study," *Soundings* 56 (1973) 446–69.
——. "The Comedy of Job: A Response," *Semeia* 7 (1977) 41–44.
Rowley, H. H. *Job.* NCB; London: Marshall, Morgan and Scott, 1976.
Scholnick, Sylvia Huberman. "The Meaning of *mišpat* in the Book of Job," *JBL* 10 (1982) 521–29.
Skehan, Patrick W. "Strophic Patterns in the Book of Job," in *Studies in Israelite Poetry and Wisdom.* CBQMS 1; Washington: The Catholic Biblical Association of America, 1971, 96–113.
Slotki, Judah J. "Job xi 6," *VT* 35 (1985) 229–30.
Snaith, Norman H. *The Book of Job: Its Origin and Purpose.* London: SCM, 1968.
Sutcliffe, Edmund F. "Further Notes on Job Textual and Exegetical [Job 6:2–3, 13; 8:16–17; 19:20, 26]," *Bib* 31 (1950) 365–78.
Terrien, Samuel. "The Book of Job: Introduction and Exegesis," *IB* 3; Nashville: Abingdon, 1954, 877–1198.
——. *Job.* CAT 13; Paris: Delachaux et Niestlé, 1963.

Thomas, D. Winton. "A Note on the Hebrew Root *NḤM*," *ExpTim* 44 (1932–33) 191–92.

Tromp, Nicholas J. *Primitive Conceptions of Death and the Nether World in the Old Testament.* Rome: Pontifical Biblical Institute, 1969.

Tur-Sinai, N. H. *The Book of Job.* Jerusalem: Kiryath Sepher, 1957.

Van der Lugt, Pieter. "Stanza-Structure and Word-Repetition in Job 3–13," *JSOT* 40 (1988) 3–38.

Vogels, Walter. "Job a parlé correctment," *NRT* 102 (1980) 835–52.

Watson, Wilfred G. E. *Classical Hebrew Poetry.* JSOTSup 26; Sheffield, England: JSOT, 1976.

Webster, Edwin C. "Strophic Patterns in Job 3–28," *JSOT* 26 (1983) 33–60.

——. "Strophic Patterns in Job 29–42," *JSOT* 30 (1984) 95–109.

Weiser, Arthur. *Das Buch Hiob.* Göttingen: Vandenhoeck and Ruprecht, 1951.

Westermann, Claus. *The Structure of the Book of Job: A Form Critical Analysis.* Philadelphia: Fortress, 1981.

Wevers, J. W. "A Study in the Form Criticism of Individual Complaint Psalms," *VT* 6 (1956) 80–96.

Whedbee, William. "The Comedy of Job," *Semeia* 7 (1977) 1–39.

Wilde, A. de. "Eine alte crux interpretum: Hiob 23:2," *VT* 22 (1972) 368–371.

——. *Das Buch Hiob. OTS* 22. Leiden: Brill, 1981.

Williams, James G. "'You have not Spoken the Truth of Me': Mystery and Irony in Job," *ZAW* 83 (1971) 231–255.

——. "Comedy, Irony, Intercession: A Few Notes in Response," *Semeia* 7 (1977) 135–45.

Williams, Ronald J. "Current Trends in the Study of the Book of Job," in *Studies in the Book of Job.* Ed. W. E. Aufrecht. Studies in Religion Supplements; Waterloo: Wilfrid Laurier University, 1985, 1–27.

Yahuda, A. S. "Hapax Legomena in Alten Testament," *JQR* 15 (1903) 698–714.

Zerafa, Peter P. *The Wisdom of God in the Book of Job.* Studia Universitatis S. Thomae in Urbe 8; Rome: Herder, 1978.

Zink, J. K., "Uncleanness and Sin: a Study of Job xiv:4 and Psalm li:7," *VT* 17 (1967) 354–61.

Index of Authors Cited

Index of Ancient Sources

Old Testament

The Catholic Biblical Quarterly Monograph Series (CBQMS)

1. Patrick W. Skehan, *Studies in Israelite Poetry and Wisdom* (CBQMS 1) $9.00 ($7.20 for CBA members) ISBN 0-915170-00-0 (LC 77-153511)
2. Aloysius M. Ambrozic, *The Hidden Kingdom: A Redactional-Critical Study of the References to the Kingdom of God in Mark's Gospel* (CBQMS 2) $9.00 ($7.20 for CBA members) ISBN 0-915170-01-9 (LC 72-89100)
3. Joseph Jensen, O.S.B., *The Use of tôrâ by Isaiah: His Debate with the Wisdom Tradition* (CBQMS 3) $3.00 ($2.40 for CBA members) ISBN 0-915170-02-7 (LC 73-83134)
4. George W. Coats, *From Canaan to Egypt: Structural and Theological Context for the Joseph Story* (CBQMS 4) $4.00 ($3.20 for CBA members) ISBN 0-915170-03-5 (LC 75-11382)
5. O. Lamar Cope, *Matthew: A Scribe Trained for the Kingdom of Heaven* (CBQMS 5) $4.50 ($3.60 for CBA members) ISBN 0-915170-04-3 (LC 75-36778)
6. Madeleine Boucher, *The Mysterious Parable: A Literary Study* (CBQMS 6) $2.50 ($2.00 for CBA members) ISBN 0-915170-05-1 (LC 76-51260)
7. Jay Braverman, *Jerome's* Commentary on Daniel: *A Study of Comparative Jewish and Christian Interpretations of the Hebrew Bible* (CBQMS 7) $4.00 ($3.20 for CBA members) ISBN 0-915170-06-X (LC 78-55726)
8. Maurya P. Horgan, *Pesharim: Qumran Interpretations of Biblical Books* (CBQMS 8) $6.00 ($4.80 for CBA members) ISBN 0-915170-07-8 (LC 78-12910)
9. Harold W. Attridge and Robert A. Oden, Jr., *Philo of Byblos,* The Phoenician History (CBQMS 9) $3.50 ($2.80 for CBA members) ISBN 0-915170-08-6 (LC 80-25781)
10. Paul J. Kobelski, *Melchizedek and Melchireša'* (CBQMS 10) $4.50 ($3.60 for CBA members) ISBN 0-915170-09-4 (LC 80-28379)
11. Homer Heater, *A Septuagint Translation Technique in the Book of Job* (CBQMS 11) $4.00 ($3.20 for CBA members) ISBN 0-915170-10-8 (LC 81-10085)
12. Robert Doran, *Temple Propaganda: The Purpose and Character of 2 Maccabees* (CBQMS 12) $4.50 ($3.60 for CBA members) ISBN 0-915170-11-6 (LC 81-10084)
13. James Thompson, *The Beginnings of Christian Philosophy: The Epistle to the Hebrews* (CBQMS 13) $5.50 ($4.50 for CBA members) ISBN 0-915170-12-4 (LC 81-12295)
14. Thomas H. Tobin, S.J., *The Creation of Man: Philo and the History of Interpretation* (CBQMS 14) $6.00 ($4.80 for CBA members) ISBN 0-915170-13-2 (LC 82-19891)
15. Carolyn Osiek, *Rich and Poor in the* Shepherd of Hermes (CBQMS 15) $6.00 ($4.80 for CBA members) ISBN 0-915170-14-0 (LC 83-7385)

16. James C. VanderKam, *Enoch and the Growth of an Apocalyptic Tradition* (CBQMS 16) $6.50 ($5.20 for CBA members) ISBN 0-915170-15-9 (LC 83-10134)
17. Antony F. Campbell, S.J., *Of Prophets and Kings: A Late Ninth-Century Document (1 Samuel 1–2 Kings 10)* (CBQMS 17) $7.50 ($6.00 for CBA members) ISBN 0-915170-16-7 (LC 85-12791)
18. John C. Endres, S.J., *Biblical Interpretation in the Book of Jubilees* (CBQMS 18) $8.50 ($6.80 for CBA members) ISBN 0-915170-17-5 (LC 86-6845)
19. Sharon Pace Jeansonne, *The Old Greek Translation of Daniel 7–12* (CBQMS 19) $5.00 ($4.00 for CBA members) ISBN 0-915170-18-3 (LC 87-15865)
20. Lloyd M. Barré, *The Rhetoric of Political Persuasion: The Narrative Artistry and Political Intentions of 2 Kings 9–11* (CBQMS 20) $5.00 ($4.00 for CBA members) ISBN 0-915170-19-1 (LC 87-15878)
21. John J. Clabeaux, *A Lost Edition of the Letters of Paul: A Reassessment of the Text of the Pauline Corpus Attested by Marcion* (CBQMS 21) $8.50 ($6.80 for CBA members) ISBN 0-915170-20-5 (LC 88-28511)
22. Craig Koester, *The Dwelling of God: The Tabernacle in the Old Testament, Intertestamental Jewish Literature, and the New Testament* (CBQMS 22) $9.00 ($7.20 for CBA members) ISBN 0-915170-21-3 (LC 89-9853)
23. William Michael Soll, *Psalm 119: Matrix, Form, and Setting* (CBQMS 23) $9.00 ($7.20 for CBA members) ISBN 0-915170-22-1 (LC 90-27610)
24. Richard J. Clifford and John J. Collins (eds.), *Creation in the Biblical Traditions* (CBQMS 24) $7.00 ($5.60 for CBA members) ISBN 0-915170-23-X (LC 92-20268)

Order from:

The Catholic Biblical Association of America
The Catholic University of America
Washington, D.C. 20064